CONTEMPORARY DOCUMENTARY

Contemporary Documentary offers a rich survey of the rapidly expanding landscape of documentary film, television, video, and new media. The collection of original essays addresses the emerging forms, popular genres, and innovative approaches of the digital era.

The anthology highlights geographically and thematically diverse examples of documentaries that have expanded the scope and impact of nonfiction cinema and captured the attention of global audiences over the past three decades. It also explores the experience of documentary today, with its changing dynamics of production, collaboration, distribution, and exhibition, and its renewed political and cultural relevance.

The twelve chapters—featuring engaging case studies and written from a wide range of perspectives including film theory, social theory, ethics, new media, and experience design—invite students to think critically about documentary as a vibrant field, unrestricted in its imagination and quick in its response to new forms of filmmaking.

Offering a methodical exploration of the expansive reach of documentary as a creative force in the media and society of the twenty-first century, *Contemporary Documentary* is an ideal collection for students of film, media, and communication who are studying documentary film.

Daniel Marcus teaches media and documentary studies at Goucher College in Baltimore, Maryland. He is the author of *Happy Days and Wonder Years: The Fifties and the Sixties in Contemporary Cultural Politics* and editor of *ROAR! The Paper Tiger Television Guide to Media Activism.*

Selmin Kara is an Assistant Professor at OCAD University. She is interested in digital aesthetics and sound in post-cinema and documentary. Her work has appeared in *Studies in Documentary Film*, *The Oxford Handbook of Sound and Image in Digital Media*, and *Music and Sound in Nonfiction Film.*

CONTEMPORARY DOCUMENTARY

Edited by
Daniel Marcus and Selmin Kara

Routledge
Taylor & Francis Group

LONDON AND NEW YORK

First published 2016
by Routledge
2 Park Square, Milton Park, Abingdon, Oxon OX14 4RN

and by Routledge
711 Third Avenue, New York, NY 10017

Routledge is an imprint of the Taylor & Francis Group, an informa business

© 2016 selection and editorial matter, Daniel Marcus and Selmin Kara; individual chapters, the contributors

The right of Daniel Marcus and Selmin Kara to be identified as the authors of the editorial material, and of the authors for their individual chapters, has been asserted in accordance with sections 77 and 78 of the Copyright, Designs and Patents Act 1988.

British Library Cataloguing-in-Publication Data
A catalogue record for this book is available from the British Library

Library of Congress Cataloging in Publication Data
Contemporary documentary / edited by Daniel Marcus and Selmin Kara.
pages cm
Includes bibliographical references and index.
1. Documentary films—History and criticism. 2. Documentary television programs—History and criticism. I. Marcus, Daniel, 1958–, editor. II. Kara, Selmin, editor.
PN1995.9.D6C557 2015
070.1'8—dc23
2015010716

ISBN: 978-1-138-84952-5 (hbk)
ISBN: 978-1-138-84954-9 (pbk)
ISBN: 978-1-315-72549-9 (ebk)

Typeset in Bembo
by Taylor & Francis Books

CONTENTS

LIST OF FIGURES

NOTES ON CONTRIBUTORS

Jaimie Baron is Assistant Professor of Film Studies at the University of Alberta and the author of *The Archive Effect: Found Footage and the Audiovisual Experience of History* (2014). She is also director of the Festival of (In)appropriation, a festival of experimental found footage films.

Ib Bondebjerg is Professor of Film and Media, Department of Media, Cognition and Communication, University of Copenhagen. He is on the advisory board of *Studies in Documentary Film*. He has published widely on documentary. His latest book is *Engaging with Reality: Documentary and Globalization* (2014).

Kris Fallon is the Mellon Visiting Assistant Professor at the University of California, Davis. His research focuses on documentary practices across photography, film, and digital media. He is currently working on a book titled *Where Truth Lies: Digital Media and Documentary after 9/11*.

Craig Hight is an Associate Professor in Screen and Media Studies at the University of Waikato, New Zealand. His current research focuses on the relationships between digital media technologies and documentary practice, especially the variety of factors shaping online documentary cultures.

Annabelle Honess Roe teaches film studies at the University of Surrey. She has contributed chapters to a number of books and published articles in *Animation: An Interdisciplinary Journal* and the *Journal of British Cinema and Television*. Her book, *Animated Documentary*, was published by Palgrave Macmillan in 2013.

Helen Hughes teaches and researches in film studies at the University of Surrey. She is the author of *Green Documentary* (2014), the co-editor of *Deutschland im*

Spiegel seiner Filme (2000), and a co-translator of Alexander Kluge's *Cinema Stories* (2007) and *History and Obstinacy* (2014).

Selmin Kara is an Assistant Professor in Film and New Media at OCAD University in Toronto. She has contributed to *The Oxford Handbook of Sound and Image in Digital Media*; *Music and Sound in Nonfiction Film*; *Post-Cinema: Theorizing 21st-Century Film*; and *Studies in Documentary Film*.

Ohad Landesman teaches in the Film and Television Department at Tel Aviv University and in the History and Theory Department at Bezalel Academy of Art and Design in Jerusalem. His recent publications have appeared in *Studies in Documentary Film* and *Animation: An Interdisciplinary Journal*.

Daniel Marcus teaches media and documentary studies at Goucher College in Baltimore, Maryland. He is the author of *Happy Days and Wonder Years: The Fifties and the Sixties in Contemporary Cultural Politics* and editor of *ROAR! The Paper Tiger Television Guide to Media Activism*.

Heather McIntosh is co-editor, with Lisa M. Cuklanz, of *Documenting Gendered Violence* (2015). Her research focuses on documentary production, distribution, and representations. She is Assistant Professor of Mass Media at Minnesota State University, Mankato.

Bill Nichols is the author of the widely used *Introduction to Documentary* (2nd ed., 2010). He is also the author of the first general introduction to the cinema to stress film's social significance, *Engaging Cinema* (2010), as well as several other books.

Siobhan O'Flynn's research and practice have focused on interactive narrative design since 2001. She mentored over 70 prototypes at the Canadian Film Centre's Media Lab and has given master classes and keynotes across the globe. She teaches at the University of Toronto Mississauga.

Laurie Ouellette is Associate Professor of Communication Studies at the University of Minnesota. She is author of *Viewers Like You? How Public TV Failed the People*, co-author of *Better Living Through Reality TV: Television and Post-welfare Citizenship*, and editor of several anthologies, including *A Companion to Reality Television*.

Pamela Wilson teaches in the Communication program at Reinhardt University, near Atlanta, Georgia. Her research interests focus upon the cultural politics of media, particularly in relation to indigenous and minority groups. She is the co-editor of *Global Indigenous Media: Politics, Poetics and Practice* (2008).

FOREWORD

Bill Nichols

Before long, the most important work of any given moment slips into the folds of history. Contemporary now, historical soon. This may appear to be a natural process of temporal progression: things happen, priorities change, new work arrives before us and demands attention. But it is not quite so natural as it may first appear. Of all the things we experience in a given day, only a handful of these things remain actively remembered weeks, months, and sometimes years later. The same is true of new contemporary work of any kind. Much emerges, much disappears. It is the unusual and remarkable, the inspiring and sometimes imitated work that stands the test of time.

And which work is that? Many factors contribute to the answer, but one of them is the active dialogue and debate that surrounds new work. Which works and tendencies command attention? How compelling a case is made for a given direction, an emerging voice, a distinctive film? To what extent does a work speak not only to its ostensible subject but also to large questions and issues that hover around it, be they aesthetic or political, technological or institutional?

This volume poses such questions. It joins the task of separating wheat and chaff, the potentially enduring from the certainly ephemeral, the galvanizing from the soporific. It contributes to the larger process of framing issues and identifying achievements that will help determine which contemporary works come to be seen as landmarks, turning points, prototypes, models, and harbingers. Readers, as they respond to these essays and carry their ideas and assertions forward, will also contribute to shaping our common understanding of how what is happening now will belong to a larger, yet to be written history. *Contemporary Documentary* invites us to join in a dialogue to identify the achievements, tendencies, and innovations that will become part of an evolving history.

We might ask, for example, if this is a new, distinct period in documentary filmmaking. To me, the strongest argument for that claim is the enormous proliferation of new ways to make, structure, and distribute documentaries. This transformation is not unique to documentary, of course, but a function of dramatic changes brought about by digital and, especially, online media production generally. It does, though, have distinct ramifications for documentary, as Ib Bondebjerg's essay on globalization and Heather McIntosh's on crowdsourcing indicate. Recognizing this shift in the means of production, distribution, and exhibition—or viewing patterns—is clearly one primary impetus for creating this book in the first place. It links to another remarkable change brought about by the digital revolution: new forms of open-ended, interactive works that function no longer as completed texts but as nodal points, taking multiple forms based on the ways in which individual users engage with them. Interactive websites and web docs will no doubt become an area of increasing attention in the years ahead.

Given that changes brought about by the rise of a digital culture have had enormous impact across our entire culture, I see this change less as the marker of a distinct, new period in documentary production than as a sign of a broad cultural shift that has caught documentary film up within it. All forms of communication have experienced a transformation in how they function, from the rotary dial telephone of old to the cellphone and from the cloth-bound edition of a book to its intangible electronic counterpart. Documentaries—once distributed as strips of 16mm film, wound onto large reels and projected onto the screen—become transformed into thin slivers of plastic known as DVDs or into digital arrays of data, available for download or streaming from the Internet and viewable from screens of all sizes, from IMAX to handheld cellphones. These changes alone do not explain why documentaries have gained far greater attention in the last two or three decades than ever before. Printed newspapers have lost circulation and appeal, but documentaries have gained both wider distribution and popular acclaim.

In other words, documentary films continue to enjoy a golden age of production that began in the 1980s despite as well as because of the massive changes brought on by the digital revolution. The 1980s were when bold, innovative films shook free of the observational and participatory modes that arose in the 1960s and began to reassert a fluid, no holds barred approach to documentary production.[1] Observational and participatory documentaries stressed the moment of encounter between camera and subject, with the filmmaker's presence actively asserted, in the participatory mode, or rendered more invisible, in the observational mode. Films like *Chronicle of a Summer* by Jean Rouch and Edgar Morin, in which the filmmakers interact with a small group of individuals in Paris over a summer, demonstrate the former, whereas the films of Frederick Wiseman, such as *High School*, which compiles a variety of observed moments in a Philadelphia high school, without interaction or commentary by the filmmaker, illustrate the latter. Engaging as these films were, they also had limitations in that the historical past, and often the voice or stylistic presence of the filmmaker, were neglected or subordinated to the subject matter.

Then something happened. Filmmakers turned in other directions, exploring past events in vividly engaging ways or asserting their own voice and vision in boldly compelling ones. Paradigmatic of this shift are Marlon Riggs's *Tongues Untied*, a richly poetic, politically powerful celebration of black gay male identity as told through the story of the filmmaker's personal experience; Michael Moore's *Roger & Me*, with its irreverent, very personal, and highly charged confrontation with the smug, callous, and extremely greedy tactics of General Motors; and Errol Morris's *The Thin Blue Line*, a stunning, galvanizing tale of social injustice in the form of a detective story that was able to free a man wrongfully accused of murder. Kris Fallon's essay on Errol Morris here helps us see how work like this initiated the current golden age by taking documentary in bold new directions that led to a surge in theatrical exhibition and a renaissance in the form itself.

Just drawing from the innovative qualities of *The Thin Blue Line*, we can see that these new directions include: 1) the use of special effects and animation as powerful tools to add an evocative, subjective dimension to representations of reality as understood by specific individuals, 2) an emphasis on music and sound effects to give added depth and complexity to documentary representation, even though these acoustic elements, like the specific stylistic features of the image, derive from the creative filmmaking team rather than from reality, 3) a shift from direct, didactic claims and arguments, in this case about who really killed a Dallas policeman—a form highly characteristic of the expository mode of documentary that arose in the 1930s—to an emotionally dense, suspensefully told narrative that only presents its proof of the true killer's identity at the film's dramatic conclusion, 4) the use of reenactments to represent not what really happened—the classic goal of historical narrative—but what various individuals believe happened, and to do so in stylistically exaggerated ways, reminiscent of *film noir*, 5) to present real people as characters who, despite having putative status as experts, victims, perpetrators, or witnesses are seen as complex, contradictory, sometimes self-destructive figures capable of deception as well as self-deception (qualities more commonly found in fiction films), 6) a fresh emphasis on performance and self-presentation as fraught ground in which masks, deceptions, delusions, and beliefs play as important, if not more important, a role as truth claims and evidential assertions, and 7) a mixing of modes that allowed participatory staples like interviews to be married to the more expressive, stylistically free-form qualities of the performative documentary. Morris also hired a production designer for this film and shot in 35mm, giving the film a polished, captivating look, an approach not universally adopted since, but a clear sign that the range of representational strategies was wide open, from the grainiest of catch-as-catch-can cinematography to the most sumptuous of visual feasts.

These qualities have been so widely adopted, in such diverse ways, that they may no longer seem as striking as they did in 1988. That can readily be a sign of just how influential Morris's film has been to the initiation of the current golden age of documentary as it now spills into the domain of new technologies and fresh opportunities. These qualities also spotlight some of the trends that other filmmakers have made even more apparent in the work that has emerged in the 1990s and the early part of the twenty-first century. I will point out four such trends that are with us, and note another that is less a trend than a side current of some significance.

The first of these revolves around the questions of performance and its representation. This is where we encounter questions about people's motives and intentions, their levels of awareness and self-awareness, their abilities to deceive, manipulate, and convince others and sometimes themselves about the nature of reality. A vivid and relatively straightforward example is Alex Gibney's *Enron: The Smartest Guys in the Room*. Gibney shows us the rope the executives of Enron fashioned for themselves in terms of their public statements and claims, presenting the corporation as an emerging giant in the energy field, only to undercut their public claims with vivid evidence of deception, manipulation, and lies. On a radically different level, Rithy Panh's *S-21* and Joshua Oppenheimer's *The Act of Killing* explore the mentality of state sanctioned guards and killers, in Cambodia and Indonesia respectively. The filmmakers allow the perpetrators of terrible crimes the opportunity to represent themselves as they wish, in lurid reenactments of their torture and execution tactics in the case of *The Act of Killing*. Their consciousness does not appear to embrace the idea of guilt; the viewer boggles at their rationalizations, their tunnel vision, their amorality. Reenactments, which had faded from the scene in the 1960s, return in compellingly innovative forms, carrying the innovative departures noted in *The Thin Blue Line* to new heights.

We have come a long way from the world of Nanook and other realist heroes of documentary who live their lives with some measure of integrity and dignity. Documentary filmmakers have learned to look into the heart of darkness and to help us understand the layers of deception and self-deception that operate in what might otherwise seem an ultimately unproblematic reality. As Laurie Ouellette's essay, *"True Life*: The Voice of Television Documentary," demonstrates, these lessons have spilled over into reality television in many different forms. Ouellette focuses on an MTV series that mixes first-person testimonial and third-person commentary as it explores the lives of young people confronting specific challenges, from homelessness to coming out. The series mixes elements of type-casting and topical issues with portraits of complex, highly distinct individuals. It therefore manages to convey much more of the complexity with which real people confront large questions than the more traditional documentary's focus on exemplary figures and abstract claims that mainly serve to reinforce the broad thematic goals of the filmmaker.

Craig Hight's essay, "The Mockumentary," and Ohad Landesman's essay, "Lying to Be Real: The Aesthetics of Ambiguity in Docufictions," take questions of performance and representation to another level as they investigate how various films throw into question the representational claims of the documentary form itself. Here we see how some films can increase our awareness of how much that passes for claims about reality is, in fact, a function of conventions that can be mocked or played with in fictional form, in the case of Hight's essay, or rendered profoundly ambiguous in their effect, in the case of Landesman's. From *This Is Spinal Tap* to *Borat: Cultural Learnings of America to Make Benefit Glorious Nation of Kazakhstan*, some films play, gleefully, with the solemnity of the traditional documentary. These works share a desire to shake up conventions and confound viewers. They call our assumptions about documentary as a form into question. We can no longer sort out actual situations and events from their cinematic representation, the fictitious from the factual, with any true certainty. Some works not only invite us to question the implications of this conundrum for documentary itself, they also attest to the vitality of a form that can call its assumptions into question and be all the stronger for it. Documentaries can entertain and confound as much as they can inform and inspire. What is possible, and what can be said about what is possible, has expanded dramatically since the 1980s.

A second trend clearly present in *The Thin Blue Line* is the turn to special effects and animation to expand the range of how documentaries can give representation to the historical world. These are resources commanded by the filmmaker; slow motion and rotoscoping, for example, modify the indexical link between an image and what it refers to, a link that has, rightly or wrongly, played a large role in giving the documentary film its sense of authenticity. A milkshake not only flies through the night sky, perfectly illuminated and in slow motion, in one of *The Thin Blue Line*'s reenactments, but its presence does nothing to clarify who killed the policeman. It seems thematically gratuitous but aesthetically engaging, and yet it is part and parcel of Morris's indirect, evocative style, which gives a sense of how people see their world and retrieve their memories in a subjective, inconclusive way that we must assess from our own standpoint. Animation contributes mightily to the effort to convey not only what comprises reality at a factual level but also what it feels like to inhabit that reality in a particular way or to see it with the distinctive eye of a filmmaker. It expands the evocative power of the documentary form and is, therefore, as Annabelle Honess Roe's essay, "Animated Documentary," demonstrates, a resource used increasingly often and with greater acceptance than ever before.

A third trend, well underway for some time, involves the use of archival footage. Finding footage that stems from earlier sources has long been of value to the documentary filmmaker who wants to address historical subjects. In many cases, archival footage can simply play an evidential role, showing what it was really like at an earlier time, as it routinely does in Ken Burns's films, from *The Civil War* to *The Roosevelts*. But it can do much more. Films, like those of Péter Forgács, take home movies and convert them into a powerful form of "private history." His *Maelstrom*, for example, uses the home movies of a Jewish Dutch family from the 1930s and 40s to chronicle their slowly worsening situation as the Nazis occupy the Netherlands and pass one anti-Semitic law after another. Without a voiceover commentary to give us the larger historical picture but with many special effects, compelling music, and a suspenseful, real life story, Forgács's remarkable work stands as one example of how much life remains in found footage that has already served one purpose but can continue to serve many more.

Jaimie Baron's essay, "The Ethics of Appropriation: 'Misusing' the Found Document in *Suitcase of Love and Shame* and *A Film Unfinished*," takes us into the domain of the archive and its uses from an ethical perspective and adds another dimension to questions of how to reuse preexisting material. As Baron demonstrates, many recent films not only raise questions about the uses and misuses of archival footage, they also prompt us to ask what ethical challenges arise for the filmmaker when she draws our attention to sounds and images from the past. What might have been personal and private no longer is; what was understood as authentic can be exposed for the distortions and manipulations beneath its surface. These are matters of considerable importance when the visual so often serves as evidence and yet is, like the documentary form itself, open to fabrications that may not be immediately obvious.

A fourth trend, evident in many recent works, is a shift away from information and advocacy for a specific position on an issue to the subjective and experiential, an awareness of what it feels like to live in the world in a particular way. This trend runs counter to the tradition of the documentary as a political tool in a direct sense, a vital element of the form, from the patriotic call to duty embedded in *Why We Fight*, the series of films directed by Frank Capra made to explain America's entry into World War II, to the compelling attack on the Bush administration's use of 9/11 as the rationale for an unjustifiable war against Iraq in Michael Moore's *Fahrenheit 9/11*. A large part of the appeal of *Nanook of the North* was its claim to depict life in the Arctic at an immediate, intimate level by telling the story of Nanook's struggle for survival for himself and his family. Pressing social issues—from the consolidation of power in the new Soviet Union to the ravages of the Great Depression, and from the fight for freedom and democracy during World War II to the battle against Communism in the Cold War—drew the documentary into the trenches of numerous conflicts and confrontations. The poetic, romantic voice of Robert Flaherty seemed a reminder of a distant, more idyllic age.

But not for everyone. Although not following in Flaherty's footsteps directly, and clearly inspired by the wide range of alternatives arising in the 1980s, many documentary filmmakers took a renewed interest in how they could convey what it feels like to live in the world in a particular way or to see the world from a distinct perspective. The 1980s harbinger of this trend, preceding *The Thin Blue Line* by some six years, is Godfrey Reggio's *Koyaanisqatsi*. This film is an astonishingly poetic view of the world in its natural and human-altered states; without commentary of any kind, but with a mesmerizing musical score by Phillip Glass, it is a vivid warning against the kind of environmental devastation that has only become a more pressing issue since.

More recent, paradigmatic examples of a poetic, experiential emphasis in documentary are the two most recent films of Lucien Castaing-Taylor, *Sweetgrass* and *Leviathan*, co-directed by Ilisa Barbash and Verena Paravel, respectively. Although described as products of the "Sensory Ethnography Lab" at Harvard, they are far more sensory than ethnographic in any customary sense. The stress is on what sheepherding and commercial sea fishing are like at an experiential level rather than in environmental, economic, or sociological terms. The imagery, especially in *Leviathan*, possesses an eerie, mysterious quality in which the human figure, let alone any distinct individual, is difficult to recognize. The stress is on the sounds and images that emanate from a fishing boat like specters from a mysterious, nocturnal, aquatic world. Like the archive-based films of Péter Forgács, such work reminds us that documentaries have a strongly affective dimension that can see the world with fresh, invigorating eyes, leaving much of the socio-political explanation and problem-solving argumentation for other occasions.

Discussion of these and other trends is well represented in this volume. The essays not only see the trends I mention here as significant ones, they also tackle the question of globalization and its representation, the uses of crowdsourcing as a new production tool, and the many ways in which indigenous media have sought to address less the ethnographic distinctiveness of a given people than the complex imbrications of ethnicity, gender, and sovereignty in negotiations between indigenous peoples and a not always attentive dominant culture. Collectively, the essays take the pulse of documentary today and suggest directions in which it is headed.

If there is a blind spot, it is one common to the field of documentary criticism generally: the place of a conservative, even at times fundamentalist wing to documentary production. Dinesh d'Souza's feature-length and high-grossing film *2016: Obama's America* is a prime example. It has been ranked as the fourth highest-grossing documentary ever in the United States, and yet few of the most regular documentary followers have seen it and fewer still have commented on it. It belongs to a different universe in some ways, circulating largely among conservative groups and in theaters outside the major coastal cities, and on DVD (Netflix carries it). The conservative documentary, like mockumentary and docufiction, serves a valuable function, outside its basic social purpose: it reminds us that the codes and conventions, the models and modes that go to make up the documentary tradition are not necessarily in the service of progressive ends, and do not assure any such end in and of themselves.

The same qualities that make for a great documentary with a progressive agenda such as *Enron: The Smartest Guys in the Room*, *The Thin Blue Line*, *The Act of Killing*, or *The Gleaners and I* can readily be turned to radically different political ends. That there are relatively few conservative documentaries is testimony less to any intrinsic quality found in documentary—though we may sometimes be prone to assume such a quality exists—than to the dominance of a conservative agenda in so much of the mainstream media. It is a perspective that does not need the more personal and more artisanal dimension documentaries contribute when conservatism has the resources of so much of the news and entertainment media at its disposal, in the form both of work that adopts a conservative perspective and of work that, as "just entertainment," distracts and placates rather than disturbs and agitates. This is an area that invites a study of its own.

Meanwhile, these essays help bring into sharper focus trends and directions giving shape to a wide swath of documentary production today, with its broad range of technological, aesthetic, social, and political perspectives. How we will regard these trends and this work in future decades remains to be seen, but the initial groundwork for those future assessments lies here, and now, in this pioneering look at the work and issues that matter today.

Note

1 I discuss the modes of documentary—the specific forms documentaries adopt—along with the models—from essays and diaries to news reports and written histories—in *Introduction to Documentary*, 2nd ed., Bloomington and Indianapolis: Indiana University Press, 2010.

INTRODUCTION

Situating Contemporary Documentary

Selmin Kara and Daniel Marcus

Accounting for documentary in the twenty-first century is no simple task. Like any other attempt at periodization, trying to fit the emergent qualities, tendencies, and aesthetics of a heterogeneous filmic practice under the banner of "contemporary" makes us miss one of the guiding principles behind documentary altogether: that for the pioneers and the most celebrated delegates of the form, documenting the world through new audiovisual technologies has always been about finding new ways to engage with reality, giving even the earliest films an indelible seal of contemporaneity. To echo the sentiments of Werner Herzog, there is a sense in which every documentary has aspired to take the viewer on a one-way-ticket journey to see the world through a fresh lens, from which there might be no return, as a reflective response to social and technological change. While putting together this anthology, we have been deeply aware of this fact; yet, as documentary media scholars and instructors ourselves, we also feel the need to confront the rapidly changing face of the field in the post-cinematic era, in which emerging technologies (not necessarily cinematic in origin) and the global socio-political order give rise to new forms of sensibilities.

Under the new media regime of the twenty-first century, which is governed by the extra-cinematic (such as the data culture, social and locative media, immersive technologies, video games, animation, and graphic and experience design, to name a few growing influences), documentary seems to have preserved if not increased its popularity, redefining itself as a type of connector or creative hub among vast fields of media activity. Producers such as Michael Moore and Morgan Spurlock have become well-known figures far beyond the traditional circles of documentary viewers, and filmmakers like Patricio Guzman, Pedro Costa, and Abbas Kiarostami have made crossovers between fiction and nonfiction filmmaking a common phenomenon. New forms of documentary have emerged; while narrative and artists' films have been enjoying a much-hailed "documentary turn," nonfiction projects have been further hybridized with fictional narratives and the mingled aesthetics of various media. In the meantime, documentary media studies has reached a certain level of maturity since its inception in the 1960s and disciplinary growth in the 1990s, allowing scholars and historians to respond to the accelerated transformations in the form at a faster, more propitious rate. The growing number of monographs, edited volumes, conferences, and journal issues dedicated exclusively to the field, and work undertaken in documentary-specific new media research labs as well as graduate academic and production programs, are testament to its coming-of-age.

This anthology, then, stems from a desire to provide readers (scholars, practitioners, students, and enthusiasts of documentary) with an entry point to some of the stylistic, aesthetic, and conjectural developments that have been central to documentary filmmaking in the early stages of this century, in order to highlight the creative evolution of the form without losing sight of its history. We hope that the reader will find in the forward push and expansive outlook of "contemporary documentary" both a momentum and a continuum, without being merely attracted by the promise of the new in the current.

For practical reasons, what we call contemporary in this anthology refers to post-1985 documentary, with an emphasis on digital forms and aesthetics. This kind of periodization is becoming more commonplace in academia with the increasing number of undergraduate courses that are specifically designed to focus on recent history. We acknowledge that it often privileges a specific kind of lineage (locating in the "self-reflexive" turn an all-too-often-articulated decisive moment for the revival of documentary in the late 1980s), yet it also allows room for making an argument against technological determinism in understanding current trends. It stays clear of the digital turn as an alternative determining moment. In focusing on digital forms and aesthetics, we wish to neither go against the legacy of documentary self-reflexivity nor hail the shift to digital technologies as the single most note-worthy watershed point in history. Bracketing contemporary documentary within these two moments at times leads to a dismissal of the influence of important documentary movements, such as guerilla, television, feminist media, and video activism dating back to the 1960s, that paved the way for various contemporary developments; therefore, the 1980s in this collection is not an absolute marker. Rather, it functions as a bookmark that facilitates a conversation about certain emerging forms and tendencies, with constant reminders to the reader throughout the text of precedents and connections to these forms in the broader documentary tradition.

Instead of offering an all-inclusive study, the anthology invites the reader to scout the vast terrain of contemporary documentary through chapter-length studies of some of the more established forms that employ digital technologies widely, such as interactive documentaries, crowd-sourced documentaries, appropriated films, animated docs, auteur docs, and reality-TV-inspired documentaries. These chapters serve to offer an entry point to larger discussions about what documentary means today—not to be bogged down once again by the tired quest for definition but as a means to map some of the ways in which film and media makers have been expanding the future's horizon. Each chapter provides a broad introduction to a documentary subject, followed by case studies of two or three documentary works that constitute innovative or evocative examples. We have paid special attention to including chapters that are diverse in terms of not only their topics and examples, but also their methodologies and geographical focus. The reader will find that the chapters draw from a wide range of approaches to documentary, including but not limited to film theory, social theory, political theory, ethics, new media, and experience design. The collection includes a chapter based on interviews with documentary makers (Heather McIntosh's take on crowdsourcing), and another that highlights practice-based knowledge as well as theory (Siobhan O'Flynn's analysis of experience design in interactive docs). By not making categorical distinctions between these methodologies, we want to encourage an interdisciplinary dialogue, in which documentary frees itself from the necessity of gatekeeping and enjoys an open field of play. As for the geographical focus, the case studies extend to documentary works that engage with issues and production contexts in various countries, continents, and indigenous territories. Ib Bondebjerg's analysis of the promotion of cosmopolitan dialogues in multi-platform collaborative projects among independent filmmakers from countries as culturally distinct as Bolivia, China, Denmark, Egypt, Pakistan, Liberia, and Russia, and Pamela Wilson's mapping of indigenous media production across the "Fourth World" (indigenous communities in Canada, New Zealand, Australia) demonstrate the spread of production and distribution opportunities and the importance of seeing current developments as global phenomena.

The use of multiple short case studies in most chapters reflects the contemporary diffusion of production resources through video and digital technology, the sense of ongoing experimentation and conversation among documentary producers today, and the variety of works that are subsumed within the concept of documentary in the twenty-first century. At the same time, limiting the number of examples in each chapter enables us to introduce specific works with sufficient context and analysis to promote serious understanding of their significant features and importance to the field. This resonates with our appreciation for analyses that value close readings and attention to details, continuing on the path opened by some of the earlier anthologies in the field, such as Barry Keith Grant and Jeanette Sloniowski's now updated *Documenting the Documentary*. In the same spirit with which Jaimie Baron takes up found-footage and appropriation films that stem from a deeply seated passion for the found document, the case studies serve to "illuminate the multiple layers of interpretation involved" in the reception of contemporary documentary.

Lastly, we have organized the chapters in the anthology under two sections, not because they lend themselves to clear, thoroughly separate categorizations, but in order to provide the readers with two lenses through which they can approach the subjects covered. Accordingly, the first section brings together chapters on emergent or newly popular documentary forms, genres, and innovations in the twenty-first century, while the second takes up older forms of documentary that have found new contexts in the digital era. In his chapter on docufiction, Ohad Landesman analyzes films "that blur or simply ignore the distinctions between fiction and nonfiction," drawing attention to the fact that in light of the significant number of internationally acclaimed filmmakers that have leaned toward crossovers since the 2000s, formal hybridity and a foregrounding of the fact–fiction continuum have become increasingly acceptable and cherished, especially in world cinema. As Landesman argues, digital (camcorder or DV) aesthetics often becomes the mediating factor in docufictions, rendering it easier to give fictional or performative sequences an immediately recognized documentary look, while filmmakers such as Jia Zhangke use high-definition cameras to make the distinction between real and fictional indiscernible as an alternative strategy. Taking up another hybrid format that is sometimes confused with docufiction, Craig Hight looks at the emergent trends in mockumentary, a fictional form that is known for its extensive application of documentary conventions. What he detects in examples as diverse as *The Office* franchise, supernatural horror films like *Paranormal Activity*, and satirical faux documentaries like *Borat* is a naturalization of the mockumentary discourse with new trends like mocusoaps and mockumentary hoaxes in the contemporary era. Annabelle Honess Roe, Heather McIntosh, and Siobhan O'Flynn look at more technology-specific genres in their chapters on animated docs, crowd-sourced docs, and interactive documentaries, also frequently referred to as i-Docs, respectively. The last chapter in this section is on a form that can also be considered an older mode of filmmaking that finds a new context in the digital era: indigenous filmmaking. However, as Pamela Wilson points out, the phenomenon of indigenous media has developed within the context of globalization and the introduction of indigenous cultural groups to the technical tools of modern communication and media technology; therefore, indigenous media making belongs to the logic of emergent media more than traditional cinematic paradigms, themselves always being in flux.

Section two deals with documentary practices and activity that rub against other cultural phenomena, as well as the reformulation of older forms of documentality within new contexts, brought about by technological, socio-political, cultural, and economic change. Laurie Ouellette looks at the transformation of factual/reality television in recent decades, especially in the context of MTV's transition from a music video channel toward reality-television-style documentary programming, and questions what it means to represent "documentary voice" today. Kris Fallon and Helen Hughes investigate the contemporary status of the auteur documentary in two contexts: that of documentary auteur Errol Morris engaging with new media as archival documents, and directors like Werner Herzog, Agnès Varda, and Spike Lee offering new strategies of survival to independent filmmakers through delineating new venues of authorship and their multi-media engagements. Also questioning the archive in the digital era, Jaimie Baron discusses the changes in attitudes and approaches toward found footage films, analyzing the ethical dimensions of appropriation, use, misuse, and abuse of found footage within a contemporary framework. Lastly, Ib Bondebjerg and Daniel Marcus revisit the political role and functions of media and documentary, by contextualizing transnational collaborative documentaries that promote cosmopolitanism and activist documentaries within contemporary global realities.

Undoubtedly, the subjects and sections outlined above map the terrain of contemporary documentary in a non-exhaustive fashion, leaving much room for further exploration. In his foreword, Bill Nichols writes about the regrettable lack of chapters on conservative documentary, which has been a very strong trend in both the televisual and the theatrical realms as well as on the Internet. In the same spirit of an appreciation for all emergent forms of documentary, we would like to point the readers to various other trends that this anthology does not cover but that we find evocative of the future of the field, such as:

- Documentary games for change: This is a documentary form that aims to raise awareness about socio-political, cultural, or environmental issues through blending documentary footage with interactive or gaming components, and utilizing gaming engines and mobile apps. It can be seen as a by-product of the media industries' move toward cross-platform or transmedia projects, especially in the last two decades. The crossover between documentary and gaming is dynamic. There has been a significant surge in interest and funding in the field for the development of games for change, with venues like The Games For Change Festival (G4C) bringing together media makers, funders, corporations, international and government agencies, NGOs, and educators to facilitate strategic partnerships. Recent examples such as indigenous-owned games company Upper One Games' 2014 puzzle-platformer *Never Alone*, which allows players to explore the culture and the traditional lore of the Alaska native peoples, show the level of creativity the form has reached.
- Technology-driven experimental documentary forms like sensory ethnographic films and drone documentaries: These forms highlight the use of emerging technologies with a capacity for audiovisual documentation in diverse projects that often decenter human-centered vision by problematizing the agency behind the camera. The multi-sensory research labs established in academic institutions, such as Harvard's Sensory Ethnography Lab and MIT's Open Documentary Lab, help expand the boundaries of documentary by foregrounding the role of the senses beyond merely vision and audition in perception, as well as the role of technologies in changing our phenomenological relationship to the world.
- Locative, wearable, and mobile media docs: Technologies such as global positioning systems, motion-sensing input devices and wearable computers that can be integrated into clothing, accessories, or prostheses, and portable devices like smartphones are also creating amorphous forms of documentary. Producers, coders, hackers, the maker communities, artists, and performers collaborate to give an expression to location-based and embodied experiences of subjects while creating new, mediated social spaces.
- 3D stereoscopic vision and IMAX documentaries: These are documentaries that challenge the boundaries of the frame and analogue cinema's 2D vision. While high-frame-rate cinema brings fiction films closer to a documentary aesthetic in terms of their look, contemporary documentaries experiment with technologies

like 3D and IMAX, which have been transforming fiction cinema, to provide more immersive forms of storytelling.

- Virtual and augmented reality documentaries, or what International Documentary Film Festival Amsterdam (IDFA)'s DocLab calls "documentary storytelling in the age of the interface."
- Live cinema documentaries that blend VJ software-facilitated simultaneous editing of documentary footage, audio, and music by video performance artists and musicians in multiscreen exhibition venues.
- Installation and expanded documentaries.
- Experimental and avant-docs.
- Culture jamming and art activist documentaries that take advantage of data manipulation, visualization, and curation.
- Documentaries such as *Zidane: A 21st Century Portrait*, which draw from the stylistic techniques of sports television (instant replay, bipolar lens shifts, multiple cameras trained on a single subject) to turn hypermediated realities into hypnotic meditations.

The diversity of such forms attests to the rapidly changing visage and future potential of documentary as a media art practice that easily finds a home outside the confines of the cinematic in a post-cinematic era. The anthology aims to provide paths to follow while readers delve into this open field of possibility, and induce curiosity about contemporary documentary in its various incarnations, changing forms, and latent capacities.

We would like to thank Natalie Foster and Sheni Kruger at Routledge for their support and assistance, and Dorie Chevlen for her copy editing of one portion of the volume. We would also like to thank our colleagues at OCAD University and Goucher College, and all of the contributors to this book.

PART I

Forms, Genres, Innovations

1

LYING TO BE REAL

The Aesthetics of Ambiguity in Docufictions

Ohad Landesman

> Man is least himself when he talks in his own person. Give him a mask, and he will
> tell you the truth.
>
> (Oscar Wilde)

Introduction

One of the most striking developments in recent documentary cinema is the
emergence of films that blur or simply ignore the distinctions between fiction and
nonfiction, staking out instead what Robert Koehler describes as "the zone of the
cinema free of, or perhaps more precisely in between, hardened fact and invented
fiction" (2009). In films from different geopolitical contexts, such as *Ten* (Abbas
Kiarostami, 2002), *Ford Transit* (Hany Abu-Assad, 2002), *The Roof* (Kamal Aljafari,
2006), *Our Beloved Month of August* (Miguel Gomes, 2008), and *Alamar* (Pedro
Gonzales Rubio, 2009), truth and fiction are systematically intermingled, compos-
sible from the very beginning. Such a strategy of documentary and fiction hybridity,
the result of which I will refer to here as "docufictions,"[1] produces a lingering
bafflement about definition. Docufictions allow a viewer to simultaneously adopt
different attitudes and embrace distinct modes of engagement toward them, without
these necessarily conflicting with one another. By doing so, they tap into a viewer's
familiarity with contemporary paradigms of representation, and take advantage of
this knowledge to expand and challenge any prescribed and rigid understanding of
what constitutes a film as a documentary. Such a viewing mode of instability, an
ongoing state of uncertainty about the possibility of placing a film within definitive
and familiar categories, is not merely the result of a playful hoax, but the function
of mixed intentions of the filmmakers that invite contradictory expectations from
an audience. To paraphrase Noël Carroll, the ambiguity produced between fiction
and nonfiction makes difficult a distinction "between the commitments of the
texts," and not just "between the surface structures of the texts" (1996: 287).

While only limited attention to the docufiction has been given in academic texts, such a strategy of commingling fact and fiction has been gaining a lot of buzz lately in critical circles. Dennis Lim speaks of films that "could be said to blur or thwart or simply ignore the distinctions between fiction and nonfiction, staking out instead a productive liminal zone in between" (2012). Analyzing recent docufictions such as *Our Beloved Month of August*, which fluctuates between "a musical, a travelogue," and a "quasi-incestuous family melodrama," or *Alamar*, where a real-life father and son embark on a fishing trip conceived and organized for the purposes of the film, he points to how "impure forms" are invented in order to match "impure content." With a similar interest, and focusing on other works such as *La Libertad* (Lisandro Alonso, 2001) and *Sweetgrass* (Lucien Castaing-Taylor and Ilisa Barbash, 2009), Koehler recognizes this phenomenon as a contemporary and important moment in film culture. "We have been living through an incredible period of the cinema of in-between-ness," he observes (2009). Finally, in his book about cinema in the twenty-first century, J. Hoberman makes a reference to docufictions and characterizes works such as *The Libertad* and *Paraguayan Hammock* (Paz Encina, 2006) as "successors to the short-lived Dogme movement in the form of modestly produced motion pictures" (2012: 23). Neither pseudo- nor mock-documentaries, these films are categorized by Hoberman as "situation documentaries," films that mark their (digital or analogue) media-specific realness "through the use of long takes, minimal editing, behavioral performances, and leisurely contemplation of their subjects or setting. Drama is subsumed in observation. Landscape trumps performance" (2012: 23).

My interest in this chapter is to broaden this discussion academically, and to outline the blurry contours of the docufiction, analyze its strategies, and contextualize it both historically and theoretically. The two case studies I will focus on are the penetrating study of poverty *In Vanda's Room* (Pedro Costa, 2000) and the mnemonic journey to modern-day China *24 City* (Jia Zhangke, 2008), hybrids of fictive and documentary storytelling made with digital technology. How does digitality, I will ask, play into their efforts to creatively mediate truth and craft performance? The spotlight put on new technologies is not meant to suggest any notion of deterministic evolution in documentary, or to reduce the formal tendency discussed to a cinematic trend made possible by technical means only. The role of the digital within the construction of docufiction aesthetics is inseparable from a complex web of other historical, economic, and political factors, among which the evolutionary trajectory of documentary is of major importance. Therefore, in the following sections, I will account for this important context, and further explore the notion of camcorder aesthetics and the effect of medium variations, address the important role a viewer may take in recognizing and defining a filmic text as a documentary, and question the notion of documentary performance.

Historical precedents and the mockumentary paradigm

Surely, there is nothing essentially groundbreaking here. Documentaries have a long history of putting together fiction and reality that the modest scope of this chapter could not sufficiently address. A few early examples include the recourse to fiction in order to iterate a daily activity in *La Terra Trema* (Luchino Visconti, 1948) and *Nanook of the North* (Robert Flaherty, 1922), the performative agit-props of Michael Moore, and the meticulously stylized reenactments by Errol Morris. "Every documentary representation," as Michael Renov clearly points out, "depends upon its own detour from the real, through the defiles of the audio-visual signifier" (1993: 7). Nonetheless, the degree to which fiction and documentary are having their way with each other nowadays is quite striking, inviting further discussion on this formal and thematic mix.

Instead of providing a comprehensive list of historical precedents, I wish to briefly point to how the docufiction has been often bordering and flirting with another format of formal hybridity, the mockumentary. Despite the difficulty in drawing clear lines between the two, an effort to highlight those blurry edges is relevant here. Mockumentaries (or mock-documentaries) are first and foremost fictional texts that mimic and exhaust documentary codes and conventions, requiring the viewer to momentarily disavow their fictional fakeness. Docufictions, on the other hand, invite a viewer to welcome and embrace their aesthetic hybridity as a formal strategy meant not so much to dupe, mislead, or mock, but *to offer a different tactic that exists along a fact–fictional continuum*. In other words, although mockumentaries emphasize the fabrications of truth, their documentary facet seems to be largely sacrificed to the fictional. Docufictions, on the other hand, displace that skepticism by foregrounding relationships with both fictional and factual discourses, and distill truth even from a constructed narrative.

Two early exemplars for such a blurred distinction between mockumentary and docufiction, made at roughly the same time during the tumultuous 1960s, are *David Holzman's Diary* (Jim McBride, 1968) and *Medium Cool* (Haskell Wexler, 1969). While both exploit the aesthetics of *cinéma vérité*, the privileged cinematic idiom during the time of their making, it is the former that levels a satirical comment on its conventions to fabricate an illusion of authenticity, while the latter embraces the strategy of infusing reality into a fictional story. *David Holzman's Diary*'s main character is a young man presenting himself to the viewer as David Holzman, an obsessive filmmaker documenting his life in New York City over the course of a week with a 16mm Eclair camera. Holzman is filming inside his apartment, introducing us to his girlfriend and friends, and intimately sharing with us every aspect of his unfolding life. A fictional character played out by Kit Carson, Holzman is acting on Jean-Luc Godard's famous statement according to which "film is truth 24 times a second" (*Le Petit Soldat*, 1963) and pretending that the only thing giving meaning to his life is the act of recording it with his camera. *David Holzman's Diary* is a satirical fiction posing as a documentary, one that deconstructs the aesthetics of *cinéma vérité* down to its individual components (sync-sound recording, grainy black-and-white shooting, and a handheld camera) in order to expose their artificiality. In *Medium Cool*, however, it is never clear where the partly scripted narrative begins and where the reality that unfolds in the background engulfs it. The relatively superficial plot focuses on a television news cameraman who grows fond of a single mother whose husband has left for uncertain reasons. What makes the film remarkable is how it places its fictional characters in real situations during a strong political upheaval of counterculture in the United States, infusing reality into a fictional story. Such hybridity becomes all the more dominant during the final sequence, when footage from the real-life events of the 1968 Democratic National Convention in Chicago penetrates the fictional story of the cameraman's love affair.

Another early example that similarly thwarts clear boundaries between fiction and nonfiction is *Daughter Rite* (Michelle Citron, 1979), a film that explores the position of women in a nuclear family by looking at the relationship between two women and their mother. *Daughter Rite* is essentially acted, but the characters' roles and dialogues in it are drawn from research and real interviews. It encourages the viewer to question whether the home movie footage represents real images of the narrator's relationship with her mother or not, and if the narrator's voice is indeed the filmmaker's. In fact, *cinéma vérité* segments sometimes relate to the footage or the voice, while other times they do not. As in *Medium Cool*, strategies of hybridity walk a thin line between producing a mockumentary effect of deception for the purpose of deconstruction and embracing a more advanced strategy of documentation.

Within the unwritten history of contemporary docufictions, nothing serves as a better illustration of how the aesthetics of ambiguity are manufactured through new modes of production than the first provocative films of the Danish Dogme 95 group. Armed with a teasing manifesto, advocating both earnestly and jokingly an alternative film practice aiming to counter escapist illusion with gritty realism, Dogme filmmakers Lars von Trier and Thomas Vinterberg scribbled (in less than 45 minutes) a taxonomy of aesthetic restrictions in hope of eliciting a new creative freedom in film. The document, publicly known as "The Vow of Chastity," is in the tradition of the fierce attacks by French New Wave and Italian neo-realist filmmakers on stagnant mainstream cinema. *The Idiots (Idioterne)* (Lars von Trier, 1998), a compelling expression of those restrictions, is a film that cleverly exploits the look and feel of DV to produce a docufiction that borders on a mockumentary. It focuses on an anarchist group of avant-garde pranksters who are playfully faking mental disability, and tells their story in both a scripted and an improvised manner. While the group's behavior targets the hypocrisy of bourgeois culture and seeks to shamelessly subvert its middle-class values, the style of the film defies not only traditional Hollywood filmmaking, but also the possibility of making any clear distinction between its fiction and documentary tenets. To put it differently, the act of "spassing/spazzing" in the film (the faking of disability) formally weds with the attempt to manufacture a documentary style.

Strategically, the film never really provides a definitive "recipe" or a template of formal cues (traditional credits, for example) for how to read it. It manufactures inconsistent and contradictory suggestions that are partly structured around our familiarity with filmic codes and conventions. Talking head interviews made post facto, shaky and sloppy handheld camerawork, loosely bordered shots that go in and out of focus, jump cuts that disrupt continuity, and degraded video quality that results from the DV-to-film transfer all connote a documentary mode of engagement and highlight photographic presence. Since *The Idiots* deals mainly with role-playing, its

FIGURE 1.1 *The Idiots* (*Idioterne*) (Lars von Trier, 1998): exploiting the look of DV for manufacturing a documentary style.

central indeterminacy lies within specific moments of performativity that make it particularly difficult to decide if what we are watching is real or not. The film's playful employment of documentary conventions and strategic use of DV aesthetics would become highly influential in the years to come for other filmmakers engaging with the docufiction format.

Both mockumentaries and docufictions help to expand our understanding of what constitutes a documentary, the former by means of parody or pure fakery, and the latter by forming a troubled relationship with the real. Such an understanding of both modes, which are not always easy to separate from each other, enables us to recognize in them a strong documentary dimension, or at least one that stems from a certain aspiration to document, without splitting hairs in making a clear distinction between the two.[2] In the docufictions I will discuss below, it is fiction that is diffused into reality without the risk of shattering the essence of the text as being partly a documentary, or the experience of it as such. The skepticism it infuses into the documentary structure, I argue, works to expand its epistemological value and not necessarily compromise it.

"Judgment comes easy in documentary": *In Vanda's Room* and the need to play oneself

Ossos (1997), *In Vanda's Room* (2000) and *Colossal Youth* (2006) are three films made by the Portuguese filmmaker Pedro Costa. Referred to by critics as "The

Fontainhas Trilogy," they focus on a neighborhood in Lisbon that does not exist anymore, a place that was completely demolished between the years 2000 and 2005. As such, the films chronicle the life of Fontainhas's inhabitants, a community of native Portuguese and immigrants from Portugal's former colonies, who were relocated to public housing after bulldozers tore down their homes. *In Vanda's Room*, the second installment in the trilogy, marks an important turning point in Costa's method of filmmaking and use of technology. While the previous film, *Ossos*, was a fiction film shot professionally on 35mm, *In Vanda's Room* involves no set or professional actors, and features low-budget digital filmmaking that takes place in one location only. Costa spent over six months with the people living in Fontainhas, and used a small Panasonic DVX 100 camera to shoot more than 150 hours of footage. *In Vanda's Room* is therefore not only a remarkable shift from the fiction of *Ossos* toward a unique documenting strategy, but also a change of scale, a transition from "working under 'professional' conditions to working in small communities akin to family contexts" (Pantenburg 2010: 56). Costa abandoned traditional, tightly crafted filmmaking because he felt it would not do justice to the community of despair he was trying to represent in Fontainhas. His pursuit of cinematic authenticity clearly resonates with the provocations of the Danish Dogme 95 movement at the turn of the millennium. It also perpetuates the premise of the Italian neo-realists, who were advocating in the 1940s the use of smaller shooting crews in real locations with no artificial lighting.

Costa was shooting in Fontainhas on a daily basis, capturing the everyday while subtracting himself as much as possible from the reality he documented. With his DV camera he remained unobtrusive, helping his subjects slowly forget his presence (or at least become oblivious to it), and accept him "not as a film-maker but as a trustworthy fellow inhabitant" (Pantenburg 2010: 58). However, while *In Vanda's Room* may look and feel like a straightforward documentary for most viewers, most of the scenes in it are rehearsed and were taken using multiple takes. In fact, it was Vanda who urged Costa to transform her from a predetermined fictional character in *Ossos* (Clotilde) to a destabilized documentary subject in the second film, in order to better reflect her true self. Accordingly, Costa decided that the neighborhood's residents would *play themselves* and become characters in a movie about their life. The two main characters, sisters Vanda and Zita Duarte, are mostly seen sitting on a bed in a dark and cramped room, smoking heroin and talking endlessly about almost nothing. The stories that they report to us in a confessional mode are assembled from daily events with no made-up additions.

Costa often speaks freely about blurring the boundaries between fiction and documentary. He admits:

> When I went with *In Vanda's Room* to documentary film festivals [...] the thing was: is it documentary or fiction? Where does fiction end? Are they smoking real drugs? [...] The film doesn't matter, really, since cinema doesn't matter for these people. Judgment comes easy in documentary.
>
> *(Samin and Sturgeon 2011)*

FIGURE 1.2 *In Vanda's Room* (Pedro Costa, 2000): Vanda and Zita Duarte.

Hybridity for Costa is an act of provocation and challenge leveled toward the viewer and the film industry. In a lecture given at the Tokyo Film School in March of 2004, Costa speaks about his films as containing "a closed door that leaves us guessing." He writes:

> the more I close the doors, the more I hinder the spectator from taking pleasure in seeing himself on the screen—because I don't want that—the more I close the doors, the more I'm going to have the spectator against me, perhaps against the film, but at least he will be, I hope, uncomfortable and at war.
>
> *(Costa 2007)*

In other words, Costa is not interested in encouraging identification or creating empathy with his characters, but wishes to keep a viewer restless and troubled. "For me," admits Costa, "the primary function of cinema is to make us feel that something isn't right" (2007). A viewer watching *In Vanda's Room* is deprived of the usual pleasure associated with satiating an appetite for continuity: conversations between characters are captured without reverse shots, are framed within claustrophobic spaces, and unfold with no camera movement. The unflinching and direct gaze of the fixed camera does not spare the viewer any discomfort. On one occasion, Costa's DV camera remains fixed on Vanda's face while she is coughing up phlegm for over a minute. This not only creates a sickening and alienating effect on the viewer, but also provides an indisputable evidentiary reminder of Vanda's poverty and drug addiction.

In Vanda's Room takes place in a relatively small space that is divided into two sections: Vanda's room and the surrounding neighborhood. However, there is no clear audial separation between the two, and one can clearly hear sounds through the thin walls separating them: voices from the kitchen, sounds of children chattering or noises of bulldozers demolishing the neighborhood. These offscreen sounds penetrate what lies within the frame and intermingle with the dialogues of characters sitting in the room. In fact, it is the fixed and rigid framing of shots that further calls attention to those sounds and to what lies beyond the frame, outside the bedroom or the house. Such spatial confinement, observes Jean-Louis Comolli, is "an opening, a call to the non-visible" (2010: 64). In that sense, framing in Costa's film emphasizes what is left outside, "*the site of what remains*: what remains to be shown, to be acted out, to be experienced. A reserve, a surplus, a beyond" (65; emphasis in original). In other words, by creating a space clearly separated by vision, rather than by sound, Costa reassembles the real from its leftover traces, creating a world that includes what conventional cinema may consider "off-topic" or a digression.

By making the off-screen space present through audio, Costa merges indoor and outdoor spaces. "Every narrow street becomes a hallway," observes Vered Maimon, "and every enclosed space is simultaneously a house, a business and a social meeting space" (2012: 339). These spaces form two sides of the same reality in which Vanda is trapped, and from which she cannot escape. *In Vanda's Room* is a film that offers no redemption or catharsis, and everyone in it speaks about an impending death. Since Vanda's tragic daily existence is inseparable from the neighborhood that shapes it, Costa crafts no clear territory of what may be seen as a home or a place to which to run away. Surely, Vanda does not hope for a better future, and there is nothing that we can do for her as a character: "It's the life we want," she assures herself; "that's how I see it." The world in which such a fatalistic character lives is painted with no optimistic colors, shaped as a claustrophobic space where suffocating Vanda is entrapped.

Vanda is underprivileged, a drug addict whose life is merely a leftover of an exploiting economic system. Thus, she is a subject often excluded by film, neglected by a medium that has not yet found the appropriate means to represent her. Costa is well aware of that, and turns away from the trap of exploiting her misery cinematically. His choice of using long takes, chiaroscuro lighting (with only candles or light emerging from the windows), and minimal movement of the camera are all stylistic decisions that adhere to anti-naturalism. Poverty and misery may be represented with a distinguished cinematic style here, but they never look attractive. Costa's decision to patiently observe Vanda without interfering in her conversations is an ethical choice that creates a space of equality in which subjects are never judged but only judge themselves.

Self-introspection is granted to Costa's subjects by way of allowing them to *play themselves* in a performance rather than simply be themselves (Maimon 2012: 343). Such a subversive strategy of representation entails important political ramifications by opening up for the people in Fontainhas the possibility of imagining a new form of subjectivity. Instead of predetermining their identities in advance, Costa facilitates a dynamic political process of becoming, where the unfixed performed identities of Zita, Vanda, and the other subjects, placed in the liminal zone between fiction and reality, allow for a new way of telling stories of a struggle against inequality.

Soliciting the viewer: documentary redefinition and camcorder aesthetics

The need to tag, categorize, or name the object of our viewing experience is a common spectatorial pleasure in film. However, such an appetite to engage with well-defined artifacts with clear boundaries, traditionally encouraged by both the genre system and the auteur tradition, cannot be easily satisfied by the docufiction. As Costa's case clearly illustrates, the docufiction is a text whose ambiguous structure grants none of this pleasure of certainty. In fact, it provocatively works against it. The invitation to adopt an attitude simultaneously of faith and of skepticism toward the knowledge gained from an image or sound leaves a viewer with what may seem to be a paradox in need of a resolution: does what is shown or heard need to be trusted or suspected? Do we, as viewers, choose to embrace a documentary mode of engagement or prefer to play the game of fiction?

Strategies of hybridity may also contest and challenge Noël Carroll's under-standing of the process of indexing in documentary as a "tagging" mechanism taking place *before* the viewer enters the theater: "We don't characteristically go to films about which we must guess whether they are fiction or nonfiction." Writing more than 30 years ago, Carroll argues that "they are generally indexed one way or another" (1983: 24). Carroll believes in a solid ontological definition that differentiates between these two modes based on the intended function of the text. However, many films today are never really tagged in one way or another (e.g. in festival programs, film reviews, etc.) to make possible a clear-cut classification, but simply encourage the vagueness of that distinction to linger on long after the viewer enters the theater.

As I argue elsewhere, the documentary facet in the docufiction becomes lately "less of a clear genre indicator, and more of an *aesthetic strategy* by which a film-maker can choose to indicate familiar notions of authenticity, or solicit the viewer to embrace a documentary mode of engagement" (Landesman 2008: 41; emphasis in original). This invitation is predicated on the assumption that our relationship to various cine-matic objects is never completely determined a priori, but is always also dependent on our engagement with these objects during the experience of watching them. The idea of "framing" a text according to how it uses familiar filmic conventions is explained by Dirk Eitzen: "the form of a text can cause viewers to 'frame' it in a specific way; poor lighting, a shaky camera and bad sound may suggest cinéma vérité, but it doesn't have to be!" (1995: 91). This strand of thinking about defining a doc-umentary according to the viewer's engagement with it responds to the limits of more traditional attempts to define a documentary solely on the basis of its textual components.

John Grierson's classic definition of documentary as "the creative treatment of actuality" (1993: 8) has stood well the test of time, mainly because it accounts for the two opposing poles in each documentary film: the inseparable tie that the recording holds between representation and reality, and the necessary component of creativity that is added by the translation of such reality to the screen. Broad enough to contain almost any cinematic text, Grierson's definition still poses a serious challenge: how much actuality remains after the creative treatment is over, and what difference does it really make for the viewer? While any documentary film blurs boundaries between what is real and what is staged, an answer to this question matters tremendously because there is still quite an important difference between treating a film as a work of fiction and a documentary. As Michael Renov clarifies, "fiction is oriented toward *a* world, nonfiction toward *the* world" (2004: 22; emphases in original). Even if Renov admits elsewhere that fiction and nonfiction are two domains that "inhabit one another" (1993: 3), such a distinction is worth holding on to if we are to understand a documentary as a filmic text that makes important assertions about the real world. Noël Carroll proposes to differentiate documentaries from fiction films by seeing the former as "films of the presumptive assertion," in which the filmmaker intends that the audience entertains the propositional content of the films as asserted (1997: 186).

Such an understanding of documentary as dependent on the author's intentions encompasses the audience response as a necessary component. It is important not only that the filmmaker *intends* that the text is received in a certain way, but also that the textual cues that signal this intention are *received* in such a way by the audience. An attempt to define the documentary by shifting focus from the properties of the text itself (which may very well be of either fictional or documentary-style content) toward the viewer's engagement with it is crucial, in my opinion, to better understand complex strategies of hybridity in documentary today. Dai Vaughan, one of the strongest proponents of this line of thinking, argues:

> The term "documentary" properly describes not a style or method or a genre of filmmaking but a mode of response to film material [...] a crucial fact about the definition of documentary as a mode of response is that it places the attribution of documentary significance squarely within the province of the viewer.
>
> *(1999: 58)*

Emphasizing further the spectator's role in the process, Vivian Sobchack provocatively holds that the term documentary "designates a particular *subjective relation* to an objective cinematic or televisual text," and therefore is "less a *thing* than an *experience*" (1999: 241; emphases in original). Since every spectator "is an active agent in constituting what counts as memory, fiction, or document," and carries a certain conscious attitude toward the cinematic object, fiction films and documentaries, according to Sobchack, can never be taken as discrete objects or fixed categories. Thus, "a fiction can be experienced as a home movie or documentary, a documentary as a home movie or a fiction" (253). Sobchack's receptive strategy is moving the focus further away from the inherent documentary components found within a film text, and toward an understanding of how texts are *read*.

Obviously, relying too heavily on the spectator as the agent who can make any film a documentary can lead to strong subjectivism, and seems to imply too slippery a slope for regarding any work of fiction as a documentary. Some kind of a middle ground between a textual definition and a reception-based understanding of documentary may be more productive here. Carl Plantinga traces such a territory by claiming that the "distinction between fiction and nonfiction is not based solely on intrinsic textual properties, but also on the extrinsic context of production, distribution, and reception" (1997: 16). Paul Ward similarly holds that the realization of whether one is watching a documentary or a fiction film is "something that is socially negotiated" (2005: 30). Such an attempt at definition, which I side with, is focused on intentional solicitation of the viewer according to both textual (aesthetic conventions) and extra-textual (reviews, publicity material) cues, along with a reception component based on the viewer's interpretations.

Further, I want to suggest that digital technology plays an important role in constructing textual cues for the viewer watching docufictions. These cues in turn solicit the viewer and encourage her to embrace, even if momentarily, a documentary mode of engagement. "As digital media make all too apparent," clarifies Bill Nichols, "fidelity lies in the mind of the beholder as much as it lies in the relationship between a camera and what comes before it" (2010: xiii). Digital cameras, technologically refining older lightweight equipment (16mm, Hi-8, Betacam), enter into an already developed and familiar tradition of camcorder aesthetics. As I have previously argued elsewhere, two of the most notable docufictions made during the first years of the previous decade, the Iranian car journey *Ten* and the Pakistani immigrant road trip *In This World* (Michael Winterbottom, 2002), use digital cameras strategically to achieve a strong degree of intimacy and immediacy that connote a mode of documentary. They form an associated aesthetic of drabness that grants credibility to the image (Landesman 2008: 42). In fact, many of the early practitioners of DV in cinema took advantage of the technical differences that distinguished it from film back then. They invited viewers to think of DV in relation and opposed to celluloid film, and to define it against cumbersome and obsolete 35mm technology.

Nicholas Rombes observes that such an aesthetic of early DV cameras in cinema results in what he calls "DV humanism," by which traces of "humanness, in the era of digital cinema, are preserved in the imperfections—deliberate and accidental—that reveal themselves in the rough, spontaneous aesthetics of DV cinema" (2009: 27). As *The Idiots* case clearly shows, the signs of presence that DV helps to establish (imperfect framing, superficial multi-focus, shaky camerawork, etc.) are merely pointers alluding to a realist style that may connote a documentary mode of engagement, but *by no means function as guarantors for truth*. In other words, neither DV realism in particular nor documentary realism in general necessarily provides epistemological evidence. The only thing that documentary realism truly validates, as Bill Nichols points out, is "the authenticity of the representation itself" (2010: 185). Nourishing such difficulty in obtaining a clear understanding of what is being represented, whether a fictional character or a real documentary subject, becomes the key strategy of ambiguity that my next case study seeks to maintain. *24 City* shows how these digital aesthetics of indeterminacy, achieved through a more precisely crafted digital frame shot with a hi-def camera (rather than the earlier DV models used by von Trier and Costa), make a distinction between real and fictional unattributable or indiscernible.

A trip down memory lane: personal testimonies of national memory in *24 City*

Jia Zhangke, one of the leading figures of the Sixth Generation movement in Chinese cinema, has often made use of digital technology to segue between documentary and fiction. Jia's body of work formulates an attempt to counter and subvert the official image that China works hard to communicate to the rest of the world through government-controlled media. By merging narrative strategies within a direct cinema mode in *The World* (2004), a meditation on urban life in Beijing, or staging scenes in a documentary setting in *Useless* (2007), a ruminative essay on clothing in Chinese society, Jia refuses to see China's sweeping economic progress as miraculous, and examines the scars it leaves on individuals from the margins of society. He is interested in documenting the effects of transition in Chinese society, those who are left unrepresented, and his films, as Jiwei Xiao observes, "reveal a 'time lag' between the fast and furious economic transformations and the slower-moving changes in people's behavior and mentality" (Xiao 2011).

In *24 City* (2008) Jia further explores how personal life changes constitute the real transformation in China, and examines how one individual's psyche can be affected by an oppressive state. He charts the history of the Chengfa Group, a large military compound that is facing a process of demolition due to the Chinese reform program. Established at the end of the 1950s as a huge government facility for manufacturing military aircraft engines ("Factory 420"), the factory has been sold to a private company that is now planning to build on its ground a gargantuan and luxurious apartment complex ("24 City"). Jia's film consists of nine long and eloquent talking-head monologues delivered by both retired and present-generation factory employees, which together narrate a personal, but multifaceted, history of modern China from the 1950s until the present. Each oral testimony is singular, never interspersing with the others, and is shot in a few digital long takes carefully composed over a deep-focus background. Without the use of reenactments or voiceover, the flow of each interview is only disrupted with either short fades to black that eliminate overly dramatic moments or cutaways to footage showing the factory as it is being demolished.

While *24 City* consists of nine interviews with factory residents who tell us about their personal memories, four of those are fictionalized accounts played out by professional and well-known actors in China. Those performances encompass a more universalized narrative that leaves a space for local viewers to project their own experiences into the stories. In fact, Jia interviewed around a hundred and thirty workers initially, with the intention of making a more conventional documentary. The decision to turn to a hybrid format only came later and was easily accommodated by digital technology that did not require him to restructure the budget.[3] Digital also makes the effect of doc-fiction hybridity smoother, since by capturing

Chengdu in hi-def images that are overly sharp and pristine, everything is interspersed seamlessly: the real interviews feel suspiciously staged, while the fake ones are made to look entirely real and convincing. Jia invests his images with the precision and clarity we would normally associate with cinematic fiction, and complements this with the language of film itself, employing tracking shots and two-shots in a professional manner that goes beyond Costa's modest aesthetics of digital intimacy.

The four actors in the film represent three generations of workers, from the 1950s to the present, and include Lü Liping (playing Dali, a woman who lost her child on her trip to Chengdu), Joan Chen (playing Gu Minhua, a Shanghai girl who is nicknamed after a character in a film), Chen Jianbin (playing Su Weidong, a character growing up during the Cultural Revolution), and Zhao Tao (playing Su Na, a representative of the youngest generation). While Jia's decision to cast professional actors may have been made for the purpose of boosting the film's box-office appeal, and may constitute "an act of compromise, betraying the independent movement for commercial success," it is nonetheless joined by a slow pace, a plethora of long takes, and an insistence on static images that may, in fact, work in the opposite direction and repel mainstream audiences (Lee 2009: 46). Whatever the case may be, using famous Chinese actors is a clever strategy that allows Jia to target a very specific local audience. Such viewers may be in on the joke and may recognize the characters onscreen as universalized surrogates for China's three generations of workers. The most playful fictional interview in the film is made with Xiao Hua (played by Chinese actress Joan Chen), a factory worker who is named after a character that Chen herself played in Zheng Zhang's *Xiao Hua* (1980). She tells us that her first love was for a fighter pilot, and that someone once wrote love letters to himself in her name and showed them to his co-workers. Are these stories real or fabricated? We never really find out, but such a complex chain of representation becomes an even more exclusive joke when the character is shown watching a replay of Zheng's film on television, and the act of separating fiction from reality is made highly dependent on the viewer's subjectivity.

Like many other films made by Jia, *24 City* is situated in the present, where a lingering state of urgency, the demolition of the factory, demands an immediate documentation of social and economic changes. Half-jokingly, Jia justifies his use of digital cameras for documenting China's tempestuous transition to a capitalist economy by claiming that changes become so rapid that they require flexible and relatively lightweight equipment to record them. "With the directness of documentary I can catch up with the changes we are experiencing as they happen," Jia confesses; "but what is funny is that even as I shift to documentary I become more aware of the importance of fiction. A very complex contradiction I'm experiencing right now" (Nochimson 2009: 413). In fact, since *24 City* constantly refers to the past and uses first-person recollections as oral testimonies of national memory, its employment of fiction seems almost necessary. Jia is very much aware of how collective memory is always narrativized and constructed, and therefore cannot be easily represented with conventional documentary strategies that allude to a past, like a voiceover or a flashback. He thus juxtaposes the *cinéma vérité* interviews with temporal ellipses (repeatedly fading to a black screen for a few seconds), frame stylizations (making symbolic analogies between characters and objects in the mise-en-scène), inserts of poetry (quoting W. B. Yeats and various Chinese poets in the intertitles), and long silences. "Every interviewee gave me the urge to imagine the rest of his story," admits Jia; "there were words unspoken, and sentences half-finished. I thought I could only fully comprehend these real people's feelings through imagination" (Lee, qtd. in Deppman 2014: 189). While digital long takes capture facial gestures and psychological nuances, extreme emotions of resentment and anger are still repressed and kept beyond the frame, outside the ethical limits that Jia formulates for *cinéma vérité*.

Such cinematic restraint is used in the story of Hao Dali (played by Lü Liping), a factory worker who sacrificed everything to the factory, including her own son. Dali is first seen carrying an IV drip bottle and walking across a field where military MiG 15 fighter jets are parked. She then steps into a small office and sits across a desk in front of a new employee who calls her "Aunty." "You should really call me Granny," corrects Dali, in what feels like a scripted moment meant to mark the decisive generational gap between them. The next scene shows Dali being inter-viewed inside a shadowy room in a small apartment. She sits before a window with a bleak view and tells a heartbreaking story about losing her three-year-old son on a rest stop during a boat journey from Shanghai to Chengdu during the 1950s. Alienated from us in the frame, she makes excuses for the inconceivable act of deserting a child. "When the siren sounded," she explains, "it was like an army bugle. We simply had to go." Jia lingers on this painful moment by resorting again to a long silence, and then cuts to another staged moment as Dali is shown watching an old propaganda film on television. Whether her incredible story is real, drama-tized, or entirely fictional we do not know, but it nonetheless exemplifies how nationalist urgency and military obligations could displace family obligations and scar an individual forever.

Dali's story contrasts significantly with the final confession of Su Na (played by Zhao Tao), a wealthy young woman who represents the voice of the new gen-eration in China. An image of her face emerges out of the ashes of demolition,

FIGURE 1.3 Hao Dali (Lü Liping) in *24 City* (Jia Zhangke, 2008).

followed by a long sequence in which she is shown driving a white Volkswagen Beetle and chattering with her girlfriends on her cellphone. She talks about how determined she is to make things better for her mother, who was laid off from the factory in 1995, and her father, who is now retired and unhappy. She has decided to make a lot of money and buy her parents an apartment in the new complex 24 City: "I can do it," she exclaims; "I'm the daughter of a worker." The film culminates with an optimistic image that shows Su Na standing on a high balcony, facing the high-rise buildings in the background. The camera slowly pans from right to left and exposes the endless skyline of Chengdu. The future suddenly seems promising.

With this docufictional mode Jia maintains an equivocal and ambivalent stance toward the economic reform and the transformation of urban landscape in modern China. As Deppman succinctly observes, Jia's

> evolution from a postsocialist realist to documentarian to docufictionist manifests a restless search for new and better cinematic languages, each of which he has needed at different times to meet the demands of his dual position as anxious inside-outsider and creative, responsible witness to China's changing realities.
>
> *(2014: 206)*

Instead of lamenting the destruction of the past by national forces, Jia intervenes in the process of personal remembering and reimagines new ways in which film can represent it. *24 City* is not merely a subversive indictment of state propaganda, but a hopeful experiment in storytelling that expresses hope for the future of a nation.

Conclusion

Docufictions, as I have shown in this chapter, both manifest their markers of fabrication and gloss over their signs of artificiality. They openly acknowledge their manipulative and deceptive facets, but at the same time emphasize their ability to hold informative and evidential value. In other words, the strategies of fiction I have been discussing here are not meant to simply deconstruct documentary's modes of address by undermining its sobriety, but work to find alternative rhetorical strategies within the documentary mode for making a stronger and more nuanced argument about reality. The spectator is left not with a vacuum of epistemological value, but with an understanding of how knowledge can disseminate through both fiction and nonfiction tropes.

If documentary, as Linda Williams famously suggests, should indeed be defined "not as an essence of truth but as a set of strategies designed to choose from among a horizon of relative and contingent truths" (1993: 9), then the docufiction may function as the recent manifestation of such an unstable structure, seeking to grasp a more slippery sense of truth. In these kinds of cinematic texts, and with this type of understanding, we can possibly speak about a more complex disposition to believe in documentary filmmaking, where there is room for both doubt and faith, suspension and trust. Such a spectatorial position becomes inseparable from the ways we understand reality and our experience of it in terms that resonate with ambiguity, complexity, and indeterminacy.

Notes

1 Referring to films that strategically avoid easy categorizations or definitions, I borrow the term "docufiction" here from an anthology carrying the same name, edited by Gary Don Rhodes and John Parris Springer (2006). The concept will be understood both formally (marking the inseparability between fiction and documentary films) and epistemologically (blurring truth and deception), and should not be confused with other types of hybridity that may be present in contemporary documentaries as well, such as the hybridity between modes of production or exhibition. The same category of films that I am discussing here has also been referred to, among many other options, as "hybrid documentaries" (Jones 2005; Landesman 2008) and "fictional factions" (Rodríguez-Mangual 2008).

2 I am indebted here to Alisa Lebow, who problematizes the assumption that mockumentaries "respond to the 'real' or 'true' original documentary" (2006: 224). Since documentary, as Lebow suggests, may not at all be a "discrete and defensible category," it is not necessarily clear which one precedes the other, and "the legitimation of the category of mockumentary as distinct from documentary" should be accordingly contested (228).

3 Such a process echoes Ari Folman's methodology in *Waltz with Bashir* (2008). Folman interviewed more than a hundred veterans of the first Lebanon war about their experiences, and decided to eventually include only eight of those real interviews in his animated film. In a similar strategy of doc-fiction hybridity, Folman used the voices of actors in two of the interviews but presented their epistemological value as equal to the rest.

Bibliography

Barnouw, Eric. 1993. *Documentary: A History of the Nonfiction Film*. New York: Oxford University Press.

Carroll, Noël. 1983. "From Real to Reel: Entangled in the Nonfiction Film." *Philosophical Exchange* 14: 5–45.

——. 1996. "Nonfiction Film and Postmodernist Scepticism." In *Post-Theory: Reconstructing Film Studies*, ed. David Bordwell and Noël Carroll. Madison: University of Wisconsin Press. 283–303.

——. 1997. "Fiction, Non-fiction, and the Films of Presumptive Assertion: A Conceptual Analysis." In *Film Theory and Philosophy*, ed. Richard Allen and Murray Smith. New York: Oxford University Press. 173–202.

Comolli, Jean-Louis. 2010. "Frames and Bodies: Notes on Three Films by Pedro Costa." *Afterall* 24 (1): 62–70.

Costa, Pedro. 2007. "A Closed Door That Leaves Us Guessing." *Rouge* 10. Available online at www.rouge.com.au/10/costa_seminar.html.

Deppman, Hsiu-Chuang. 2014. "Reading Docufiction: Jia Zhangke's *24 City*." *Journal of Chinese Cinemas* 8 (3): 188–208.

Eitzen, Dirk. 1995. "When Is a Documentary?: Documentary as a Mode of Reception." *Cinema Journal* 35 (1): 81–102.

Grierson, John. 1993. "The Documentary Producer." *Cinema Quarterly* 2 (1): 7–9.

Hoberman, J. 2012. *Film after Film: Or, What Became of 21st Century Cinema?* New York: Verso.

Jones, Kent. 2005 "I Walk the Line: Hybrid Cinema." *Film Comment* 41 (1): 30–3.

Koehler, Robert. 2009. "Agrarian Utopias/Dystopias: The New Nonfiction." *Cinemascope* 40. Available online at http://cinema-scope.com/features/features-agrarian-utopiasdystopias-the-new-nonfiction.

Landesman, Ohad. 2008. "Digital Video and the Aesthetics of Realism in the New Hybrid Documentary." *Studies in Documentary Film* 2 (1): 33–45.

Lebow, Alisa. 2006. "Faking What? Making a Mockery of Documentary." In *F Is for Phony: Fake Documentary and Truth's Undoing*, ed. Alexandra Juhasz and Jesse Lerner. Minneapolis: University of Minnesota Press. 223–37.

Lee, Kevin B. 2009. "24 City." *Cineaste* 34 (4): 44–6.

Lim, Dennis. 2012. "It's Actual Life. No, It's Drama. No, It's Both." *New York Times*, August 22. Available online at www.nytimes.com/2010/08/22/movies/22hybrid.html?_r=0.

Maimon, Vered. 2012. "Beyond Representation: Abbas Kiarostami's and Pedro Costa's Cinema." *Third Text* 26 (3): 331–44.

Nichols, Bill. 2010. *Introduction to Documentary*. 2nd ed. Bloomington and Indianapolis: Indiana University Press.

Nochimson, Martha. 2009. "Passion for Documentation: An Interview with Jia Zhangke." *New Review of Film and Television Studies* 7 (4): 411–19.

Pantenburg, Volker. 2010. "Realism, Not Reality: Pedro Costa's Digital Testimonies." *Afterall* 24 (1): 54–61.

Plantinga, Carl. 1997. *Rhetoric and Representation in Nonfiction Film*. New York: Cambridge University Press.

Renov, Michael. 1993. "Introduction: The Truth about Non-Fiction." In *Theorizing Documentary*, ed. Michael Renov. New York: Routledge. 1–11.

——. 2004. *The Subject of Documentary*. Minneapolis: University of Minnesota Press.

Rhodes, Don Gary, and John Parris Springer, eds. 2006. *Docufictions: Essays on the Intersection of Documentary and Fictional Filmmaking*. Jefferson: McFarland & Company.

Rodríguez-Mangual, Edna. 2008. "Fictional Factions: On the Emergence of a Documentary Style in Recent Cuban Films." *Screen* 49 (3): 298–314.

Rombes, Nicholas. 2009. *Cinema in the Digital Age*. London: Wallflower Press.

Samin, Jeanette, and Jonathon Kyle Sturgeon. 2011. "Costa in Indiana." *n+1*, February 2011. Available online at https://nplusonemag.com/online-only/film-review/costa-in-indiana/.

Sobchack, Vivian. 1999. "Toward a Phenomenology of Non-fictional Film Experience." In *Collecting Visible Evidence*, ed. Jane Gaines and Michael Renov. Minneapolis: University of Minnesota Press. 241–54.

Vaughan, Dai. 1999. *For Documentary: Twelve Essays*. Berkeley: University of California Press.

Ward, Paul. 2005. *Documentary: The Margins of Reality*. London: Wallflower Press.

Williams, Linda. 1993. "Mirrors Without Memories: Truth, History, and the New Documentary." *Film Quarterly* 46 (3): 9–21.

Xiao, Jiwei. 2011. "The Quest for Memory: Documentary and Fiction in Jia Zhangke's films." *Senses of Cinema* 59. Available online at http://sensesofcinema.com/2011/feature-articles/the-quest-for-memory-documentary-and-fiction-in-jia-zhangke's-films/.

2

THE MOCKUMENTARY

Craig Hight

Introduction

A mockumentary (or mock-documentary) is popularly understood to be a fictional audio-visual text, such as a feature film or television program, which looks and sounds like a documentary. These texts feature fictional characters and events which appear to have been "captured" on location and through interviews by a documentary film crew, compiled together with other forms of evidence familiar to documentary productions, such as archival footage and photographic stills. The term "mockumentary" itself was first widely used to describe the fake rockumentary *This Is Spinal Tap* (Rob Reiner, 1984), and is often assumed by commentators to refer only to similarly parodic or satiric material.

Because of the range of material that now falls under this label, however, it is more useful to consider mockumentary as a *discourse*: a broadening set of textual strategies characterized by the *appropriation* of codes and conventions from the full *continuum* of nonfiction and fact–fiction forms. A mockumentary, then, might refer to a text that borrows from the codes and conventions of documentary, or from hybrid texts such as nature documentary or animated documentary, from the wide variety of factual-based television formats such as reality game shows and doc-usoaps, or from traditional nonfiction forms including newsreels, news bulletins, and current affairs programs.

Mockumentary discourse, in other words, has closely paralleled developments within documentary proper, broadening to appear across a wide range of media forms and platforms as mediations of reality themselves have inflected every part of the mediascape. Mockumentary entails a call to play (rather than documentary's assumed appeal to social and political engagement) and in part is symptomatic of a more problematic and challenging environment for documentary's more traditional "discourses of sobriety," as described by Bill Nichols (1991). A feature of broader documentary culture is a variety of forms of what might be termed "playful hybrids," a label encompassing documentary comedy, mockumentary, and the more reflexive strategies of engaging with the world. Mockumentary discourse is important, in part, because it embodies a playful and less reverential approach toward nonfiction media than was the case in the early decades of the twentieth century (certainly in comparison with films cited as exemplars as documentary became codified into a genre). Most crucially, mockumentary demonstrates the ease with which nonfiction can be faked, which offers an immediate challenge to audiences' expectations toward these forms, and potentially has broader implications for the extent to which audiences remain willing to put their trust in documentary, news, and other nonfiction media.

As documentary aesthetics and agendas have been appropriated by more ethically problematic hybrid forms (such as reality TV) and the nature of indexicality itself is questioned within a digital environment, mockumentary contributes and appeals to more varied modes of reading which contemporary audiences must have in encountering mediations of reality. Mockumentary is part of a broader set of trends, serving to reshape how we as audiences view the realities appearing on our screens. The discourse draws from and has contributed to a more complex and conflicted set of expectations about how documentary and a host of related hybrid productions are created, focused particularly on the agendas of both producers and the people who appear within the continuum of fact-fiction material.

Some mockumentaries, such as the Belgian black comedy *C'est arrivé près de chez vous* (*Man Bites Dog*) (Rémy Belvaux, André Bonzel, and Benoît Poelvoorde, 1992), about a documentary crew following a serial killer, are less playful than explicitly antagonistic toward the variety of assumptions and expectations associated with documentary practices. Such examples of mockumentary are deliberately *reflexive* toward the nonfiction form, which they appropriate. In the terms meant here, reflexivity involves a foregrounding of how and why a text has been put together. In a conventional documentary, these moments might inadvertently appear when a cameraperson is caught reflected in a mirror, a boom mike floats into frame, or gaps appear in the authority of the voiceover narration. Mockumentaries in general are reflexive toward the production practices, textual strategies, and range of audience expectations and interpretations which characterize documentary and reality-based media, precisely because they encourage their audiences to consider how *constructed* these kinds of media are. The producers of mockumentaries play to a *knowing* audience, one which is assumed to be familiar with a variety of nonfiction and related aesthetics, to immediately recognize the specific types of nonfiction which are being referenced, and to be willing to engage with a more playful exploration of these in the service of different kinds of storytelling.

Given their playfulness toward nonfiction codes and conventions, a key aspect of any mockumentary is the *degree* to which it flags to its audience that it is fictional. Some mockumentary texts, like *Spinal Tap*, are intended to be immediately recognized by viewers as fake. Their pleasure derives from the ways in which they might reference ideas from popular culture, play with typical or iconic scenes from documentary culture, or provide the traditional entertainments of narrative. Other mockumentaries are more deliberately ambiguous, aiming to leave it up to the viewer to make up their minds whether what they are viewing is real or not. A key example here might be *The Blair Witch Project* (Daniel Myrick and Eduardo Sánchez, 1999), a horror film that was convincingly promoted as a real documentary about three missing student filmmakers. It is no coincidence that *Blair Witch* relied on online marketing for its impact—the production of mockumentary has flourished within the more playful spaces of online video, where it can be more difficult to determine whether or not a text is fictional.

Mockumentary has been employed as an innovative approach to storytelling across a wide range of media, including popular cinema (as with the science fiction, horror, and superhero genres), television genres, and any number of experimental forms of media production that pursue a more critical agenda toward representations of reality. Mockumentary is also not limited to audio-visual productions; an early example of mockumentary is the infamous 1939 radio version of *War of the Worlds*, developed by Orson Welles's theatrical troupe, which transformed H. G. Wells's science fiction classic into an apparent breaking news bulletin. The broadcast continues to be an inspiration for producers in perpetrating media hoaxes. It is also an example of mockumentary used as a stunt or to create novelty within a more conventional series, as has been done with one-off episodes of the popular television programs *M.A.S.H.* (1976), *ER* (1997), *X-Files* (2000), and *The West Wing* (2009). Each of these move out of their series' aesthetics in order to present their fictional characters apparently engaging with a television documentary crew, or to ground their fictional worlds in a more plausible version of reality.

In the last two decades, however, mockumentary has also broadened and diversified, as it has established itself as a distinctive and at times innovative approach to storytelling. The remainder of this chapter explores in greater detail three examples of contemporary media texts that employ mockumentary discourse. Collectively, these illustrate some of the variety of ways media producers have explored its storytelling potential, aiming to develop innovative media content referencing broader currents within visual culture. They especially play to viewers assumed to have rich and layered forms of media experience. These are the superhero feature film *Chronicle* (Josh Trank, 2012), the UK and US versions of the mockusoap *The Office* (UK, 1997–2000; US, 2005–13), and independent feature film *I'm Still Here* (Casey Affleck, 2010).

Chronicle: documenting the superhero

Chronicle is one of a number of examples of "found footage" mockumentaries,[1] a grouping that includes *The Blair Witch Project*; *Zero Days* (Ben Coccio, 2003), presented as the video diary of the perpetrators of a Columbine-style high school massacre; *Cloverfield* (Matt Reeves, 2008), the home movie of an alien invasion; *Diary of the Dead* (George A. Romero, 2007), from the long-running zombie franchise; the *Paranormal Activity* (2007–) supernatural franchise; and the teen/

drama/comedy *Project X* (Nema Nourizadeh, 2012). The range of genres covered in just this selective listing is illustrative of the number of film producers who are interested in using mockumentary to revitalize generic conventions. As is discussed below, there are a number of advantages in adopting a "found footage" approach (Heller-Nicholas 2014) particularly for lower budget feature films, and *Chronicle* is illustrative of this strategy, with first-time filmmaker Trank looking to approach very familiar generic terrain while escaping from the demands of CGI-laden superhero spectacles.

Most of these found footage examples also fit more broadly within a pattern of dramatic mockumentary, which includes the early classic *David Holzman's Diary* (Jim McBride, 1967); *Hard Core Logo* (Bruce McDonald, 1996), a punk Canadian derivation of *This Is Spinal Tap*; and a couple of "documentary" investigations of assassinations, *Nothing So Strange* (Brian Flemming, 2002) and *Death of a President* (Gabriel Range, 2006). These last two films play with the possibilities of examining "assassination tapes," of Bill Gates and George Bush respectively, drawing inspiration from the endless debates surrounding the Zapruder film of the assassination of President John F. Kennedy in Dallas in November, 1963. In these mockumentaries, the footage is forensically examined by experts, who debate its relevance and possible insights into broader conspiracies. (Unsurprisingly, there are overlaps here with the wealth of conspiracy documentaries that proliferate online.)

As with other contemporary found footage films, *Chronicle* is presented largely as edited amateur video footage, from digital camcorders, camera phones and similar devices, but it also references broader video and surveillance cultures (especially CCTV and police surveillance practices). There are also constant references, visually and in the dialogue, to prank videos and other familiar YouTube tropes. The variety of material which is edited together here provides its own commentaries on the ubiquity of video-capturing devices within contemporary society, how easily these are carried into every social space, and how quickly video footage is distributed through social networks and digital media. As with all mockumentary, its style is symptomatic of its time; the core of its aesthetic is directly linked to the image-gathering technologies available at the time of its production.[2]

Chronicle's lead characters are non-professional filmers trying to capture events as they are unfolding (we constantly hear them exclaiming "Look at that!" and similar comments). At the core of the film is an extended video diary for main character Andrew Detmer (Dane DeHaan),[3] who eventually employs a number of cameras to document himself and his friends testing out suddenly acquired superpowers. Andrew is closely attached to his cameras, preferring to use his devices as confidantes rather than reveal his feelings to his family and friends. While early in the film he uses a camcorder as an extension of his arm, eventually his cameras become extensions of his telekinetic abilities.

There are also significant reflexive moments throughout the film. There are frequent moments when the act of filming is captured in a mirror, and instances in which multiple cameras document each other, especially later in the narrative. Everyone is aware of being filmed, and reacts to and/or performs for the camera.

There are scenes in which Andrew is abused because people assume he is filming illicit behavior or just because having a camera on all the time is "creepy." Andrew's constant filming of others marks him out early as an outsider, and while he is initially uncomfortable with appearing in frame himself, he eventually takes self-surveillance to disturbing extremes. The broader sense of surveillance that pervades the film also allows it to make reference to familiar examples of domestic video surveillance. At one point Andrew positions a camera in his room and captures his father physically abusing him (which echoes the practice of anxious parents secretly filming their children's care-givers to capture moments of possible abuse).

The use of a first-person camera has clear advantages in positioning the film within generic boundaries. A common characteristic of found footage films is the ways in which they allow filmmakers to plausibly constrain and interrupt the amount of narrative information that is conveyed to audiences, usually in order to build dramatic tension. New York partygoers in *Cloverfield*, for example, are initially confused about what is going on, and while they attempt to document an apparent disaster unfolding, they only slowly gain evidence and glimpses of the alien monster which is assaulting the city. This effectively delays the moment of the monster's "reveal" to the audience. In contrast, *The Blair Witch Project* has a more dichotomous aesthetic, as the filmmakers searching for the Blair Witch oscillate between employing the formal conventions of filmmaking for their documentary and more casually videoing themselves behind the scenes. The limited frame of their video camera is used here as a key generator of horror, as we cannot see beyond the constraints of the camera's gaze. The film commits to this, denying even a final revelatory reveal of the supernatural forces that appear to be targeting the filmmakers.

For *Chronicle*, the effect of a handheld camcorder aesthetic is to ground the superhero narrative in a more personalized perspective.[4] For the bulk of the film we see more or less what the main characters see, supplemented by their commentaries directly to the audience in the form of video diary confessionals or their overheard discussion and arguments. This approach revitalizes well-trodden parts of every superhero narrative, such as the "origin" scene, in which Andrew and his two closest friends, cousin Matt Garetty (Alex Russell) and popular Steve Montgomery (Michael B. Jordan), encounter an extraterrestrial object and mysteriously acquire powers. The moment when the boys encounter a (possibly radioactive) meteorite is hidden, as the camera image distorts into static, the soundtrack becomes chaotic, and we are left just with impressions of what might have happened.

Employing a first-person video narrative also allows the film to jump into other scenes and perspectives, as the footage cuts quickly from camera to camera, from Andrew's personal diary to footage captured by other people. We see, for example, the footage captured by Matt's girlfriend, Casey Letter (Ashley Hinshaw), for her blog. The jumps in the narrative appear natural because they are simply when the boys or other characters were too busy to turn the cameras on or were interrupted in their filming. When they have a close encounter with a plane while testing their newfound flying abilities, the footage turns into the familiar tropes of accidental disaster footage. The camera tumbles to the ground and lies on an angle. They move closer to peer into the lens and rejoice on discovering it is operating ("please tell me you got that!").

The manner in which footage is captured is also character-driven, meaning that each character tends to employ slight differences in style or approach. Andrew is somewhat dictatorial with his camera(s); he takes control and has his camera(s) zooming in and out, floating around him and his friends in ways that they find uncomfortable and cannot control, which reflects in part his lack of social sensitivity. This visually suggests his sense of superiority and isolation from them, and ultimately the camera becomes an extension of his disturbed personality, his filming a reflex and habit he cannot give up. When he is alone with his terminally ill mother, however, they hand the camera back and forth to each other, in gestures that form part of an intimate conversation as they take turns recording their exchanges and questioning each other. Matt and Casey's relationship begins as they accidentally film each other. It is notable that she makes a point of asking if she can film (in the narrative's only examples of conventional filmmaking ethics). Their video encounters are more equal, and their mutual filming almost serves as foreplay (importantly, again, they make a point of not filming when they have sex).

The variety of camera angles gradually expands as well over the course of the film, initially as Andrew starts to use his abilities to send his camera out to get mid and long shots, including aerial shots, but also because his superior telekinetic abilities allow him to have two cameras floating around him (see Figure 2.1). As he gradually becomes overwhelmed with the sensations and emotions he is experiencing, his filming also becomes more chaotic and expansive. By the time of the climactic final scenes, an inner-city battle sequence between Matt and Andrew, he grabs any number of cameras from bystanders who are trying to record what is happening.

By this stage, there is a constant tension between the self-imposed limitations of the found footage frame and the expansion of the aesthetic to include a broad

FIGURE 2.1 Andrew, Steve, and Matt debate what to do with their newfound superpowers.

range of video sources. The perspective cuts rapidly between police surveillance footage reminiscent of reality programming such as *COPS* (1989–) (complete with time code and garbled police radio), inner-city CCTV cameras, cellphone footage from a number of bystanders (including some presumably uploaded immediately to YouTube, Facebook, or another platform), and footage from a cloud of devices that are appropriated by Andrew. The effect is similar to the variety of angles that are typical of mainstream action films, with some shots from behind or through buildings capturing glimpses of action, some extremely shaky and including bad focus and flash pans, while the surveillance footage appears more stable and static. Although overall it mimics the frenetic editing approaches of action montage sequences, in a broader sense it also provides a visual representation of the expanding, proliferating, and fracturing of means of documentation in contemporary society.

The Office and the emergence of the mockusoap

The UK and US versions of the television series *The Office* are exemplars of "mockusoaps," a key recent development in mockumentary. They draw inspiration from the prevalence of docusoaps, a distinctive hybrid television format of documentary and soap opera, which gained popularity in the 1990s. Mockusoaps are evidence of the manner in which television producers have become increasingly confident of using mockumentary discourse to revitalize and reorient sitcom conventions in particular.

Docusoaps focus on the everyday, on the perspectives and activities of the "common people," and have been used as a relatively inexpensive form of prime-time television programming, a kind of "documentary lite" which build their appeal around distinctive and idiosyncratic individuals within local and national contexts rather than around investigating social and political issues (which would attract a more elite audience). Docusoaps have been a popular televisual reality-based format for over 20 years, helping to reestablish nonfiction programming within primetime schedules while also complicating the relationship between audiences and documentary discourse. Together with trends toward satirical television programming (such as *The Daily Show with Jon Stewart* and numerous satirical news programs), such hybrid formats have contributed to a naturalizing of reflexivity toward core issues of documentary representations of the social world. In particular, docusoaps impart to viewers a critical awareness of how participants of these programs manage their behavior in the presence of a camera. Instead of capturing social actors in the natural performance of their everyday social roles (the pretense of direct cinema), reality TV forms inevitably create tensions between the ways in which participants are encouraged to act (within highly constructed contexts), how they articulate their actions, and instances when their more deliberate performances are inadvertently revealed.

In addition to their narrative concerns, docusoaps tend to have a distinctive aesthetic, one that is derived from observational documentaries but adapted to suit the tighter and more intimate frame of the television screen. Mockusoaps draw directly from the handheld immediacy of direct cinema, pretending to document the everyday dramas of a collective of characters within specific locations, and providing a distinctive addition to the long-established traditions of sitcom production. Many mockusoaps dispense entirely with even such standard sitcom conventions as a laugh track, aiming for a more subtle and ambiguous form of comedy. Some draw directly from the common docusoap practice of a voiceover narrator (for example, *That Peter Kay Thing* (2000) uses Andrew Sachs, who has actually served as a docusoap narrator) to introduce each character, link scenes together, and generally provide rational, deadpan counterpoint to whatever is happening on the screen.

The need for characters to respond to and anticipate the presence of an apparent documentary crew opens space for new forms of sitcom performance. As with mockumentary feature filmmaking, it is common practice in mockusoaps to develop characters and comedic situations through improvisational rehearsal, creating performances that rely on subtle gestures that can be amplified by the intimacy of the television screen. Final episodes are then structured and polished through post-production.

Mockusoaps draw from and exaggerate the slippage between the different forms of social performance offered by (fictional) characters that are "captured" by cameras. Their comedic effect builds particularly from contrasts between what characters tell each other, what they will reveal directly to camera in interviews, and what they are caught doing by cameras that often film from around the corner of buildings or through windows without their knowledge (all familiar conventions of a mockumentary narrative style). Mockusoap humor, in other words, is embedded within the different forms of knowledge that are provided to the viewer. These gaps are made obvious especially through the juxtaposition between interview and observational sequences, as individual or joint interview segments overlap with footage that adds telling details to their narratives, generating unexpected observations on how they might be performing in different contexts, or capturing the moments when their performance fails.

There are layers of complexity here, however. As is also common with docusoaps, there are typically many reflexive moments throughout a mockusoap series, scenes in which characters demonstrate that they are well aware of the presence of the camera, of the manner in which it might be framing and capturing their behavior, and especially of the impact that an appearance on television could have on their lives. Many characters are actively performing for the camera, or continually commenting on its presence, either warning others to behave correctly while it is on or complaining about its presence. On the other hand, mockusoap characters are often presented as being unaware of how the confessions of their private lives might appear on the small screen. They will confide a great deal in an (unseen) interviewer, and especially reveal to the camera much more than they intended.

Across mockusoaps there are a variety of more specific styles and approaches, but usually a series will aim for a stylistic consistency across an entire season. The more interesting examples look to sustain storylines and characters across entire series (as compared to earlier, more episodic mockumentary television series such as *People*

Like Us (1999–2001) or *Human Remains* (2000)). In the process, mockumentary discourse has become naturalized on the small screen, emerging as a familiar but distinctive storytelling style available for television producers (although to date this has been applied almost exclusively in comedic formats).

There are subtle variations in mockusoap across national production cultures. Australia, for example, is the site for mockusoap auteur Chris Lilley, who plays multiple characters in a number of series: *We Can Be Heroes: Finding the Australian of the Year* (2005) and its part-sequel *Summer Heights High* (2007), *Angry Boys* (2011), and *Ja'mie: Private School Girl* (2013). Lilley is as much a mockumentary auteur as Christopher Guest is in feature films.[5] Each of his series strives to replicate docusoap style extremely closely, not just in eschewing laugh tracks and relying on deadpan performances, but also in minimizing reflexive moments in order to create as close a pastiche of docusoap form as possible. These mockusoaps flag their fictionality to viewers through Lilley's multiple appearances as a variety of characters (of various ages, genders, and ethnicities) and the sharpness of their satirical insights into Australian culture. *Wayne Anderson: Singer of Songs* (2005), a New Zealand mockusoap, went a step further in constructing ambiguous performances, the main actor using his own name and appearing in character in interviews to promote the series, leaving many of its viewers confused about whether or not it was fiction.

The Comeback (2005), in contrast, is a high point in reflexive mockusoap, a series which foregrounds the reflexive potential of mockumentary. The lead character is Valerie Cherish (Lisa Kudrow), a former sitcom actor attempting to revive her career. The series uses a show-within-a-show premise, as Cherish stars in her own reality TV series about her efforts to turn a small part in a new sitcom into a launching pad for a new career. The key innovation of the series, one that no other mockumentary seems to have attempted, is to present itself as a pre-edit of the footage captured by the reality TV crew. What we see is the rough cut of the apparent docusoap, before it has been edited to broadcast standard—including the crew and director repeatedly caught in frame or in negotiation with Valerie over what they should and should not film. The result is that the series partly operates as the "making of" a docusoap. HBO revived *The Comeback* in 2014, with Valerie now playing a fictionalized portrait of herself in a series based on the making of the sitcom featured in the original version.

Within this broader context of mockusoap developments, the British and American versions of *The Office* have served as exemplars and templates for mockusoap production (much as *This Is Spinal Tap* is invariably cited as inspiration by contemporary mockumentary filmmakers). Both have enjoyed popular and critical success, helping to reshape sitcom development in their respective countries, but also providing a ready-made template to be adapted and revised by different national broadcasters.[6] Despite beginning with the same basic premise and largely employing the same mockumentary textual strategies (an aesthetics referenced to popular docusoap formats), the two series are distinct in some important ways.

The original British *Office* was created by Ricky Gervais and Stephen Merchant, inspired in part by *This Is Spinal Tap* and earlier British mockumentary series such as *People Like Us* and *Operation Good Guys* (1997–2000). The series is focused on a small number of key characters in the local branch of a paper company under threat of closure in the depressed industrial area of Slough, Berkshire. Gervais and Merchant took great pains to sustain the consistent premise that everything we are watching is the product of a documentary crew's encounters with the core cast members. They experimented initially (in their pilot) with the use of a voiceover narrator, using an experienced docusoap narrator, and briefly considered the possibility of making the documentary crew openly incompetent (Walters 2005: 16). However, they soon developed a distinctive approach, one that relied on tightly written scripts rather than improvisation. Almost all of the action occurs within the uncomfortable environment of an open-plan workplace, and centers on the generally banal everyday activities of an office (even to the extent of occasional long and close-up shots of a bubbling water cooler, or the mechanical operations of a photocopier, within an otherwise soundless environment).

The series otherwise closely references a docusoap aesthetic, using naturalistic lighting and sound, and developing a layered set of representations of each of the characters and their interactions with each other within the confines of their apparent workplace. In classic mockusoap fashion, scenes are constructed from individual partly confessional interviews with characters, observational sequences in which the characters are obviously highly conscious of the presence of the camera, and more surreptitious filming in which the camera quietly lurks in semi-surveillance mode behind office equipment or outside doorways or windows to capture the employees at their most natural and with their guard down. This layered aesthetic is central to our understanding as viewers of what is happening and how these characters operate. As noted above, the interplay between these layers of narrative information closely informs our understanding of the differences between their private thoughts and feelings and those they offer to other people.

The employees within the office are generally uncomfortable with each other, partly because they seem to have little in common apart from their shared space, and partly because that space is made more excruciating by both the presence of the cameras and the behavior this prompts from the office manager, David Brent (Gervais), who is the dominant character in the series. Alone among the subjects of the documentary camera, he appears delighted at its presence. He is constantly disrupting the everyday activities of the office to perform in a self-created role as a beloved leader and entertainer. He appears familiar with (British) docusoaps himself and notes how many have propelled their subjects into instant stardom. He has not understood how a documentary camera might also capture character flaws. Brent hovers constantly into view, ready to interrupt his employees as they are being filmed, and insists on being the focus of attention. The comedic tension that his presence creates is between his assumptions that he is able to control how he appears on camera and the precision with which the camera is able to reveal his ambitions and his naked desire to be at the center of everything. When his expectations of positive reinforcement of his sense of humor or his assumed status are not forthcoming, there are moments of uncomfortable silence—heightened by the presence of the camera, and often exquisitely prolonged through editing by slightly delaying a cut to the next shot or scene. As is characteristic of docusoaps themselves, reflexivity is naturalized here; people make no attempt to ignore the camera, and there are many moments in which characters look into the camera lens, directly to the audience, in a shared moment of horror over a Brent-inspired moment of embarrassment.

The only positive relationship we see is the frustrated budding romantic relationship between salesman Tim Canterbury (Martin Freeman) and receptionist Dawn Tinsley (Lucy Davis). Dawn is engaged to another character, but the mutual attraction between her and Tim is suggested through suggestive body language, fleeting facial expressions, and their shared rapport in enduring the everyday boredom of their workplace (see Figure 2.2). Their relationship is hidden from the other characters but not from the camera crew, as they capture the fleeting moments of intimacy between Tim and Dawn. Their sexual tension is heightened in part because they have not openly declared their attraction to each other, and in part because it is glimpsed indirectly by the cameras, caught through surreptitious filming through windows and around office plants.

Almost uniquely among mockusoap producers, and deliberately breaking with sitcom tradition, Gervais and Merchant decided to acknowledge a sense of broadcast and audience feedback. They used the second season to suggest how viewers might have responded to the "docusoap" about the little paper company office, and how those reactions impacted upon the characters themselves. Likewise, they used a Christmas special at the end of the second season to give narrative closure to *The Office*'s narrative arc, which again is unusual within the more perpetual fictional worlds of sitcoms. Both are key differences between the British series and its more conventional American descendent.

FIGURE 2.2 The subtle and tentative *Office* flirting between Tim and Dawn in the original series.

The American series is also much less bleak, toning down the satirical bite of the original series to create more of a sense of the office characters as a surrogate family. As the American *Office* progressed it expanded its roster of secondary characters, exploring their office and personal lives in action over a larger social geography. The broader production environment of American television also imposed some structures onto the American *Office*. Unlike the condensed narratives of the six-part British version, the American seasons provided a longer season of twenty-three episodes, but shorter episode lengths of only twenty-two minutes. These helped foster a faster-paced style, virtually eliminating the quieter moments that are so distinctive of the British *Office*.

The American *Office* was also produced within a more deliberately improvisational approach (more directly drawing upon practices common to mockumentary filmmaking), with episodes carefully crafted and structured in post-production. Finally, a key difference emerged through this series' use of the camera, which was allowed a more dynamic and collaborative series of relationships with key characters—they would talk directly to the camera/crew, and the camera would occasionally nod or shake "no" in response, in contrast to the more distanced and objective position of the UK *Office*'s fictional documentary camera crew. This meshed also with a generally more confessional style of interview segment, which accorded in turn with a more confessional television culture in the American context. As there was no suggestion that early seasons had actually been broadcast, members of the US *Office* are never confronted with what their colleagues have said about them, or what the camera crew has been able to document about their relationships. The overall result is that the US *Office* operates in more conventional sitcom territory, with characters living in complete ignorance of the kinds of knowledge that the docusoap of their professional lives reveals to viewers.

I'm Still Here and mockumentary hoaxes

In contrast to the found footage constructions of *Chronicle* and docusoap pastiche of *The Office*, *I'm Still Here* suggests the potential of the discourse to provide more ambiguous and challenging forms of media experience. At the heart of this film is a stunt: it "documents" the year which follows Joaquin Phoenix's 2008 announced intention to retire from Hollywood acting in pursuit of a music career, all apparently filmed by his brother-in-law and fellow actor Casey Affleck. The majority of the film's scenes play out in hotel rooms, limousines, and other claustrophobic spaces, with Phoenix shadowed by personal assistants and Affleck's camera. Phoenix quickly falls into depression in the face of indifference and hostility to his efforts in musical creativity, and his failed pursuit of Puff Diddy (Sean Combs) as producer for his hip-hop album. He becomes more bellicose and incomprehensible, mumbling in long monologues and increasingly abusive toward those around him. Throughout, he has encounters with representatives of the press, who question him on whether he is serious about his retirement and about persistent rumors that his year-long sabbatical is all a sustained hoax. Included is actual footage from Phoenix's

FIGURE 2.3 Joaquin Phoenix's infamous appearance on *The Late Show with David Letterman.*

infamous appearance on *The Late Show with David Letterman* on February 11, 2009, in which he appeared antagonistic and unresponsive in the face of an openly irritated Letterman, and extracts from a variety of tabloid television news reports on his strange public behavior (see Figure 2.3). After a disastrous gig in a Miami night-club, in which he abuses and physically attacks hecklers, he retreats in confusion and melancholy to a childhood haunt in Panama.

I'm Still Here falls into an occasional pattern of mockumentary hoaxes in which media producers have attempted to employ nonfictional codes and conventions to convince an audience of the validity of a fictional character and/or events. *The War of the Worlds* radio mockumentary is an early example here, and *The Blair Witch Project* (for its convincing marketing campaign, particularly centered on a number of online resources), as are a smattering of television mockumentary hoaxes, including *Alternative 3* (Christopher Miles, 1977), which reported on a Cold War conspiracy to establish a base on the moon; *Ghostwatch* (Lesley Manning, 1992), in which a super-natural entity appeared to use a live television investigation of a haunting to attack watching television viewers; *Forgotten Silver* (Costa Botes and Peter Jackson, 1995), which detailed the discovery of a long-lost pioneering New Zealander filmmaker; and the presentation of video evidence of alien visitation at the center of *Alien Abduction: Incident in Lake County* (Dean Alioto, 1998). Not all of these hoaxes were artistically or popularly successful, but all looked to exploit an ambiguity in performance to help generate enough credibility as nonfiction to challenge the expectations of viewers.

There are broader precedents for this kind of media production: everything from April Fools' Day news reports (when real reporters present outrageous stories with a straight face) to the series of mondo exploitation films produced by Paolo Cavara, Franco Prosperi, and Gualtiero Jacopetti from the 1960s, which blended the real and the staged, and the faked murder that ends *Snuff* (1976). Orson Welles engaged in a film hoax with *F for Fake* (*Vérités et mensonges*) (Orson Welles, 1973) as he detailed an apparently real narrative about fakery before ultimately revealing the latter half of the film is fiction. The same stunt impulse informs Sasha Baron Cohen's performances in *Borat: Cultural Learnings of America for Make Benefit Glorious Nation of Kazakhstan* (Larry Charles, 2006), which combines mockumentary sequences with footage that documents encounters between Cohen's "Borat" persona and unwitting participants.

I'm Still Here was something of a critical and commercial failure. It is not an exemplary example of mockumentary or filmmaking more generally, but the reasons for its failure provide useful insights into the nature and future of mockumentary discourse more broadly. The film itself tries to build an intimate and poignant perspective of Phoenix's decline into depression and confusion as his intended music career stalls and he regrets his decision to retire from acting. Its narrative, however, does not build toward a compelling climax but meanders from one public/social disaster after another involving Phoenix, and repetitive scenes capturing his poor management and communication skills, particularly in engaging with his staff, whom he tends to blame for his own failures. His character is not particularly likeable; he is boorish, tedious, and increasingly uncomfortable to watch. Crucially, we are never invested in his troubles or possible redemption (something which distinguishes Ricky Gervais's character in the UK version of *The Office*). The best mockumentaries, those which reward repeated viewing, tend to be layered in their narrative, taking pains to develop characters with which the audience can identify, and building a narrative arc which provides dramatic highpoints and a cathartic conclusion. The pleasures of watching the television hoax *Forgotten Silver*, for example, are actually enhanced with the knowledge that this is a carefully crafted pastiche of historical biography and contemporary investigation.

Part of the reason *I'm Still Here* is uncomfortable to watch is also that if it were real, it would demonstrate some ethically suspect practices on the part of Affleck himself. Phoenix seems to be so obviously self-destructive that we are increasingly uneasy with Affleck's commitment to the act of filming over and above any real concern or care for his own brother-in-law. Affleck's lack of empathy does not appear plausible here.

The reception of the film was complicated by the release at a similar time of films which confused audiences and critics over whether to read their constructions as fiction or nonfiction—most notably *Exit Through the Gift Shop* (Banksy, 2010) and *Catfish* (Henry Joost and Ariel Shulman, 2010). Of these, only Phoenix's film is an openly declared mockumentary, as he and Affleck acknowledged immediately after the film's premiere that Phoenix's whole public persona during the year of production, and improvised behavior within the film, had been part of an elaborate piece of performance art (inspired in part by the exploits of performance artist and comedian Andy Kaufman, who engaged in deadpan public acts that played out ove a number of years). Because of the public debates over its possible hoax status during production, Affleck and Phoenix apparently decided they had no choice but to include extracts from some of those commentaries, and have Phoenix appear outraged in response. This dissipates rather than deepens the ambiguity around his performances, eroding any playful challenge the film might have provided for viewers. Affleck and Phoenix apparently intended the film as a commentary on the suffocating excesses of celebrity culture and surveillance, but critics tended to agree that this message was lost in the face of its meandering narrative.

In a larger sense, however, *I'm Still Here* serves as a reminder of the challenges of any filmmaker (documentary or otherwise) in engaging with contemporary visual culture, which encourages such fluid boundaries between the real and fiction and critical forms of engagement from audiences.

The naturalization of mockumentary discourse

Parodic and satiric mockumentary in particular has proliferated since the 1990s, and its recent popularity within film and television has some key implications for the future of mockumentary discourse. It has become increasingly hard to fool most audiences, either to use mockumentary to perpetrate a hoax or to engage with unwitting participants in faux documentary style, as Sasha Baron Cohen achieved for key scenes within *Borat*. Media producers have needed to move beyond using mockumentary as simply a stunt or novelty style, and are compelled to carefully craft textual material which explores the reflexive, layered, and playful potential inherent to its appropriation of the fact–fiction continuum. The widespread application of mockumentary as a storytelling style across a range of genres and media forms, including blockbuster feature film production and primetime televisual programming, also suggests that it has less potential to be subversive, diluting its essentially reflexive stance toward documentary and related forms. As a more naturalized storytelling style within contemporary film and television media, mockumentary's playful appropriation of nonfiction aesthetics both draws upon and sits comfortably with the full range of texts that mediate reality.

Notes

1 Not all of these types of films are sustained exercises in mockumentary. The classic Italian horror film *Cannibal Holocaust* (Ruggero Deodato, 1980), for example, includes elements of this, as does *District 9* (Neill Blomkamp, 2009), but both move in and out of a pretense that what we are watching has been captured by a documentary camera.

2 Just as *David Holzman's Diary* appropriates direct cinema and *cinéma vérité* filmmaking practices which developed around the emergence of black-and-white handheld film cameras and synchronous sound technologies in the 1960s.

3 There is an early direct visual reference to *David Holzman's Diary* as he films himself talking into a mirror to explain what he is doing and why.

4 This is very similar to Kurt Busiek's comic book miniseries *Marvels* (1994), which centers on the perspective of a photographer who tries to capture more than just a glimpse of superheroes in action (and may have been an inspiration for *Chronicle*'s scriptwriters).

5 Guest is co-writer and co-star for *This Is Spinal Tap* and its sequel, and co-writer and director for mockumentaries *Waiting for Guffman* (1996), *Best in Show* (2000), and *A Mighty Wind* (2003), all of which draw from the same stable of actors.

6 *The Office* itself has been remade in France, Germany, Canada (French language), and Israel, and as of this writing there are versions planned in China and Sweden.

Bibliography

Heller-Nicholas, Alexandra. 2014. *Found Footage Horror Films: Fear and the Appearance of Reality*. Jefferson: McFarland.

Hight, Craig. 2008. "Mockumentary: A Call to Play." In *Rethinking Documentary: New Perspectives, New Practices*, ed. Wilma de Jong and Thomas Austin. Maidenhead: Open University Press. 203–14.

———. 2010. *Television Mockumentary: Reflexivity, Satire and a Call to Play*. Manchester: Manchester University Press.

Higley, Sarah L., and Jeffrey A. Weinstock, eds. 2004. Nothing That Is: Millennial Cinema and the "Blair Witch" Controversies. Contemporary Approaches to Film and Television Studies. Detroit: Wayne State University Press.

Juhasz, Alex, and Jesse Lerner, eds. 2006. *F Is for Phony: Fake Documentary and Truth's Undoing*. Visible Evidence Series. Minneapolis: University of Minnesota Press.

Nichols, Bill. 1991. *Representing Reality: Issues and Concepts in Documentary*. Bloomington and Indianapolis: Indiana University Press.

Plantinga, Carl. 1998. "Gender, Power and a Cucumber: Satirizing Masculinity in *This Is Spinal Tap*." In *Documenting the Documentary: Close Readings of Documentary Film and Video*, ed. Barry K. Grant and Jeannette Sloniowski. Detroit: Wayne State University Press. 318–32.

Roscoe, Jane. 1997. "*Man Bites Dog*: Deconstructing the Documentary Look." Metro Education 13: 7–12.

Roscoe, Jane, and Craig Hight. 2001. *Faking It: Mock Documentary and the Subversion of Factuality*. Manchester: Manchester University Press.

Torchin, Leshu. 2008. "Cultural Learnings of *Borat* Make for Benefit of Glorious Study of Documentary." *Film & History* 38 (1): 53–63.

Walters, Ben. 2005. *The Office*. London: British Film Institute.

3

ANIMATED DOCUMENTARY

Annabelle Honess Roe

Introduction

Documentaries propose to tell us something about the real world. But what if a documentary maker wants to tell us something about the real world that cannot be filmed with a camera? There are many aspects of reality that evade live-action film: events that predated the invention of the camera (such as prehistoric life), things that are too far away for a camera to reach (such as the outer reaches of the solar system), and things that we experience that may not be visible whilst at the same time being very real (such as emotions and other psychological experiences). There are also aspects of reality a documentary filmmaker may not want to film, for ethical or other reasons. For example, documentary interviewees may need to remain anonymous for their own safety. Just because these things cannot be filmed, or in some cases even seen at all, does not make them any less a part of the real world as it is lived and experienced by its inhabitants.

Documentary has traditionally adopted several strategies in situations in which it is not possible to capture live-action footage of the events concerned. An early approach, adopted in the first film labelled as a documentary, Robert Flaherty's *Nanook of the North* (1922), is to ask documentary subjects to reconstruct events for the camera. A standard means of keeping an interviewee's identity secret is to film them in silhouette and perhaps also to use an actor to speak their words, so that all identifying traits are removed from the film. More recently, animation has become a popular choice to overcome the limitations of live-action filming. Animation is being explored also for its own expressive potential within a nonfiction context. For example, the Australian short film *It's Like That* (Southern Ladies Animation Group, 2003) animates little knitted bird puppets to evoke the innocence of incarcerated child asylum seekers held in detention centers. In Brett Morgen's *Chicago 10* (2007), a comic book or video game animation aesthetic becomes a metaphor for the farce-like legal trial of Abbie Hoffman and other members of the Yippie movement accused of "inciting riot" at the 1968 Democratic National Convention in Chicago.

Using animation in documentary might initially feel problematic or even inappropriate. Where does this instinctive sense of the incompatibility of documentary and animation come from? We have expectations of documentary's relationship between the filmic (what we see on screen) and the profilmic (what took place in front of the camera). We might conventionally expect a documentary to film things as they happen, to not manipulate the order of events, and to represent reality as truthfully as possible. In turn, this implies expectations about what a documentary should look like—its aesthetic and formal qualities. In animated documentary this conventional documentary material is (usually) absent. In its place is animation, which goes above and beyond merely representing and can be thought of as a kind of formal excess, with varying styles and aesthetics that have to be contended with by viewers as they perceive and comprehend the film.

The expectations regarding documentary films are not really to do with what they should inherently or absolutely be like, but more about how we have become conditioned to think about documentary. Brian Winston has suggested that a certain idea of documentary has come to dominate due to developments in nonfiction filmmaking in the 1960s (Winston 1995: 206). At this time, two documentary movements on different sides of the Atlantic produced films within strongly articulated rhetorics about how documentaries should be made. The direct cinema filmmakers in the United States believed documentaries could best convey the truth of a situation by observing it without any intervention. In France, ethnographer Jean Rouch suggested an alternative means of uncovering the truth through *cinéma vérité*—a style of nonfiction filmmaking in which the camera was a catalyst that probed documentary participants and often included direct questioning. Even though direct cinema and *cinéma vérité* had different approaches, they were both committed to the pursuit of "truth" via documentary, a truth that was revealed by the presence of the (observing or probing) camera.

There are, of course, many limitations to the documentary as understood according to these conventional expectations. One significant limitation is that most documentaries actually fail to live up to these purist criteria. Prior to the 1960s, and the advent of lightweight camera and sound recording equipment that could capture synched image and sound on the fly, documentary techniques such as reconstruction were commonplace. Similarly, there did not really exist the demand that documentaries reveal some objective truth about the world. For example, documentary had historically been used to convince the audience of a certain point of view in films such as those made by the British Documentary Movement filmmakers of the 1930s under the auspices of John Grierson. Similarly, after the halcyon moments of direct cinema and *cinéma vérité* in the 1960s and 70s, very few documentaries have continued to aspire to their formal or rhetorical ideals. Errol Morris, for example, is roundly dedicated to the revelation of truth, but as he frequently asserts, "style doesn't guarantee truth" (Morris 2004), and his own films use a combination of interviews, archival material, and stylized reenactments to present different perspectives on events, often with great success. His 1988 documentary *The Thin Blue Line* played a significant role in overturning a wrongful murder conviction, yet it includes stylized reenactments, which are in no way objective or observational, to call into question the reliability of eyewitnesses and other figures to do with the case.

We could say that animation is only a problem for documentary if we have a too limited understanding of what a documentary is and what its relationship to reality should be like. If we return to the long-standing definition of documentary as "the creative treatment of actuality" (as stated by John Grierson in 1933), then there is no reason why animation cannot be a way of creatively treating reality. Animated documentaries also fulfill a more recent distinction, made by Bill Nichols, between documentary film and fiction film: that documentaries are about *the* world, whereas fiction film is about *a* world (2001: xi). In fact, it is probably more useful to think about animation as a solution to the limitations of conventional live-action documentary, rather than a problem. If we shake off the now outdated idea that documentary has to merely witness events like an unbiased fly on the wall, then there is no reason why animation cannot be just as viable a means of documentary representation as live-action film. Indeed, this is one of the arguments I hope to make in this chapter—that animation is a very useful addition to the documentary maker's toolbox, one that enables them to show the real world in greater breadth and depth than live action.

What are animated documentaries?

A very simple definition of an animated documentary would be something like: a nonfiction film that uses animation as a means of visual representation. But, as we will see, the relationship between documentary and animation is a little more nuanced than that. There are plenty of documentaries that use bits and pieces of animation, such as Michael Moore's *Bowling for Columbine* (2002), but that we would not label as animated documentaries. I have previously (Honess Roe 2013: 4) suggested a comprehensive definition of animated documentary as a film that "(i) has been recorded or created frame by frame; (ii) is about *the* world rather than *a* world wholly imagined by its creator; and (iii) has been presented as a documentary by its producers and/or received as a documentary by audiences, festivals or critics." Many animated documentaries combine live-action material and animation, so it is not the amount of animation a documentary contains that necessarily makes it an animated documentary. Rather, it is that the animation and live-action elements must be "integrated to the extent that the meaning of the film would become incoherent" (ibid.) were the animation to be removed.

Many scholars identify a 1918 film by American animator Winsor McCay, *The Sinking of the Lusitania*, as the first animated documentary. In this film McCay, who was an established animator, vaudeville performer, and comic strip illustrator, reveals how the British passenger liner *Lusitania* was sunk by a German submarine in 1915, a key event in bringing the United States into World War I. The animation style of the 12-minute film mimics nonfiction media of the time, such as newsreels and newspaper illustrations, and the film implicitly suggests that the use of animation to reconstruct a factual, historical event is unproblematic when, in an early intertitle, McCay tells viewers, "you are looking at the first *record* of the sinking of the Lusitania" (emphasis added). However, McCay didn't label his film an animated documentary,[1] and film scholars and historians did not start using this term until many years later. In fact, it was not until the 1990s that the animated documentary started to develop in a meaningful way.

Prior to the 1990s, however, there were several significant incidences of films that animated real-life scenarios, usually by combining animated visuals with documentary soundtracks; we might think of these short films as precursors to the animated documentary as we understand it now. Animators John and Faith Hubley made a couple of short films based on audio recordings of their young children playing make-believe. *Windy Day* (1967) and *Cockaboody* (1973) interpret the youngsters' imaginary worlds through a childlike, hand-drawn animation style. Aardman Animation, the British studio best known as creators of Wallace and Gromit, animated Plasticine figures to recordings of eavesdropped conversations or interviews from the 1970s in their BBC series *Animated Conversations* (1978) and their Channel 4 series *Conversation Pieces* (1983) and *Lip Synch* (1989). The latter included the Oscar-winning *Creature Comforts*, which gained the studio wide, international recognition and praise and, arguably, raised awareness for the creative potential of combining documentary and animation. The early and pre-history of animated documentary is discussed in greater detail in Honess Roe (2013), DelGaudio (1997), Patrick (2004), Strøm (2003), and Wells (1997).

These films by Aardman and the Hubleys are important forerunners to the animated documentary, but they are not strictly animated documentaries, as they were never labelled as such at the time by the filmmakers or their audiences. It was not until the 1980s and 90s that filmmakers began making short films that combined animation and documentary and calling them "animated documentaries." In the late 1980s and early 1990s there were a handful of animated documentaries that reached a limited audience via festivals and television (see Honess Roe 2013). Subsequently, the final years of the 1990s were a pivotal time in establishing the animated documentary as a legitimate mode of filmmaking. Several films that demonstrated the great potential and possibilities for animated documentary were made by independent animators who have gone on to influence and shape the form. In the UK, Jonathan Hodgson's *Feeling My Way* (1997) animated hand-drawn doodles over live-action POV footage of a walk through London, giving the audience insight into the walker's train of thought. In Australia, Dennis Tupicoff made an animated film using rotoscope animation[2] that was based on a radio interview of a mother talking about the night her son was shot and killed. *His Mother's Voice* (1997) is a powerful evocation of grief and loss that offers two animated versions of the interview, which we hear twice through in its entirety.

In the United States, Sheila Sofian made *Survivors* (1997), about domestic abuse, in which animation works metaphorically and illustratively in conjunction with

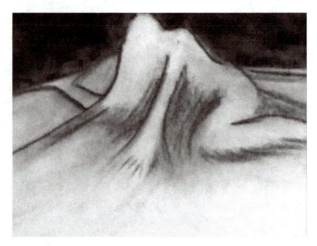

FIGURE 3.1 Animated metaphor of domestic abuse and repression in *Survivors* (Sheila Sofian, 1997).

interviews from survivors, perpetrators, and support workers. For example, at one point in the film a woman's repressive domestic situation is evoked through the representation of a female figure being smothered by the sheets of the marital bed. The animated figure strains and pulls against the bedclothes, to no avail, a metaphor for her entrapment in an abusive relationship (see Figure 3.1). Also in the United States, animator Bob Sabiston, who became known for inventing the Rotoshop digital rotoscoping software used in Richard Linklater's fiction feature films *Waking Life* (2001) and *A Scanner Darkly* (2006), first experimented with this method through animating nonfiction scenarios. He made *Project Incognito* (1997), *Roadhead* (1998), and *Snack and Drink* (1999) in quick succession, and all three films use Rotoshop to animate vox pops and encounters between the filmmaker and real people. In 1998, Sylvie Bringas and Orly Yadin demonstrated the potential for animation to deal with issues of memory and trauma in *Silence*, a short film about a Holocaust survivor that is animated by Ruth Lingford and Tim Webb in two different styles. The first half of the film, which takes place in the Theresienstadt concentration camp, uses a bleak, dark, black-and-white style of animation. The second half, after liberation, is bright and colorful.[3]

These short films were seen mostly at festivals, and one festival in particular has played an important role in establishing the animated documentary. In 1997 the German documentary film festival DOK Leipzig launched a strand dedicated to animated documentary, and the festival remains an important venue for their screening and discussion. Television, however, has also played a part in the form gaining exposure. Channel 4 in the UK supported experimental animation via its Animate project (established in 1990), in particular Jonathan Hodgson's work. Another, much more mainstream, television event during this period could also be argued as laying the groundwork for using animation in documentary. In 1999, the BBC broadcast *Walking with Dinosaurs*, a natural history documentary series that used cutting-edge computer animation to bring prehistory to life. At a reported budget of £6 million, it was the most expensive documentary series produced by the BBC and was extremely successful with audiences. The 18.9 million viewers that tuned in to the first episode made it the most popular documentary broadcast on BBC (Honess Roe 2013: 46, 54).

That 1997 to 1999 seems a particularly significant time for the production of animated documentaries is probably due to coincidence rather than to any specific event. However, it does seem that a significant, if small, global critical mass was reached around this time. Since then, the animated documentary has continued to proliferate. More shorts are produced each year, with their visibility raised through online distribution and exhibition as well as an increasing number of public viewing platforms via festivals and, occasionally, television. Animated documentaries have also made it to the big screen. Most significantly, the 2008 Israeli film *Waltz with Bashir*, in which director Ari Folman uses animation to explore repressed memories of his role in the 1980s Lebanon War, and which is discussed in more detail below, could be argued as firmly planting animated documentary on the map.

Interpreting animated documentaries

Early writing on animated documentary by film scholars in the late 1990s and early 2000s tended to attempt to interpret them within existing frameworks for under-standing and analyzing documentary, particularly Bill Nichols's "modes" of doc-umentary that he first suggested in a book published in 1991, *Representing Reality*. Paul Ward (2005), Sybil DelGaudio (1997), Gunnar Strøm (2003), and Eric Patrick (2004) have variously attributed animated documentary to the interactive, reflexive, and performative modes.

Some scholars, however, have suggested alternative typologies for grouping and understanding animated documentary. Paul Wells (1997) suggests adopting Richard Barsam's modes of documentary production to categorize the form. Eric Patrick (2004) proposes to organize animated documentary according to their "structures," or the ways in which the films tell their stories. More recently, I have suggested an alternative analysis based on asking the relatively simple question of what function the animation is serving in animated documentary: "what is the animation doing that the conventional [live-action] alternative could not?" (Honess Roe 2013: 22). To answer this question, I set out three ways animation functions in animated documentary: mimetic substitution, non-mimetic substitution, and evocation.

In the first two functions, animation is used as a stand-in for missing "conventional" documentary material, such as film footage and photographs. The reasons this material is "missing" vary. Sometimes it is for simple practical reasons, as when the events being depicted took place before cameras existed (such as with *Walking with Dinosaurs*) and are, therefore, to a certain extent speculative. There are ethical considerations which may make filming inadvisable, such as having to keep the identity of parti-cipants secret, as in *Hidden* (*Gømd*, Holborn, Aronowitsch, and Johansson, 2002), a Swedish film about a young illegal immigrant. I have classed the CGI photorealistic animation *Walking with Dinosaurs* as "mimetic" because it "strives to closely resemble reality, or rather, the look of a live-action recording of reality" (Honess Roe 2013: 24). *Hidden*'s animation, on the other hand, can be classed as "non-mimetic substitution" because it does not try "to make a visual link with reality or to create an illusion of a filmed image" (24). Instead, films of this type are using animation to stand in for missing live action (in this instance, there was no filmed record of the interview scene being depicted in the film) but are also exploiting the fact that animation "has the potential to express meaning through its aesthetic realisation" (24). In *Hidden* the illegal child immigrant, Giancarlo, is animated in such a way as to evoke sympathy for his situation. In particular, he is drawn with a childlike simplicity and has big, sad eyes that are often downcast.

The third function of animation, evocation, demonstrates how animation can make up for another, significant, shortcoming of live-action film—its relative inability to reveal or explore things that cannot be seen, such as feelings and states of mind. In films such as Hodgson's *Feeling My Way*, animation "allows us to imagine the world from someone else's perspective" (Honess Roe 2013: 25). Another significant example of the evocative function of animation can be seen in the *Animated Minds* series of short films, directed by Andy Glynne (2003 and 2009). In these two series of four short films, animation is used to evoke the experiences of living with different mental health issues, which we hear being described by anonymous interviewees on the soundtrack. The animation is a powerful way of illustrating what we hear being described, and works in an often metaphorical way to help the audience imagine experiencing life as the interviewees do by giving a visual representation to their words. For example, in *Fish on a Hook*, one of the shorts from the first series, interviewee Mike explains that his agoraphobia-induced panic attacks may make him appear, to an outsider, to be like a fish wriggling on a hook. The animation accompanying these words shows a silhouetted human figure jerking around on the end of a fishhook. Most of the *Animated Minds* films work in this way, by visualizing what is heard on the soundtrack, evoking the experiences being described by giving the audience a visual equivalent to that which is invisible or internal. This process was aided by the filmmakers encouraging the interviewees to use metaphors to explain their experiences (Glynne 2013: 74); Glynne suggests that it is the "combination of an honest and open discussion of the experiences of mental illness with well-articulated and metaphorical language [that] provided an excellent canvas on which to use animation" (2013: 75).

Each of the eight shorts from the two *Animated Minds* series is animated in a different style, sometimes using different animation techniques. In each film, an animation aesthetic most suitable to the subject matter is chosen. This reminds us that when analyzing animated documentary it is important to consider not only the way the animation functions, but also how the animation aesthetic and techniques used contribute to this function. *The Light Bulb Thing*, the *Animated Minds* short about manic depression, evokes the experience of that mental illness through its animation style, which has a washed-out look and creates a sense of open, empty spaces by avoiding the use of outlines to, for example, demarcate the edges of a room. In *Dimensions*, another short from the first series, animation is combined with live-action material to evoke the experience of psychosis. The contrasting effect of animation helps to convey the confusion of paranoid schizophrenia and the overwhelming distortion of reality.

Samantha Moore's *An Eyeful of Sound*, a film about the neurological condition synesthesia, takes the evocative function even further by eschewing a direct representation of its soundtrack, on which we hear people describing what it is like to have audio-visual synesthesia (when sound triggers other sensory responses, such as taste or sight). The film initially appears quite abstract, until it becomes clear some way into its running time that the animation is evoking the synesthetic experience through responding to the soundtrack in a similar way to how images are triggered by sound for an audio-visual synesthete. Moore finessed and fine-tuned her film through close collaboration with her documentary subjects to ensure the accuracy of the film's imagery.

Animation's evocative potential means that it can help encourage us to imagine what it would be like to experience things from someone else's point of view, even if that point of view is cognitively very different from our own. Because of this, animated documentaries have become a very useful way of raising awareness, and their production has been funded by agencies that are keen to promote this. For example, Samantha Moore's *An Eyeful of Sound* was funded by the Wellcome Collection, a charity that supports medical and science research. Moore was the recipient of an arts award, which is intended to promote public knowledge and understanding of medical and scientific issues. There is evidence that animated documentaries are successful in encouraging viewers to imagine the world from someone else's perspective. Andy Glynne, who is also a clinical psychologist, recalls a patient's response to the *Animated Minds* series as one of relief after years of trying to explain to people what their condition was like and that they could now show them the film instead (Glynne 2013: 75). Samantha Moore has had similar feedback to *An Eyeful of Sound* from one of the film's participants, who commented that her non-synesthetic husband had a better understanding of her condition after seeing the film (Honess Roe 2013: 123).

What is it about animation that makes it so successful at evoking the experiences of others? Andy Glynne (2013: 75) observes that if they had made the *Animated Minds* series "as live action films and had seen one person talking, then suddenly the film becomes about a particular individual rather than 'a condition'." Scott McCloud's writing about comic books is very useful for understanding why we more readily insert ourselves into animated stories than live-action ones. "Everyone can see him or herself in a simplified cartoon face [...], whereas arguably only a few (or just one) can identify with a photograph, or photo-realistic image, of a face" (Honess Roe 2013: 111). This might help us understand why films such as the *Animated Minds* series and *An Eyeful of Sound* are so effective at allowing us to comprehend personal, psychological experiences that might differ greatly from our own.

The three different functions of animation in animated documentary tend to imply different animation aesthetics, styles, and techniques. The mimetic substitution function usually works by virtue of the animation being photorealistic, or resembling, often as closely as possible, the look of live-action footage. Evocative animation often functions due to its symbolic or abstract style, which encourages and allows a viewer to imagine herself in the world being represented on screen. It is important to remember, however, that it is not unusual for any single animated documentary to contain animation that functions in all three ways: mimetic and non-mimetic substitution and evocation. Unlike the approaches suggested earlier by Wells and Patrick, the functions outlined above are less a way of categorizing or organizing animated documentaries than a way of understanding how the animation, and by implication the film as a whole, works to represent or evoke aspects of reality. By addressing animation's function, we can hope to answer the deceptively simple question of "What's the point?": that is, why use animation instead of live-action or photographic material?

Waltz with Bashir (Ari Folman, 2008)

It might seem unlikely that a Hebrew-language film about the post-trauma of fighting in the 1982 Lebanon War would draw such public and critical attention to the possibilities of animating documentary. However, Ari Folman's autobiographical feature-length film, with its pounding electro-pop soundtrack and vibrant, graphic-novel-style animation, was a success with audiences and film critics. The film cost $2 million to make, but grossed over $11 million worldwide. It was almost universally positively received by critics and nominated for many awards, including an Academy Award, the Palme d'Or at Cannes, and a Golden Globe (which it won). It is interesting to note, however, that the film was nominated at mainstream awards festivals such as the Oscars and Golden Globes not in the documentary or anima-tion categories, but for best foreign-language film. We can hypothesize the reasons for this, although the Academy is particularly noted for its relatively conservative sensibilities when it comes to documentary film.

As has been commonly noted (see Honess Roe 2013; Stewart 2010; Landesman and Bendor 2011), *Waltz with Bashir* is a documentary about memory as much as about the historical events of the Lebanon War. The motivating event for the film is Folman's realization that he has virtually no memory of what he did during the war. In particular, he has repressed his role in the brutal massacre of civilian Palestinian refugees residing in the Sabra and Shatila refugee camp in Beirut, who were killed by Phalangist Christian soldiers, allies of the Israelis, in misdirected vengeance for the murder of Phalangist leader Bashir Gemayel. While the Phalangists carried out the attack in the camp, their activities were aided by soldiers from the Israeli Defense Forces, including Folman, who fired flares to light up the night sky while the Phalangists took their revenge. *Waltz with Bashir* is Folman's search to reclaim his buried memories, by means of interviewing friends, acquaintances, and others who fought in the war. Folman is particularly haunted by a dream, or vision, which is shown three times in the film and becomes a kind of refrain, accompanied by an emotive and engulfing score, written by Max Richter. In this recurring scene, a young Folman is seen emerging naked from the sea with two companions. They exit the sea, pull on their uniforms and guns, and drift in a dreamlike trance through the city until they encounter a sea of wailing women wearing the hijab.

The animation style is an interesting aspect of the film to consider. At first glance, we might categorize the function of the animation in this film as simple mimetic substitution. Despite a stylized aesthetic that resembles a comic book or video game, the animation also has a strong element of realism. Most of the animated characters look like the people they represent,[4] albeit in Folman's case his animated self is a somewhat idealized, better-looking version. The film's production designer, David Polonsky, worked closely with Yoni Goodman, the animation director, to create verisimilitude in the film. When designing the animated layouts they used archival photos and film from Lebanon in the 1980s to make sure that the animated scenes resembled historical reality as much as possible. The character animation was drawn using the original video footage of the interviews as reference. The animation also functions, however, as evocation.

The film shows us three different types of events—interviews conducted by Folman in the present day, flashbacks to events that took place during and around the time of the Lebanon War, and personally subjective events such as dreams and hallucinations. It is easy to understand that animation is necessary for some of the historical scenes, because archival material of much of what we see might not exist. Dreams and hallucinations also are natural territory for animation. However, we know that the interviews that Folman conducted were filmed, with one exception. A more obvious approach to the film might have been to animate the dreams and hallucinations, to use footage of the interviews, and to use archival material for the historical flashbacks. Folman and his team actively eschewed this more conventional approach, instead deciding to animate the entire film (bar the final minutes, which are discussed below) because they did not want any one element of the film to seem more truthful than another. This choice has significance for how we interpret the film. Displaying a uniform animation style throughout the film suggests a parity of significance for present and past, witnessed and dreamt. Hallucinations are just as important as present-day interviews and past events in terms of this film's story—Ari Folman's quest to recapture his lost memory. The animation is evocative of the process of memory retrieval. It is also evocative in its "trippy" quality, conveyed in part through the orange-tinged color palate (something we come to realize as being inflected by the light of the flares). The slightly jerky character movement that is a symptom of the digital cut-out animation process also contributes to the dreamlike quality of the film—as if the characters are floating through past, present, real, and imagined.

We can question whether the film's aesthetic parity is undermined by its final, live-action coda. The end of the film represents a resolution for Folman. As he finally recalls his role in the Sabra and Shatila massacre—lighting flares from a nearby rooftop—the film's repeated refrain finally reaches closure. The last interviewee we hear from is a war reporter who was in Beirut during the massacre. As he describes the exodus of women from the camp the morning after the massacre, we see an animated reconstruction of this scene. The "camera" moves through the crowd of women and ends on the young Folman, in a shot that we have already seen three times before in the film—the final shot of his trance-like exit from the sea in his hallucination/flashback sequence. Folman stands, shell-shocked with breath heaving in his chest, as the women flood around him. What comes next is, in many ways, hard to reconcile with all that has been seen so far in the film. As we cut to the reverse shot of Folman's point of view the image switches to live-action archival footage. The camera pans around scenes of dead bodies piled in the rubble-strewn streets and stuffed into courtyards. Women wail with grief at the loss of their loved ones. A particularly haunting image of a child's hand and curly dark hair, poking out from a pile of bricks and rubble, closes the film, and it fades to black (see Figure 3.2). We have already seen this heartrending sight, just a few minutes earlier, in its animated version, which accompanies the war reporter's recollection of entering the camps (see Figure 3.3). The sight struck him because of the child's resemblance to his own daughter. Why then the need to see it again via archival footage? What does this final live-action sequence, which runs less than a minute and a half, say about the preceding hour and a half of animation? Does this

FIGURE 3.2 A final recourse to live action in *Waltz with Bashir* (Ari Folman, 2008).

FIGURE 3.3 The animated version of something we later see in live action in *Waltz with Bashir* (Ari Folman, 2008).

ultimate recourse to live action undermine animated documentary? Do we need that final bit of confirmation, or impact, to take the film seriously as a piece of nonfiction? Dave Saunders proposes that this sequence is "an afterthought, designed to wrench the viewer back into an empathetic engagement with reality" (2010: 184). Stewart, however, suggests that the final moments are "no formal recapitulation to simple verité" (2010: 62). I have previously proposed that "the truth of the experience is, for Folman, as much about its incomprehensibility and his amnesia as about what actually happened. [...] It is through the animated journey that we learn the true meaning of the war for Folman" (Honess Roe 2013: 168). While the archival news footage may reveal the "truth of the event of the massacre" (ibid.), the truth of Folman's experience of fighting, and forgetting, is much more meaningfully conveyed through the film's use of animation.

Waltz with Bashir is a film about memory, but it is also a film about guilt. The film suggests that the reason for Folman's amnesia is his guilt about his activities during the war. His guilt is particularly acute, suggests his psychologist friend Ori, because the Sabra and Shatila camps carry a memory of the Nazi concentration camps and the Holocaust and Folman is subconsciously equating his behavior with that of a Nazi guard. *Waltz with Bashir* has been accused of ignoring the real victims of the Lebanon War—the Palestinian and Lebanese civilians—and instead directing the audience's sympathy toward Folman and the other young Israeli men who fought in the Israeli Defense Forces. Saunders notes that the film has also been read as absolving Folman and his cohort of any guilt and, in this way, succumbing to the Israeli tendency of "shooting and crying" (2010: 169). That is, it depicts "the Israeli soldier as morally conflicted [...] a mechanism that allows Israelis to emerge from even their darkest episodes with their moral image intact" (Freedland 2008). That *Waltz with Bashir* has provoked so much debate can only be seen as a positive thing for animated documentary. The film's success, commercially and critically, raised the profile of animated documentary to an audience beyond scholars and filmmakers already invested in the form. The questions the film raises, about aesthetics, ethics, and the responsibility of representation, and, most fundamentally, the purposes of using animation as a representational strategy for documentary, are questions one can ask of all animated documentaries.

The present and future of animated documentary

The past 25 years have seen a marked increase in the production of animated documentary and also a growing interest in the form from film critics and scholars. There are also several indications that animation has become an accepted means of documentary representation. Animated documentary is now regularly mentioned in introductory-level books on documentary in ways that it was not prior to 2010. Bill Nichols's revised edition of his *Introduction to Documentary*, published in 2010, talks about animated documentary, whereas the original version, published in 2001, makes no mention of it. Similarly, Dave Saunders's 2010 book, *Documentary*, includes a lengthy discussion of *Waltz with Bashir*, and Brian Winston's recent compendium on documentary (*The Documentary Film Book*) contains a chapter on animated documentary by Andy Glynne (Glynne 2013).

There are other indications that animation has become accepted. As well as an increase in the number of animated documentaries being made, there has been a rise in otherwise live-action documentaries that include short animated sections. Franny Armstrong's crowd-funded climate-change activism documentary *The Age of Stupid* (2009) includes witty and pointed animated sections, created by Jonathan Hodgson, to emphasize the film's point regarding capitalism, globalization, and depleting natural resources. Michael Moore used animation in *Bowling for Columbine* (2002) to make clear his attitude toward America's relationship with firearms. A short, anarchic, *South Park*-style animated sequence paints this history as ridiculous, extreme, and founded on racist exploitation, inequality, and fear. More recently, the Russian film *Khodorkovsky* (Cyril Tuschi, 2011) uses animation with seemingly little purpose at all, but instead as just one of many filmmaking tools available. We would not necessarily call these films animated documentaries, as the animated sections make up a very small percentage of the film and one could, arguably, remove the animation without detracting too greatly from the overall meaning of the film. However, these films, and the many other recent live-action documentaries that contain animated segments, point to the fact that animation is becoming increasingly accepted as another tool, along with interviews, observational filming, archival material, and all the rest, in the documentary maker's toolbox.

Suggested viewing

Many of the films listed below are available to view online via the filmmakers' websites or other streaming sites.

A Is for Autism (Tim Webb, 1992, UK)
An early animated documentary about autism that combines live action and animation. Made in collaboration with people with autism.
Abductees (Paul Vester, 1995, UK)
Short film about alien abduction using animation and other media.
Animated Minds (Andy Glynne, 2003 and 2009, UK)
Two series of four short films about mental health issues.
Blind Justice (Orly Yadin, 1987, UK)
Four short films made for Channel 4 television, about how the law treats women.
Centrefold (Ellie Land, 2012, UK)
An awareness-raising film funded by the Wellcome Collection, about labiaplasty.
Chicago 10 (Brett Morgen, 2007, USA)
A feature film about the trial of Abbie Hoffman and other members of the Yippie movement for "inciting riot" at the 1968 Democratic convention in Chicago. Could be considered the first feature-length animated documentary.
An Eyeful of Sound (Samantha Moore, 2009, UK)
An evocative animated documentary about audio-visual synesthesia.

Feeling My Way (Jonathan Hodgson, 1997, UK)

Animated documentary that combines animation and live action to show the filmmaker's train of thoughts as he walks through London.

Hidden (David Aronowitsch, Hannah Heilborn, and Mats Johansson, 2002, Sweden)

Animated documentary about an undocumented child immigrant.

His Mother's Voice (Dennis Tupicoff, 1997, Australia)

Rotoscoped animated documentary that illustrates a radio interview.

Leonid's Story (Rainer Ludwigs, 2011, Germany/Russia)

Combines animation, documentary interviews, and archival footage to tell one family's story of the Chernobyl nuclear disaster.

Little Deaths (Ruth Lingford, 2010, USA)

An animated documentary about orgasms.

Rocks in My Pockets (Signe Baumane, 2014, USA)

Feature-length animated documentary about the mental health issues suffered by the filmmaker and other women in her family.

Ryan (Chris Landreth, 2004, Canada)

Computer-animated film about the animator Ryan Larkin.

Silence (Orly Yadin and Sylvie Bringas, 1998, UK)

Short film that uses two styles of animation (created by Ruth Lingford and Tim Webb) to tell a story of Holocaust survival.

Snack and Drink (Bob Sabiston, 1999, USA)

Rotoshopped film about the filmmaker's encounter with Ryan, a teenage boy with autism.

Survivors (Sheila Sofian, 1997, USA)

A film that uses animation to talk about domestic abuse against women.

The Trouble with Love and Sex (Jonathan Hodgson, 2012, UK)

Animated documentary about the relationship counselling service Relate, made for television.

Waltz with Bashir (Ari Folman, 2008, Israel)

Feature-length animated documentary about the 1982 Lebanon War.

Notes

1 Some might argue that "propaganda" is a more suitable term, as the film expresses a very strong opinion on the German perpetrators of the sinking.
2 Rotoscoping is the process of tracing over live-action material to create animation.
3 All these films are discussed in greater detail in Honess Roe (2013).
4 The exception here is Carmi, Folman's friend who is now living off a fortune made in the falafel trade in the Netherlands. Carmi requests that Folman not film him and his voiceover is also dubbed by an actor.

Bibliography

DelGaudio, Sybil. 1997. "If Truth Be Told, Can 'Toons Tell It? Documentary and Animation." *Film History* 9 (2): 189–99.

Freedland, Jonathan. 2008. "Lest We Forget." *The Guardian*, October 25. Available online at www.theguardian.com/film/2008/oct/25/waltz-with-bashir-ari-folman (accessed December 23, 2014).

Glynne, Andy. 2013. "Drawn from Life: The Animated Documentary." In *The Documentary Film Book*, ed. Brian Winston. London: British Film Institute. 73–5.

Grierson, John. 1933. "The Documentary Producer." *Cinema Quarterly* 2 (1): 7–9.

Honess Roe, Annabelle. 2013. *Animated Documentary*. Basingstoke: Palgrave Macmillan.

Landesman, Ohad, and Roy Bendor. 2011. "Animated Recollection and Spectatorial Experience in *Waltz with Bashir*." *Animation: An Interdisciplinary Journal* 6 (3): 353–70.

Morris, Errol. 2004. Interview with *The Believer*. Available online at www.errolmorris.com/content/interview/believer0404.html (accessed December 23, 2014).

Nichols, Bill. 2001. *Introduction to Documentary*. Bloomington and Indianapolis: Indiana University Press.

——. 2010. *Introduction to Documentary*. 2nd ed. Bloomington and Indianapolis: Indiana University Press.

Patrick, Eric. 2004. "Representing Reality: Structural/Conceptual Design in Non-fiction Animation." *Animac Magazine* 3: 36–47.

Saunders, Dave. 2010. *Documentary*. London: Routledge.

Stewart, Garrett. 2010. "Screen Memory in *Waltz with Bashir*." *Film Quarterly* 63 (3): 58–62.

Strøm, Gunnar. 2003. "The Animated Documentary." *Animation Journal* 11: 46–63.

Ward, Paul. 2005. *Documentary: The Margins of Reality*. London: Wallflower.

Wells, Paul. 1997. "The Beautiful Village and the True Village: A Consideration of Animation and the Documentary Aesthetic." In *Art and Animation*, ed. Paul Wells. London: Academy Editions. 40–5.

Winston, Brian. 1995. *Claiming the Real: The Griersonian Documentary and Its Legitimations*. London: British Film Institute.

——, ed. 2013. *The Documentary Film Book*. London: British Film Institute.

4

PRODUCING THE CROWDSOURCED DOCUMENTARY

The Implications of Storytelling and Technology

Heather McIntosh

The participation of a subject in a documentary production represents an ideal for the form's democratic and advocacy intentions, as this participation suggests a greater agency unavailable to subjects through representational strategies alone. Subject participation appears in documentary productions throughout the last century. For example, with *Misère au Borinage* (1933), Joris Ivens and Henri Storck worked with striking coal miners to recreate a protest march (Nichols 2001: 149–50). For *Chronicle of a Summer* (1960), Jean Rouch and Edgar Morin included their interview subjects' observations in a rough cut of the film as an experiment in "shared anthropology" (Spence and Navarro 2011: 90). These inclusions allow subjects to assume greater roles in the production process, thereby turning them into participants.

The modes of participation shift in online spaces, suggesting a potential for greater collective involvement through conversations, collaborations, and user-generated content production (Jenkins, Ford, and Green 2013: 154), as well as for rethinking what participation implies within documentary practice. According to Jon Dovey (2014), "Conventional film making and journalistic practices are adapting to the potentials of participation and changing, though not destroying, the forms and the address to the audience of documentary" (19). Crowdsourcing offers an opening up of the documentary production process, as it imbues a sense of deep optimism for the democratic possibilities it brings. Daren C. Brabham (2013) defines crowdsourcing as "an online, distributed problem-solving and production model that leverages the collective intelligence of online communities to serve specific organizational goals" (xix). This definition builds on *The Wisdom of Crowds* by James Surowiecki (2005), who states that a crowd carries greater overall intelligence than a series of cultivated individuals, particularly if the crowd is diverse, independent, and decentralized (22). With crowdsourcing, crowds partner with organizations on creative productions toward specific goals. For documentary production, this process suggests the introduction of decentralized crowds into a central organization, which includes the director and production team, while possible goals include not only the completion of the project but also other targets associated with social documentary production, such as raising awareness, motivating audiences, and enacting change.

Several recent documentaries incorporating crowdsourcing as part of their production processes have drawn significant attention from the press. Helmed by Ridley Scott and Kevin MacDonald, the heralded *Life in a Day* (2011) brought together footage shot from around the globe on July 24, 2010, into a theatrical film. More than 4,500 hours across 80,000 videos were uploaded to partner site YouTube and then edited into the 90-minute production ("About the Production" n.d.). The *One Day on Earth* trilogy followed a similar model in gathering footage on dates in 2010, 2011, and 2012. Cameras were distributed to participants in more than 150 countries, with the theme of each segment of the trilogy guiding them (Ruddick n.d.). Partnering with the United Nations and other not-for-profit organizations, the project claims almost 38,000 members and counting. For its interactive documentary *A Journal of Insomnia* (Kaganskiy 2013), the National Film Board of Canada recorded stories from 2,000 insomniac people between the hours of 9 p.m. and 5 a.m. to create a portrait of the sleeplessness that affects millions of people.

Each of these examples shows the possible scale of crowdsourcing through the numbers of participants, their disparate demographics and locations, and their various contributions. Another popular application of crowdsourcing is crowdfunding, which seeks support through campaigns on such sites as Kickstarter and Indiegogo. The primary goal of crowdfunding is to raise money for production and other expenses. In return contributors enjoy perks for their cash donations. For Steve James's *Life Itself*, a biopic about the late film critic Roger Ebert, the Indiegogo campaign offered private streaming, gift cards to Steak 'n Shake, DVDs, signed merchandise, fan club memberships, theatrical screenings, and social media mentions ("*Life Itself*" n.d.).

This chapter addresses the topic of crowdsourcing through the modes of storytelling and applications of new technology within contemporary documentary production. The foundations for this chapter come from interviews with five documentary makers who used crowdsourcing as part of their production processes. These directors include Elizabeth Rynecki, who is working on *Chasing Portraits*; Audrey Ewell, who co-directed *99%: The Occupy Wall Street Collaborative Film* (2013); Jeanie Finlay, who is directing *Orion: The Man Who Would Be King*; Liz Canning, who is directing *Less Car More Go*; and Yasmin Elayat, who co-created with Jigar Mehta *18 Days in Egypt*. These titles represent the diversity within the contemporary documentary landscape generally and within crowdsourcing more specifically.

The chapter begins with a brief review of crowdsourcing, looking at its definitions, motivations, applications, and outcomes with a focus on how these relate to documentary production. The following sections provide overviews of the five major projects and the women behind them, and an exploration of how crowdsourcing within these productions intersects with two major aspects of filmmaking: storytelling and technology. Overall, this chapter links these ideas through connections between online and offline spaces, between amateur and professional contributions, and between crowd potential and individual contributions.

Crowdsourcing

As a concept and a practice, crowdsourcing appears across a wide spectrum of venues and applications. Organizations using crowdsourcing include corporations, government, and not-for-profit groups, and their projects vary just as much as their vested interests. The US government regularly uses it to promote discussion toward innovations in policy through its challenge.gov website. Corporations use crowdsourcing to develop new products, packaging, and marketing schemes, such as when Anheuser-Busch developed Black Crown lager and Doritos called for fans' Super Bowl advertisements (Erickson 2012). Not-for-profit organizations use crowdsourcing to raise funds, gather information, and outsource labor. The United States Holocaust Memorial Museum, for example, seeks help from the crowd in identifying and telling the stories of the more than 10,000 schoolchildren who lived in the Lodz ghetto during World War II before most of the children perished in the Nazi concentration camps (United States Holocaust Memorial Museum n. d.). Some companies, such as InnoCentive, work with all three sectors to connect organizations and projects with the right crowds.

Crowdsourcing ideally consists of a co-production model that unites an organization's goals with a crowd's collective intelligence and skills, which suggests that the organization and the crowd work together toward these goals. Crowdsourcing distributes the control of production so that innovation and power flow in multiple directions at the same time, even though the project's goals remain within the organization (Brabham 2013: xxi). Brabham explains further:

> In crowdsourcing, the locus of control regarding the creative production of goods and ideas exists *between* the organization and the public, a shared process of bottom-up, open creation by the crowd and top-down management by those charged with servicing an organization's strategic interests.
>
> *(2013: xxi)*

The Internet allows the gathering of even larger crowds from disparate geographical locations and generally reduces the barriers to people's participation (Brabham 2013). With new platforms and media technologies added to its capacity for connectivity, Web 2.0 further supports different forms of participation (Garcia Martinez and Walton 2014: 203), although the latter term remains open to significant debate for its possibilities (Jenkins, Ford, and Green 2013) and limitations (Fuchs 2014).

Multiple intended outcomes drive the uses and applications of crowdsourcing. Brabham (2013) offers a comprehensive framework, which delineates four types: "knowledge discovery and management," "broadcast search," "peer-vetted creative production," and "distributed human-intelligence tasking" (44–5). Knowledge discovery involves locating data. For example, FoodSwitch, an Australian nutrition app, crowdsourced nutritional information for 30,000 products from its users (Dunford et al. 2014). A broadcast search seeks a broad, diverse talent pool and applies members' skills to scientific problems toward their solutions. With this method, the website InnoCentive allows companies to post problems in the form of contests and solicit potential solutions from participants. One contest called for developing solar-powered lights to keep people safe in remote African villages, and the winner, who developed the lights, pocketed a $20,000 prize ("InnoCentive Solvers" n.d.). Creative production focuses on design and creation wherein the crowd shares a vested interest in taste. The aforementioned Doritos Super Bowl ads fit this type. Human-intelligence tasking brings human skills to tasks that exceed the capacities of computational analysis. Through Amazon's Mechanical Turk, crowds might determine product categories, identify correct word spellings, or rank information. Crowdsourced tasks related to documentary productions align with knowledge discovery and creative production. The crowdsourcing used in each of the projects discussed in this chapter depended on the respective production's goals, and it was enacted at the different stages of pre-production, production, and post-production. Within all of the frameworks, however, it is important to recognize that crowd-sourcing becomes part of the production and is not the entire production (Roig Telo 2013). It is also important to recognize that levels of participation vary across crowdsourcing projects. As Antoni Roig Telo (2013) explains, "[P]opular 'crowd' terms in media, like crowdsourcing and crowdfunding, do not encompass the diversity of creative practices involved in participatory media production" (2314).

While Brabham's four types shed light on the motivations and desired outcomes of the production side of crowdsourcing, the activities and motivations of the crowd side remain important for understanding the practice as well. In his book *Here Comes Everybody*, Clay Shirky (2009) outlines three tiers of group activities within crowdsourcing and other online applications. The simplest activity is sharing, such as information or materials (Shirky 2009: 49). The next activity in complexity is cooperation, which involves aligning behaviors across a group toward common goals, such as engaging in conversation within and across online platforms (49). The most complex activity is collective action, wherein the group's cohesiveness determines the group's identity, commitment, and binding outcomes (50–1). For Liz Canning's *Less Car More Go*, for example, collective action comes from the group's identity with, commitment to, and investment in cargo bikes as alternatives to cars. Though the types of participation available in a crowdsourcing project originate with the organization and its goals, Shirky's tiers indicate how people can approach these projects depending on their levels of interest and incentive. Motivations for participation vary, and they can include wanting a sense of belonging, a belief in a cause, the connection with other people, and, possibly least so, the chance for financial reward. Other motivations include passing time, having fun, making contributions, and engaging in challenges (Brabham 2013: 68).

Production overviews

Five projects provide insight into the ways crowdsourcing becomes part of a doc-umentary production. These projects cover a range of topics, such as music, art, and social movements, but what links them is their relationship with history, in that each one creates a history about its subject through the story it tells. These projects also engage in varying levels of activism. Each person interviewed brings a unique background to the production and maintains a unique relationship to it and its subject as well. The following section offers a brief summary of each one.

Elizabeth Rynecki is a first-time documentary maker and creator of the project *Chasing Portraits*. The documentary traces the quest to recover the lost paintings of Moshe Rynecki, who painted scenes of Jewish life in Warsaw during the 1920s and 30s. As the Nazis invaded Poland in 1939, he bundled 800 of his paintings and hid them so they would not be destroyed. Moshe Rynecki died during the Holocaust, and since then family members have recovered only 120 of the 800 works. *Chasing Portraits* follows Rynecki's journey as she attempts to recover more of her great-grandfather's lost works. The film is currently in production.

Audrey Ewell founded and directed *99%: The Occupy Wall Street Collaborative Film*. Aaron Aites produced and directed the film as part of the founding team with her. Ewell previously directed *Until the Light Takes Us* (2009), a film about Norwegian black metal music, with Aites. The *99%* film followed the Occupy movements that appeared in cities throughout the United States and around the world, and it invited people at those protests to record video and submit the footage for inclusion in the film. The documentary received funding from the Sundance Documentary Institute, and it premiered at the Sundance Film Festival in 2013. Unlike Rynecki's involvement in her own story, Ewell remained outside the Occupy movement.

Jeanie Finlay is directing *Orion: The Man Who Would Be King*, about Jimmy "Orion" Ellis. An American singer who sounded like Elvis Presley and performed under the masked persona known as Orion, Ellis was shot and killed during an armed robbery at the age of 53 in 1998. Known for her documentaries about music, including *Sound It Out* (2011) and *The Great Hip Hop Hoax* (2013), Finlay learned about the story when she purchased one of his albums. Upon researching more about Ellis and his background, she decided to pursue the story, in the process connecting with Ellis's fans throughout the world. The production of *Orion* involves multiple organizations, including BBC Storyville, Ffilm Cymru Wales, and Finlay's own Glimmer Films. It is co-produced by Truth Department. It also has connections with REACT (Research and Enterprise in Arts and Creative Technology), which awarded the project money and research support through its Future Documentary Sandbox project, and with Creative England, which also offered funding. The film is currently in post-production.

Liz Canning brings her passion for cargo bikes to *Less Car More Go*, which is about the cargo bike movement that has emerged in the United States during the last 20 years. Instead of relying on cars, people adopt cargo bikes for commuting, errands, and even moving. Herself a long-time bicycle rider and inspired by the energy within the movement that she found online, Canning reached out to people who had become "fanatic evangelistic advocates," as she describes them, and recruited about 100 co-directors, who submitted footage and other materials as part of telling the story. Canning brings to this project extensive experience in editing, animation, producing, and directing in documentary and other media forms. *Less Car More Go* is still in production.

Co-creator Yasmin Elayat comes to *18 Days in Egypt* with a background as a human–computer interaction designer and creative technologist. While the other projects profiled here point toward a completed film as a final project, *18 Days in Egypt* is a collaborative, online documentary that centers on Internet users telling stories about the ongoing movements and activities in Egypt, in their own voices and using their own media. Users gather a variety of digital materials, such as moving images, stills, and audio, in order to share the stories they want to tell from their own perspectives. Viewers then come to the site and watch the stories they want to see. This approach means that *18 Days in Egypt* is evolving constantly without a definitive final product like the other four projects. Working as co-creator with Jigar Mehta, Elayat developed and revised the collaborative storytelling platform Group-Stream as the project evolved. The project received support from the Ford Foundation, Tribeca Film Institute, Sundance Institute, and Brooklyn Law Incubator and Policy Clinic. *18 Days in Egypt* is available at 18daysinegypt.com.

The roles of crowdsourcing within these documentaries vary. Each maker interviewed discussed crowdsourcing from within the specifics of her production, and offered perspectives on various issues related to handling the crowdsourcing, recruiting participants, and integrating the crowd's submissions into her project. Each maker also offered insights into managing the people themselves and accounting for the variables in their skills, preparations, and contributions. The following sections explore these intersections through documentary storytelling and technology.

Documentary storytelling

In contemporary documentary production, storytelling is an integral part of the production and the promotion processes both before and after the film's release. Linking to documentary advocacy in particular, story-driven awareness campaigns offer greater potential to connect with audiences because audiences relate more to people than to abstract ideas or truth claims (Miller 2010). The story becomes a way to unite the subjects involved, the documentary makers, and the potential crowds, who may become viewers, donors, and contributors. The relationship between crowdsourcing and documentary storytelling depends on the demands of each project. Sometimes the scale and novelty of the crowdsourcing overshadows the documentary narrative itself, as in the cases of both *Life in a Day* (2010) and the *One Day on Earth* (2010, 2011, 2012) trilogy. For most documentaries, though, the crowdsourcing activities and materials connect with the storytelling in smaller ways during all phases of the production.

The most common type of crowdsourced contribution is through materials, such as film footage and still images. All five projects involved these kinds of materials, but how each project approached them depended on the project's conception and, in part, on the makers' involvement. Rynecki and Canning in particular shared personal connections with their projects. For Rynecki, the crowd became her co-sleuths in solving the mystery of her great-grandfather's missing paintings. Canning, herself a cargo bike enthusiast, wanted to tell the story of the cargo bike movement, and she connected with and drew inspiration from the co-directors, who shared materials toward the telling of that story. For Finlay, the crowd she drew on included the adoring fans of Jimmy "Orion" Ellis and others involved with his life and career. For the *99%* film, Ewell sought footage from people who were involved in or who witnessed the Occupy movements happening around the United States, but she herself remained outside the movement. All four of these projects involve a central figure gathering these materials toward the final piece. For Elayat, who designed the platform that enabled people to create their stories, the conversation between crowdsourcing and activism shifted because the crowds shared the stories that they felt should be told in *18 Days in Egypt*. Elayat deliberately removed herself from the storytelling process, instead focusing on the development of interactive tools. By not delimiting the scope of the story in advance, Elayat and her co-director encouraged the crowd to exercise its own agency in determining what to share, how, and when through their streams on the site.

Working with the people creating materials drives crowdsourcing in documentary production in different ways. The *99%* film offered a unique way to consider crowd participation because the project called for submissions from anyone, whether a person had previous experience in film production or not. The materials provided a broader look at American life than the familiar depictions in mainstream media, with stories about poverty in Mississippi and a single mother in Minneapolis. Ewell recounted having asked the co-directors she was working with, who originated from very diverse areas, to submit all of their raw footage and assemble a pre-edit, which ran longer than the segment would run in the final edit of the film, but showed the co-directors' intentions for the story. She then provided feedback about whether to shoot additional footage that might help integrate the individual stories into the film as a whole. Ewell, Aites, and their editor then put together the film with consultation from two other directors. In the end, she said, "It's very much their stories that they wanted to tell" (Ewell 2014).

Unlike the other four directors, who served as central contact points, Elayat developed the online platform as an interaction designer for the crowd participants to submit and to view their stories. The storytelling and the people's empowerment to tell those stories drove the project's development, not the other way around. Elayat explained further,

> *18 Days* took this theoretical idea, that a country could write its own history, and documented everything in real time utilizing a variety of tools in social media, regular media, mobile phone cameras, DSLRs. Everyone was somehow documenting in their own ways, so how can you leverage that? In the beginning we kept talking about trying to document that living history, leveraging existing tools and existing technology. If the technology doesn't allow this, then you have to find something that does work. I think a lot of times people start with the technology for this kind of project and then think

about the goals. [The subject is an] afterthought, and I think you can tell in the work. I believe the technology is secondary. It's just the medium and the tool. The number one question is what is the big major goal here?

(Elayat 2014)

Elayat was also sensitive to the digital divide and bridging it, particularly with the vision of an accessible project for a country with only about 25 percent of people online. To help people who did not possess the skills to tell their stories online, the project recruited several Fellows who had the skills or were trained and could help bring in those stories. For Elayat, then, the story itself became the foundation, the common denominator, for the crowd's interactions with *18 Days in Egypt*, either as producers or as viewers.

Directors' favorite submissions demonstrate the rich variety of the submitted materials. Canning recounted how a professional documentary maker putting together a mini-documentary captured a cargo bike story of a family who moved from West Virginia to Buffalo, New York, and gave the unused footage to her. She explained that the director "wanted the footage to have a life beyond" the singular narrative of the longer documentary (Canning 2014). Ewell, on the other hand, shared an example related to the infamous police pepper-spraying incident from the Occupy movement. Officer Inspector Anthony Bologna approached a line of protesting girls, sprayed them, and walked away—an iconic moment that left an imprint on the public perception of Occupy, drew heavy criticism for being unwarranted, and resulted in subsequent lawsuits (Haberman 2012). A woman, whom Ewell called "the silver bullet," shared a recording of the incident, which had become an Internet meme (Ewell 2014; Wortham and Bilton 2011). As Ewell described her, "this lovely older woman," who "was actually one of the people who filmed the girls being pepper-sprayed," got her footage because police were hesitant to treat her as brusquely as other protesters. Elayat admitted to being taken aback by how people reacted to certain events, particularly on violent days when no one wanted to participate. She said, "No one wanted to talk. No one was in the mood. That was something that was very tricky. I don't think we anticipated the human factor" (Elayat 2014). She cited one story that did emerge from the aftermath of violence.

How the footage becomes part of the documentary and its style depends on the production's goals. Canning, who envisioned her work as part of the cargo bike movement, intended to tell its story by focusing on several key people, using the crowdsourcing materials to supplement the narrative. She explained, "I feel like most of the crowdsourced stuff will be either parts, used in montages that are sort of going to convey some stage of the movement. In some cases, there's enough stuff there to talk about the scene in a particular city or a particular trend or a particular family" (Canning 2014). Part of her rationale for this decision was that in order for the documentary to have a proper beginning, middle, and end, she needed to focus on a few key people with whom viewers could develop a close connection.

For Ewell and Finlay, the contributed materials also become part of the documentary's style. For Ewell, style—specifically, aesthetics—played an important role in documentary production in that it added "another layer of truth about the subject matter" (Ewell 2014). In *99%* the crowdsourced materials and the style of the film complemented the telling of the Occupy story and its moment in American history. Resonating with the organizational strategies of Occupy, anyone was welcome to participate in *99%*, and they received a wide range of footage from people around the country.

For *Orion: The Man Who Would Be King*, Finlay saw the mythmaking in Ellis's legend as part of the story and the crowd's contributions. Ellis for many years performed as "Orion," a masked stage persona whom people sometimes confused with the deceased Elvis Presley. Many members of the film's crowd belong to an older generation, some baby boomers and even older, and many of them are fans and collectors of Ellis-related memorabilia. Many of them offered still photographs, and Finlay described how people also gave her airline tickets, micro cassette tapes, super 8 footage, handmade T-shirts, and even the jacket from Ellis's first record, of which only 500 copies were made. Finlay recalled how the airline tickets came from a woman who was in love with him and who flew to Los Angeles and lived with Ellis for two years there. Those tickets were from her flight to go live with him. Finlay developed the story from what this array of material suggested to her. She said, "From that we animated sections and brought animators in to design, to bring parts of the story to life." With some of the other materials, the production team has been projecting them and then filming them again. Finlay stated, "It's giving an extra layer of immersion and a dreamy quality to the film" (Finlay 2014).

The crowd assisted the processes of research and story development for other films as well, which helped Rynecki's production in particular. The effort to solve the mystery of her great-grandfather's missing paintings covered three continents and multiple countries, crossed language and cultural barriers, and involved working with cultural and other institutions. Rynecki described how crowdsourcing helped her with navigating the culture of Poland; connected her with individuals who helped her with Polish, German, and Yiddish and their translations; and provided access to an online auction site based in Poland. Rynecki found great value in this kind of help. She said, "The first is that I get information that I didn't have and the second is that it becomes this detective story and people get invested in my story and it makes people want to follow along" (Rynecki 2014).

These contributions from the crowd impact the stories in terms of the construction and style of their narratives. While they pose some challenges in developing the story, they offer a rich opportunity for potential new directions. They also require a different relationship between the filmmaker and the materials. Working with crowdsourced materials requires the director, according to Rynecki, to "let go" of the story in some ways so that it can develop more organically, even though the story remains personal to her life and family (Rynecki 2014). Ewell recalls her excitement when people turned in footage that she was not expecting. That kind of footage "made us tremendously happy, because those were the times where I felt the collaboration really working," she said (Ewell 2014). Finlay compares the crowdsourced production with being an archaeologist who digs for the story through the depths of Ellis's fans and their personal archives. She said, "The film wouldn't exist if it weren't for crowdsourcing because it's all private archive" (Finlay 2014). Canning will be "showing the way that these main characters are interacting with the movement and I need the crowd source stuff to manifest the movement" (Canning 2014). For Elayat, *18 Days in Egypt* represents "technology driven storytelling" that places the people before the technology (Elayat 2014).

Technology

According to Brabham (2013), crowdsourcing requires "an online environment that allows the work to take place and the community to interact with the organization" (3). His definition, though, covers only a fraction of the technologies involved with crowdsourcing and documentary production, which in itself largely occurs through various practices including interviewing, creating B-roll, and other applications. In this regard, technologies should be understood as numerous tools performing diverse tasks, instead of defined solely by the Internet or online environments. In fact, a constant flow of tasks between online and offline spaces during communication and production occurs when crowdsourcing factors into a documentary production.

Communication drives every documentary production, but with the addition of crowdsourcing to the process, it gains another layer of importance and complexity. Part of that complexity derives from the added work of gathering the crowd, managing the larger quantity of people, and addressing its range of skills. Social networking sites such as Facebook and Twitter contribute to this process of generating interest, making connections, and maintaining connections. All five productions had a dedicated Facebook page, and all five had related Twitter accounts, such as to the specific film, to the film's maker (as in Rynecki's case), or both (as in Finlay's case). Rynecki mentioned that Twitter offered the opportunity to personalize her communications in reaching out to people, and Finlay highlighted the fact that Facebook connected her with a key figure in the Jimmy Ellis story. During the shooting that killed him, Helen King managed to survive, and Finlay found her and reached out to her through the site, which resulted in an interview. According to Finlay, "Before social media, I wouldn't have been able to find her" (Finlay 2014). Notably, Ellis fans used closed Facebook and Yahoo! groups to keep connected and talk about him.

Other productions maintained a website that served as the hub for connecting with people, such as by offering guidance on submitting footage. Canning's website offered explanations for crowdsourcing, its role in the film, and her own role as the filmmaker. It further explained where to send footage, what kind of footage to send, what technical specs to use, where to get equipment, and even how to shoot in the style wanted. In Elayat's case, the website became the documentary itself. Instead of the submitted footage becoming a separate film, it became the end-user experience for the website users. In a section titled "How to Participate," the site offered four steps for people to follow, but it also allowed people to "start a stream, contribute some media, tell us the story, invite others to fill in the gaps. You can always come back to add more or reflect on the stream" ("How to Participate" n.d.). In this case, the website platform—Groupstream—enabled the storytelling to occur.

Not all tools connect documentary makers with their audiences through social networking sites. Both Rynecki and Canning, for example, used e-mail news-letters. For crowds specifically, Ewell started a listserv, only to be overwhelmed by the volume of postings to it; she abandoned it within a week. She shifted to group e-mails by regions around the country to manage them better, and she used Google Docs and Dropbox for other collaborative tasks.

Critical to engaging audiences online is to go to where they congregate and not make them come to you (Bennett and Segerberg 2011). Jeanie Finlay in particular stressed the importance of this practice because of the demographics for Jimmy Ellis's fans, who tend to be over 60 years old and whose fandom predates the consumer availability of the Internet. Engaging these audiences also means under-standing their attitudes and limits to interacting online. While some of them used Facebook or the Yahoo! groups, some of them resisted using e-mail to send materials. Some of the users wanted to donate money to the production as part of its crowdfunding efforts, but they refused to use their credit cards online. Finlay explained, "In a way, it was easier for them to share a story or memory than it was to put money in" (Finlay 2014).

Another strategy for gathering materials came through a media-scraping company called Tint, which creates and collates hashtag campaigns across social media and offers analytics about their reach and impact. While the company sells its services to online marketing campaigns for brands and products, the company donated its services to Finlay's production. Finlay explained further that the company's tool

> allows you to pull various feeds, whether it's from any social media, Pinterest, Facebook, Twitter, Instagram, Flickr. You either pull in specific feeds or you can custom hashtag something and it'll pull it in. People can share material using their favorite social media and then it will automatically contribute it to the project, rather than making people go to a special portal that you've invented.
>
> *(Finlay 2014)*

For the documentary, contributors just needed to add the hashtag #MyOrion or #IAmOrion to any post on a public feed in order for Tint's platform to find and collect it into campaign-dedicated pages. The technology makes online audience participation in a crowdsourcing endeavor simple.

Interpersonal communication also navigated to offline technologies. Ewell mentioned how even within the flurry of online communication with people around the country, some of this communication moved to the telephone and sometimes to in person as the project progressed. For Rynecki, these offline con-nections proved instrumental in learning about key resources that hold clues to the mysteries of her great-grandfather's missing paintings. She regularly gives talks at universities and cultural institutions about her project, which she said makes for some amazing connections with people about potential leads and resources. After giving a talk at the University of Toronto's Center for Jewish Studies, Rynecki learned from an audience member about a collection in the university library that had photographs of her great-grandfather's paintings and originals of his letters. A connection after another talk resulted in Rynecki working with a Fulbright scholar in Warsaw who obtained information from the Jewish Historical Institute there for her. While online communication is important for reaching crowds and interacting with them, personal appearances also remain important for the same reasons.

The use of technology is significant not only in facilitating communication but also for production. It especially gains prominence in coordinating the submissions of material and solving problems. Because four of the five projects seek to complete films about their subjects using archival materials, the quality and consistency of the footage are important. Video-based sites such as YouTube and Vimeo allow people to connect with others through their uploading and sharing of videos, but the visual quality available through these sites remains too low for final film production. While Ewell found some potential contributors through Vimeo, for example, she still needed better-looking visuals. High-quality footage often requires digital files that exceed the upload limits for many e-mail services and even cloud-based storage services, and both the quality and the quantity of the materials required alternatives for getting the footage to the filmmakers. Canning used a DIY upload service called transferbigfiles.com. She and others also sought offline means of getting the files, such as through sharing hard drives and thumb drives. Ewell and Aites managed this process of hard-drive exchange through a system of "hard drive trees" (Ewell 2014).

One challenge that emerged in working with crowds is the wide range of knowledge about film production technologies and techniques. This issue impacted the 99% documentary in particular because Ewell and Aites invited anyone to participate, whether the person knew film production or not. Ewell noted that sometimes the production felt like running a "film school" because people knew little about the mechanics, such as time codes, frame rates, and codecs, or about the legalities, such as signed releases (Ewell 2014). They had to put together instructions and guides to help people with the processes, which the participants sometimes but not always followed. Even then surprises came up regularly. Ewell recalled one

> grandfather in Chicago who would send us some iPhone footage, which was great! He would get in touch a lot and tell us a story, and he still had no idea what even a codec is. We were dealing with people who just weren't filming [regularly], who didn't work in media, who had no idea what we were talking about.
>
> *(2014)*

Another contributor had footage in iMovie, an amateur film-editing program that made it difficult to interface with other programs. Being professional filmmakers, both Ewell and post-production supervisor James Salkind were unfamiliar with the specifics of amateur-focused editing software, and had to send the woman to an Apple Store for help. These disparities in skills reflect Ewell's philosophy of the production in that anyone could participate, but the range of issues, even ones this basic, made it difficult to thoroughly plan the production steps.

As an Internet-based documentary, *18 Days in Egypt* required a different focus when it came to technology. This project encouraged people to assemble the footage and other materials into streams for viewing on the site, so the technology's role here was not in creating or sharing footage but in curating it into stories. The footage included not only user-generated content, but also content in multiple formats such as text and audio from across the Internet. For Elayat, the challenge thus came in developing the platform to facilitate various activities. She described the process as one of trial and error as she and her co-director conceptualized the project and its intentions: "We tried a bunch of different tools, tried the linear narration approach with popups and layers, but that still didn't work because we were forced to have a narrative that we were choosing, so we threw that prototype out" (Elayat 2014). In the end, they decided to withdraw from the storytelling as much as possible and focus their efforts on developing the technologies to encourage the storytelling. They sought to discover how people would use the platform if left to their own devices. Elayat explained,

> Without giving rules, people were using the tools in different ways. We thought people would want to link to articles and blog posts. People start using it for completely different things. So that's the goal. We wanted to keep it completely open and see what people would naturally create.
>
> *(2014)*

They offered a text-entry function for people to write stories, but instead participants used it for creating titles and offering context for other types of materials. Elayat added that, more generally, "People just curate, add whatever they want, move it around and edit it. The entire story becomes archived with a geo-location, with tags" (2014).

Ultimately, technology serves as an invaluable tool within the documentary production process. With crowdsourcing, it facilitates communication for recruitment and interaction, and creates the opportunity for the generation of user-produced content. New technologies and organizational structures, however, pose three challenges for crowdsourcing and documentary production. First, while crowdsourced participation and materials potentially democratize production, they create a new set of responsibilities for the filmmakers to handle, sometimes in ways they cannot anticipate. Second, they reinforce the importance of offline communication, so that offline and online contacts can be integrated. Last, they call for a balance between thinking about individuals and about crowds as a collective in that filmmakers must consider individuals' unique contributions, skill sets, and situations against the projects' goals and outcomes.

Conclusion

Crowdsourcing offers ways to open up the documentary production process so that people can participate in it, but in the end it impacts the process more than the final product. It changes the management of a documentary production. Each interviewed director spoke about the crowdsourcing aspect as intensive and intense with its varying logistics, problems, and unpredictability. Ewell pointed out the time-intensive nature of it, with 100-hour weeks early in the production spent on managing the crowdsourcing aspect. After describing multiple speaking engagements and crowd contacts, Rynecki noted that sometimes she found the process overwhelming. At the same time, though, the crowd's energy offered some inspiration to persevere; as Canning described the momentum: "It helps to feel like you're making an impact" (Canning 2014). Rynecki similarly said, "I try to thrive on the energy and keep going" (Rynecki 2014). The directors also spoke about needing to find a balance (if possible) to all the stress, both positive and negative, that crowdsourcing brought.

Crowdsourcing offers both possibilities and limitations for documentary productions. It offers chances to include more voices within a production, either as supplementary materials or as dedicated stories. These participants may shape the overall direction of the story through their submitted materials, research findings, or networking opportunities. They may gain the chance to further their own activism by contributing to projects in which they believe with footage, paraphernalia, contacts, or financial donations. Successful crowdsourcing can demonstrate public interest in the project to funders, create built-in core audiences, and spur word-of-mouth promotion. The limitations of crowdsourcing affect the documentary makers more than the crowd members themselves. The increase in communication obligations, the range of skills of crowd contributors, and the logistics of materials exchanges add to the work already involved in the production process. The unpredictability of the crowd poses challenges for scheduling and workflow. Overall, crowdsourcing has the potential to offer much to the right kinds of productions, but it involves a significant commitment to making it happen.

Bibliography

"About the Production." N.d. nationalgeographic.com. Available online at http://movies. nationalgeographic.com/movies/life-in-a-day/about-the-production/ (accessed October 2, 2014).

Bennett, W. Lance, and Alexandra Segerberg. 2011. "Digital Media and the Personalization of Collective Action." *Information, Communication & Society* 14: 770–99.

Brabham, Daren C. 2013. *Crowdsourcing*. Cambridge, MA: The MIT Press.

Canning, Liz. 2014. Interview by author. October 2, 2014.

Dovey, Jon. 2014. "Documentary Ecosystems: Collaboration and Exploitation." In *New Documentary Ecologies: Emerging Platforms, Practices and Discourses*, ed. Kate Nash, Craig Hight, and Catherine Summerhayes. New York: Palgrave Macmillan. 11–32.

Dunford, Elizabeth, Helen Trevena, Chester Goodsell, Ka Hung Ng, Jacqui Webster, Audra Millis, Stan Goldstein, Orla Hugueniot, and Bruce Neal. 2014. "FoodSwitch: A Mobile Phone App to Enable Consumers to Make Healthier Food Choices and Crowdsourcing of National Food Composition Data." *JMIR mHealth uHealth* 2 (3): e37.

Elayat, Yasmin. 2014. Interview by author. October 4, 2014.

Erickson, Christine. 2012. "Crowd-Powered: Why Doritos Lets Fans Make Its Superbowl Ads." Mashable.com, April 5. Available online at http://mashable.com/2012/04/05/doritos-crash-super-bowl/ (accessed October 19, 2014).

Ewell, Audrey. 2014. Interview by author. September 26, 2014.

Finlay, Jeanie. 2014. Interview by author. September 29, 2014.

Fuchs, Christian. 2014. *Social Media: A Critical Introduction*. Thousand Oaks, CA: Sage.

Garcia Martinez, Marian, and Bryn Walton. 2014. "The Wisdom of Crowds: The Potential of Online Communities as Tools for Data Analysis." *Technovation* 34: 203–14.

Haberman, Clyde. 2012. "No Thank-You Note, but Several Lawsuits for a Pepper-Spraying Inspector." nytimes.com, September 25. Available online at http://cityroom.blogs.nytimes.com/2012/09/25/no-thank-you-note-but-several-lawsuits-for-a-pepper-spraying-inspector/ (accessed December 22, 2014).

"How to Participate." N.d. 18daysinegypt.com. Available online at http://beta.18daysinegypt.com/#/how (accessed October 20, 2014).

"InnoCentive Solvers Make a Difference in Rural Africa and India." N.d. innocentive.com. Available online at www.innocentive.com/innocentive-solvers-make-difference-rural-africa-and-india (accessed December 22, 2014).

Jenkins, Henry, Sam Ford, and Joshua Green. 2013. *Spreadable Media: Creating Value and Meaning in a Networked Culture*. New York and London: New York University Press.

Kaganskiy, Julia. 2013. "Where Film Goes to Be Reinvented." *The New Yorker*, April 29. Available online at www.newyorker.com/tech/elements/where-film-goes-to-be-reinvented (accessed October 2, 2014).

"*Life Itself*: A Feature Documentary Based on Roger Ebert's Memoir." N.d. indiegogo.com. Available online at www.indiegogo.com/projects/life-itself-a-feature-documentary-based-on-roger-ebert-s-memoir (accessed December 22, 2014).

Miller, Kivi Leroux. 2010. *The Nonprofit Marketing Guide: High-Impact, Low-Cost Ways to Build Support for Your Good Cause*. San Francisco: Jossey-Bass.

Nichols, Bill. 1991. *Representing Reality: Issues and Concepts in Documentary*. Bloomington and Indianapolis: Indiana University Press.

——. 2001. *Introduction to Documentary*. Bloomington and Indianapolis: Indiana University Press.

Roig Telo, Antoni. 2013. "Participatory Film Production as Media Practice." *International Journal of Communication* 7: 2312–32.

Ruddick, Kyle. N.d. "About *One Day on Earth*." onedayonearth.org. Available online at www.onedayonearth.org/about (accessed October 2, 2014).

Rynecki, Elizabeth. 2014. Interview by author. September 26, 2014.

Shirky, Clay. 2009. *Here Comes Everybody: The Power of Organizing Without Organizations*. New York: Penguin.

Spence, Louise, and Vinicius Navarro. 2011. *Crafting Truth: Documentary Form and Meaning*. New Brunswick, NJ, and London: Rutgers University Press.

Surowiecki, James. 2005. *The Wisdom of Crowds*. New York: Anchor.

United States Holocaust Memorial Museum. N.d. "Children of the Lodz Ghetto: A Memorial Research Project." Available online at www.ushmm.org/online/lodzchildren/ (accessed October 19, 2014).

Wortham, Jenna, and Nick Bilton. 2011. "Pepper-Spray Incident Spawns Remixes." nytimes.com, November 21. Available online at http://bits.blogs.nytimes.com/2011/11/21/occupy-wall-street-pepper-spray-incident-turns-into-internet-meme/ (accessed December 22, 2014).

5

DESIGNED EXPERIENCES IN INTERACTIVE DOCUMENTARIES

Siobhan O'Flynn

As media forms, webdocs and i-Docs (interactive documentaries) currently exist at the cutting edge of experimentation in new technologies and platforms. (Note that "i-Docs" is a more expansive term than "webdocs," denoting interactivity in any medium, with digital, analogue, and material instantiations.) The National Film Board of Canada (NFB/ONF), the Franco-German television channel ARTE, and the French webdoc production company Upian, among others, continue to break new ground in the creation of experiential, game-based, participatory, networked, and in-situ (installation) documentary projects. I-Docs adapt existing disciplinary practices from documentary, and film more generally, but also explore new communicative tools that support documentary makers in connecting with a potentially global audience through the Internet. As webdocs and i-Docs almost always share the goal of communicating a story and/or of providing the "interactor" with an immersive deep dive into a given subject area, the growing taxonomy of platforms, technologies, modes, and media being used has also simultaneously expanded the critical perspectives from which the narrative form of i-Docs can be understood and analyzed, including but not limited to literary studies, cinema and media studies, cultural studies, affect studies, reader response theory, and digital humanities.

Critical research and writing on webdocs and i-Docs have developed in relationship with and in response to the emergence of interactive digital documentary making as a new artistic and industry practice over the last decade. Webdocs from the early 2000s are still accessible online (Thalhofer and Soar 2009; Thalhofer and Hamdy 2004), though the audience at that time was small, and these early pre-touch-screen, pre-Flash webdocs explored the possibilities of database cinema organized via tagging algorithms and pre-planned narrative paths. The scale, visibility, craft, and innovation of webdoc production changed when the NFB/ONF, ARTE, Upian and other major, often government-funded producers entered the creative space. Social media and Web 2.0 technologies have also radically impacted how interactive documentaries are designed. As forms have evolved, scholars have been forced to play catch-up with rapidly emerging innovations in the fields of production and exhibition.

Experience design

The challenge of analysis for students of webdocs and i-Docs is that no single critical practice can adequately address the diverse and idiosyncratic components that each new project may present. Various disciplinary lenses can offer valuable insights on the structure, narrative, and interaction mechanics of a given work, yet each approach reaches a limit edge of theory in what falls outside of its disciplinary purview (gameplay in literary or cinema studies, for example). Current critical discussions can be enriched by an understanding of an area of practice known as "experience design," which has its conceptual and methodological roots in the discipline of human–computer interaction (HCI). As a practice, experience design focuses on the user experience in every aspect of a given work (cinematic, game, participatory, creative) and in the cohesion and integrity of the whole, be it as a website, hospital infrastructure, or design of a new digital platform. Experience design is "the discipline of looking at all aspects—visual design, interaction design, sound design, and so on—of the user's encounter with a product, and making sure they are in harmony" (Saffer 2009: 20). An experience design approach does not contradict or negate other epistemologies; rather, it can complement them by providing a set of assessment criteria and methodologies that underlie the design of the whole. As such, experience design can function as a paradigm for under-standing how to bring into relationship elements of analysis that are often viewed as discrete and as belonging to distinct disciplinary spheres.

Experience design is differentiated from the related field of "user experience design" by its focus on the totality of the produced environment. User experience design in computer science focuses on the quality of experience and satisfaction for an end user interacting with a system or a product. In contrast, to understand how broad experience design is as a field, it is now widely recognized as having been formalized by Walt Disney in his 360-degree attention to the environmental design of Disneyland (Dickerson 2013). As a more expansive category it includes all aspects of a designed experience, from the layout of IKEA retail outlets to Steve Jobs's control of the design integrity of the Apple experience down to the human interaction with Apple staff in-store. Experience design is a methodology that can provide insights and practical principles for students and makers of webdocs and i-Docs. Experience design addresses both form and content in the broad categories of function, utility, aesthetic, and affect and attends to the design of

1 function: purpose of the project; what the user gains through the experience; degrees of responsive vs. unresponsive interaction design
2 utility: ease of use; comprehensibility of interaction design and information architecture

3   aesthetic: immersiveness of content and engagement; expression of content themes and core concepts consistent with the communicative message of a project

4   affect: physical experience of the user beyond the intellectual comprehension of information; emotional impact; includes human-to-human interaction and calls to action.

Experience design aims to integrate the core concept for the project across all elements of design, though this is not always necessarily easy to do.

Both experience design and user experience design are informed by the advances in the field of human–computer interaction since the 1980s. HCI, broadly, is the process of the design and assessment of the digital interfaces that mediate and enable human–computer interaction. As a discipline, HCI incorporates methodologies, practices, and insights from computer science, psychology, sociology, anthropology, and linguistics. A key concept in HCI is that of mental models, or what a user understands and anticipates as to how a given system, interaction, or website will function on first encounter. Webdocs and i-Docs as media place a high value on innovation in the expressive relation of form to the content, and the value of understanding how mental models impact user experience is crucial. In this context of mental models, experience design terminology refers to the affordances and constraints of any technology, as when we expect a light switch to flip and turn lights on and off. These models can be so deeply entrenched that, for example, if we flipped a light switch and turned on audio instead of a light source, most people would experience a surprise. Consider, too, the generational divide relating to those who grew up with cassette players, rotary dial phones, and turntables, and how mystifying these technologies are now to teens and children. Frustration can easily result when the expectations of a given mental model are disrupted. Designing functional, user-friendly interfaces and understanding both the designed and the perceived affordances and constraints of digital technologies are essential for creating user comprehension and satisfaction. Every webdoc or i-Doc that attempts any kind of innovation has to be attentive to the question of the mental model the user/player will perceive. For example, the developing grammar or distinctive visual language shared by many NFB webdocs includes the constant visual presence and/or availability of a timeline or map of some kind to orient the user/player within the interactive experience.

As an expansive and inclusive practice, experience design addresses all of the physical, digital, and social interactions in which people engage. Nathan Shedroff, a leading practitioner, consultant, and theorist of experience design, steps back from disciplinary silos to a macro understanding that all interactions—digital, material, or interpersonal—can be designed in concert for optimum effect and, therefore, can be thought through in terms of how the user will experience a given project in all aspects. Shedroff (2015) defines experience design broadly as "an approach to creating successful experiences for people in any medium." The range of forms could include theater, performance art, graphic design, storytelling, exhibit design, theme-park

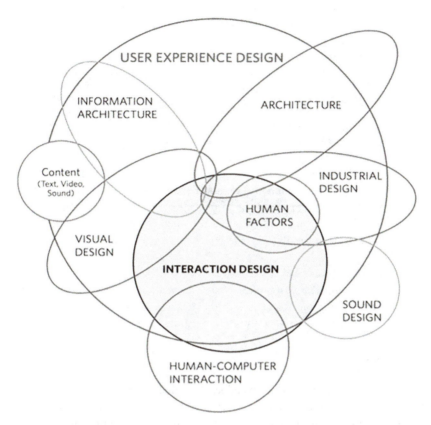

USER EXPERIENCE DESIGN

INFORMATION
ARCHITECTURE

ARCHITECTURE

Content
(Text, Video,
Sound)

INDUSTRIAL
DESIGN

HUMAN
FACTORS

VISUAL
DESIGN

INTERACTION DESIGN

SOUND
DESIGN

HUMAN-COMPUTER
INTERACTION

FIGURE 5.1 Image from *Designing for Interaction*, second edition, courtesy of Dan Saffer and New Riders.

design, online design, game design, interior design, architecture, and others. From this perspective, the shift to digital technologies and ubiquitous computing does not mark a break as a new field of practice. Shedroff and the internationally recognized design firm IDEO (Kelley 2001) argue persuasively that the design principles remain the same whether one works in material, digital, or social realms. As such, experience designers are transdisciplinary and are often required to bridge and lead team members in disparate fields. Saffer's diagram (Figure 5.1) maps the interrelated fields brought together under the aegis of experience design.

Because experience design is a human-centered practice, it provides a language and methodology that can address the limits of critical frameworks and epistemologies that are object-centered, predicated on a static, closed text. Literary and cinema studies have long histories of analyzing "texts" that are predesigned, and that exist as artifacts. Now, however, webdocs and i-Docs incorporate social media interactions and user-generated content that increasingly extend the scope of a given work. Social media's ubiquity offers entirely different measures of engagement. With online tracking software, it is possible to measure audience interaction with a given webdoc from duration of stay, degree of interaction, numbers of return visits, sharing of links, tweets, and what Henry Jenkins (2009) terms "spreadable media."

Hugues Sweeney, Executive Producer of Interactive Media at the ONF/NFB Digital Studio Montreal, describes the shift to an understanding of "a 360°-user experience":

> It's a switch of point of view from storyteller/author to the person who is living the experience of the project. [...] The big question is if a documentary is a representation of the world, how does that representation change if people are actively engaged in the experience? For me it's the foundation of everything we do, and the notion of experience comes from there. Then there are levels of participation, of collaboration; in some parts people do not create content, some parts people do, but again we really try to shape it from the POV of the user.
>
> *(O'Flynn 2014)*

A 360-degree user-centric approach is also foundational to transmedia or cross-media documentary projects that seek to move fans across platforms and to design a cohesive, meaningful experience through distributed media.

Interactivity

The critical research in studying webdocs and i-Docs has focused increasingly on interactivity as a defining characteristic distinct from the preceding linear, spectator experiences of cinematic and broadcast documentaries, with their respective long-standing artistic, critical, and investigative practices. Scholars have worked to illuminate the lines of continuity between past practices and current innovations in the field, and simultaneously to theorize innovations within responsive, supple theoretical models that offer new taxonomies (Nash 2012; Gaudenzi 2013; Dovey 2014; Gifreu-Castells 2013). Kate Nash's (2014) statement is illustrative of this approach:

> While research on film and television documentary reception explores the response of audiences to a fixed documentary text, interaction with documentary content has been widely seen as involving the audience in something distinct from interpretive engagement. [...] Whereas reception focuses on audience negotiation of documentary representations, interactivity involves the audience in the representative process.
>
> *(223)*

That is, audiences as interactors with i-Docs do not merely interpret textual elements; they arrange and create them as well, entering into the field of representations to structure, recombine, and augment content.

Interactivity from this perspective currently falls into three broad modes: 1. the user/player can impact how the "story" unfolds; 2. the user/player can play with game elements in the "story;" and/or 3. the user/player contributes to the "story." Analytical narrative readings of the first two modes have their roots in literary and cinema studies, in the distinction between "story" and "plot": the chronological "story" that is understood as events in the story world unfolding in linear time versus the plot as it is told (which may include flashbacks, flashforwards, and simultaneous parallel storylines). This model presupposes a stable, closed, finite text/story, whether it is in print, film, or database form. Barthes's notion in *S/Z* (1974) of the distinction between readerly and writerly texts is also relevant in terms of understanding the challenges of theorizing interactivity. The readerly text demands little cognitive engagement of the reader, who can easily understand the narrative, which is usually linear, conventional, and realist. Meaning is usually unambiguous and allows the reader to be a passive consumer of a "story." Writerly texts such as Joyce's *Ulysses* or Nabokov's *Pale Fire*, in contrast, often are nonlinear and ambiguous, foreground the mechanics of writing, and require the reader's active cognitive engagement in the production of meaning. This active reader has a parallel in cinema in scripted films such as *Memento* (Christopher Nolan, 2000), which demands the viewer's rapid mental recomposition of scenes into a unified narrative as the film unspools in the backward order of events (O'Flynn 2006). In all of these works, however, the text remains a static artifact that does not change its contents.

Despite the possibilities, instabilities, and ambiguities of the text, the meaning of which is generated through the active narrative stitching or closure of gaps (Barthes 1977; McCloud 1994), interactivity in a closed database remains narrative-based, no matter how many variations a hypertext may offer through a range of navigations. A reader/user cannot change the text's essential form as a previously authored artifact, no matter how many versions they generate from, for example, Borges's "The Garden of Forking Paths" or Jonathan Harris's webdoc *Whale Hunt* (2007). Discussions of meaning-making in this context continue a logic based on the reader/user/interactor relating to the text as artifact. Understanding how both closed and open interactive works produce variant experiences of the content or narrative is fundamental to the study of webdocs and i-Docs; what is needed now is greater examination and assessment of interactivity specifically as a process/action-based experience with distinct characteristics.

In her discussion of participatory documentaries, what Sandra Gaudenzi (2013) has termed "live documentaries" exist in a significantly different register from that of closed webdocs in which the primary interactivity or agency is one of choosing the iterative order of fragments as constrained by the database software (Gaudenzi 2013; O'Flynn 2012). Live documentaries can be "conversational" and "relational," providing the framework for audience engagement as co-creators and collaborators in a documentary project that unfolds over time (Gaudenzi 2013: 83). The two forms, the closed database and the live documentary, share a fundamental component as interactive works, the goal of producing an intended response and potentially an action in the audience. The success of live documentaries as intentional, generative systems can be measured by assessing the degree of engagement in user/fan-generated content and the distinct characteristics of that content in meaningful relation to the originating prompts. It is also possible to monitor fan engagement with content in online blogs and social media or content-sharing platforms such as Pinterest, Tumblr, and YouTube. Fan-generated art, story extensions, parodies, and memes constitute important responses to contemporary innovations in documentary form.

As an area of research addressing a parallel to this recent phenomenon in documentary practice, game studies provides a useful model for prioritizing user/ interactor engagement as a disciplinary focus. Theorists of game studies, often self-designated as ludologists, have argued for the need to attend to the distinct character-istics of games as games, rather than "reading" games through a narratological lens (Juul 2003; Frasca 2003; Salen and Zimmerman 2003, 2005). They have asserted that games have to be understood in their own terms, as systems of rules with outcomes that unfold over time, impacted by player engagement. Ludology's emphasis can be used in conjunction with other analytic frames to provide a more comprehensive understanding of users' experiences with i-Docs.

Earlier literary and cinema-based approaches become inadequate for addressing four distinct aspects of interactive documentaries, all of which can be traced to specific technological innovations and which can be studied via experience design. The first concerns the aspects of design and interaction that are distinct to the digital interface(s) supported by mobile and desktop computing. The second draws on gaming and immersive theater, leveraging audience engagement in the digital and physical realms, as co-producers and collaborators in the "text." Further, responsive and improvisational performances by audience members extending the narrative as experience are similarly difficult to critique via earlier theoretical models. The fourth variable has emerged with the proliferation of Web 2.0 technologies and the ubiquity of the social web as a networked many-to-many communicative platform. Underlying all four is the destabilization of the object of study, as web-docs and i-Docs shift from closed to open and from static or finite to processual, unfolding over time and co-created with the audience as participants and emergent publics (Dovey 2014).

Many recent critical works address interactivity in a range of ways that dance around the core insights and methodologies of experience design. In the introductory essay to a special issue of the *Journal of Documentary Studies* (2012), Aston and Gaudenzi view "interactivity as a means through which the viewer is positioned within the artefact itself, demanding him, or her, to play an active role in the negotiation of the 'reality' being conveyed through the i-doc" (Aston and Gaudenzi 2012). Kate Nash (2014) has examined the effects of "interactive/interpretative strategies" on players of the National Film Board's *Bear 71*, noting the importance of idiosyncratic knowledge and expectations in the meaning-making user experience. Each of these inquiries has contributed significantly to the field and offers viable strategies for ongoing investigations. In the introduction to their 2014 anthology, Nash, Hight, and Summerhayes note that the intention of the title, *New Documentary Ecologies*, is to draw attention to "emerging documentary platforms as situated within a complex media environment" (2014: 2) and that "[f]rom this perspective the media object can be thought of as a pattern of interaction as much as an apparently tangible object" (2014: 2–3). Taken together, the critical perspectives in this emerging field articulate a range of useful taxonomies for understanding the distinctive qualities of webdocs and i-Docs as emergent art forms. Audiences, too, bring their past experiences in gaming and online transmedia experiences to their interactions when they "play" with webdocs and i-Docs.

To explore the usefulness of experience design and other approaches that can incorporate deeply interactive elements in their understanding, I will look at three significant projects of recent years. *Gaza/Sderot, Bear 71*, and *Fort McMoney* illustrate the variety of innovations that have marked webdocs and i-Docs as at the cutting edge of twenty-first-century documentary production.

Gaza/Sderot

Alexandre Branchet's webdoc *Gaza/Sderot: Life in Spite of Everything* (ARTE, 2008) is illustrative of the approach to content as a finite database with multiple navigation paths through the content, although the design elements that make it distinctive and innovative fall outside of the story architecture purview and can be addressed from an experience design perspective. *Gaza/Sderot* documents the lives of two communities on either side of the Israeli/Palestinian border. There is a limited database of cinematic content and a number of modes that reorganize the display of the content, "Time, Faces, Maps, Topics." As Peter Lunenfeld (2002: 147) notes in "The Myths of Interactive Cinema," the widespread adoption of computers "fueled a hunger for interactivity as an end unto itself. […] The privileging of the interaction between user and machine became a grail of computer-based media." This view of the user as an agent participating in the production of meaning, playing with a finite database that produces a new text, is rooted in the approach to narrative and story dominant in interactive cinema in the 2000s and earlier, when the goal and distinctive experience of an interactive movie (DVDs or CD-ROMs) was letting the user edit his or her own film (Serrano, qtd. in Droganes 2007). What Lev Manovich termed "database cinema" relies on the existence of a stable, closed "text" with a set of elements (scenes, audio, etc.). Early webdoc examples such as *Diamond Road* (2008) make this explicit on the home page: "Four Continents. Fifteen characters. Hundreds of video clips. A documentary you direct." Many webdocs use this model, from early (2000s) experiments with Florian Thalhofer's Korsakow open-source software such as *Seven Sons* (Thalhofer and Hamdy 2004), to contemporary works such as *Hollow: An Interactive Documentary* (2013) and the Warsaw Rising Museum's webdoc *Warsaw Rising* (2014). In this version of the webdoc as "choose your own adventure," the user's input into the system, as a choice made in clicking, swiping, or typing, may change the plot, but the story or "story field" of content remains the same.

In practice, the challenge of this model for creating a cinematically satisfying artifact is that intercutting between scenes can be aesthetically problematic, especially in terms of audio and visual design. Much creative energy has been expended on the question of how to create interactive works with the integrity of design we expect in film or literature. *Gaza/Sderot* uses this static-content form but adds design elements that deepen the affective experience of the user and reflects upon the content in distinctive ways. The experience of "schism" is communicated through all design elements—interface, interaction, and content. The home page is designed with a responsive timeline that "splits" on a slant through the webpage, always remaining as a border demarcating the two collections of videos, of Israel and Gaza. Moving our cursor from side to side determines which video plays and which side freezes, the latter instantly grayed over with a reduction of color intensity and the addition of a minimalist point grid. The schism between these two communities is expressed as a visual motif in the interaction design—the divided lives and the divisive border are then replicated and reinforced in the choice and interaction of the user. Choose one video clip from one community and we subordinate the other community. Choice grants voice and agency and enforces silencing and immobility, in a simple, elegant interaction and interface design.

Bear 71

The NFB's *Bear 71* (2012) has won numerous awards as a groundbreaking documentary webdoc and installation piece. The project follows the life of a tagged female grizzly in Banff National Park in Canada. *Bear 71* is structured as a finite database through which we can choose our path through the visual content, but the interface foregrounds its digital construction and our manipulation of data in the use of an artistic rendering of the landscape as a responsive, shifting grid. Immersion is not meant to be easy; nor is narrative fulfillment. The design aesthetic counters expectations of a traditional cinematic immersion, as do the embedded videos of surveillance camera footage of the animals in the park, both of which reinforce the theme of surveillance and control (see Nash 2014 for a discussion of the surveillance effects).

One way of thinking through the experience design component of this work is to consider that both the webdoc and the installation mediate the "story" of Bear 71 through a series of technological filters that begin with the recording of the bear's movements via GPS and surveillance camera footage. These layers of data are then mediated through the interface, which gives us some choice as to how to follow the bear. Content nodes signal their accessibility with color, scale, and proximity shifts, and clicking opens up surveillance video windows, putting the viewer in the position of visual mastery. The viewer's desire for an immersive emotional experience, however, a meaningful connection with the story of the bear, is always frustrated by the intervening layers of technology, which reestablish a perceptual distance between the consciousnesses of viewer and grizzly bear. The distributed panopticon effect strongly suggests the entrapment of the bear as an object of the gaze continuously monitored in the "wild." However, the meditative aspect of the work also reflects back on the viewer, who is inversely trapped in a technological interface and system as well. That we do not gain immediate or consistent access to the bear is perhaps as it should be, given the gaps between human and ursine experience.

Loc Dao, NFB executive producer, in reference to the ten-day installation of the i-Doc at the 2012 Sundance Film Festival, states that

> Online the user faces the disconnect from nature by the very form they are using—sitting in front of their computer. Similarly, at the installation the viewer is out of their element, being in a public space, and like many of us who live our lives through iPhones and digital cameras, the user at the installation experiences the grandiose 24-foot wide digital grid world of Bear 71 through a tablet app, limiting their view of the bigger picture and giving them safe distance from what's happening in front of them.
>
> *(Aziz 2012)*

Dao's comment provides insight as to how the production team intentionally designed the user's experience of disconnection from the content via the mediation of the technical interface and interaction. In situating the viewer as the viewed, the installation design suggests a resonance between two states of entrapment and the pathos of the bear's condition is amplified, which is reinforced by the "mother bear's" voiceover narration, describing the challenges of existence in a human-mediated landscape. In the webdoc, the problem of audio disruption when shifting visual content is solved by the voiceover, which runs continuously whether one clicks or not, and a musical score of evocative instrumental and vocal tracks. If the design intention is to create a user experience of alienation and tension, then the participant reaction in Nash's study commenting on the tension and disjunction between the linear audio narration and the nonlinear visual content indicates success in achieving the intended effect.

The un-syncing of the voiceover and the visual/video content can also be read as a solution to the problem of audio disruption that occurs in webdocs when voiceovers are paired with specific video content, so that choosing what to see then results in audio breaks or disruptions in narrative threads. In terms of Dao's stated frame, the tension between linear audio narration and the open exploratory engagement with visual content also works to enhance the distancing of the user from that video content, as the voiceover provides a consciously problematic attempt at narrative unity. Sound design is tremendously important in interactive works because of the pros and cons of these decisions. Additionally, visual transitions between "narratives" in *Bear 71* are managed with fade-ins and fade-outs, creating shifts between the narrative threads, further disrupting a user's sense of masterly immersion.

Our separation from the protagonist and our uneasy relationship with the content was collapsed in the live performance I saw in Montreal in November, 2013. In a live concert hall space, Jeremy Mendez and Leanne Allison played a director's cut of the webdoc, leading the audience through one iteration of Bear 71's story, accompanied by a live cellist. What we lost in our positioning as spectators was offset by the physical enhancement of the live cello accompaniment, though the immersion I experienced had much to do with the scale of the projection and the cinematic quality of the unfolding narrative. Here the experience was designed for spectators, rather than interactors, and each iteration of *Bear 71* (web-based, installation, performance) intentionally creates different effects and affects. Understanding this design intention from the producer's perspective provides the analytical tools for a complete "reading" of a given work.

Fort McMoney

When the critical focus is on how the audience changes the plot of an interactive story, the focus is primarily on the story architecture. What is elided from the discussion is a contemplation of the distinctive characteristics and qualities of the webdoc as a digital responsive artifact, which should include a consideration of how the interface can influence the user/player's experience and understanding of documentary. In the instances in which webdocs incorporate game mechanics, such as the NFB/ONF's *Fort McMoney* (2013), the interface and user experience design's use of game mechanics is foregrounded and critical readings can draw on a "game grammar" of ludic structures that define types of gameplay (Koster 2010), and the discursive conventions of game studies. As a docu-game, *Fort McMoney* invited global players to debate and decide on the fate of Canada's oil-sands industry and explore the implications for the future of the oil industry. The project was launched with French, English, and German interfaces. *Fort McMoney*'s game mechanics fell into the spectrum of gamification, collecting hidden objects, missions, and yes/no competition dynamics in surveys and votes. It did not use first- or third-person shooter gameplay. *Fort McMoney*'s trilingual engagement over two set periods of play created an opportunity to envision likely future possibilities in order to intentionally craft a better future. From that perspective, the curation and design of the docu-game explicitly encouraged dialogue and the testing of points of argument and proposed strategies. In his director's statement, David Dufresne writes, "The game serves to focus interest. It's the lever that opens the door to debate, a tool for confrontation" (Wohlberg 2013).

 Fort McMoney utilized an open participatory model in which users could contribute user generated content (UGC) to the webdoc database or social media platform, extending and building on the existing narrative. Here, the conceptual model of the interactive documentary operates with an ethos of collaborative, co-created, crowdsourced content generation, and a participatory media engagement with an issue-based story or topic area. The "call to action" that explicitly invites or implicitly leads to audience contributions is of central concern in the development and production process. Participation and content creation do not just happen organically. Understanding how to prompt engagement beyond the "Like" button is a central concern of the digital producers who build webdocs and i-Docs. *Fort McMoney* encouraged UGC by explicit invitations to comment and exchange on new issues via internal discussion forums. While the full degree of player interaction is likely still being assessed by the ONF/NFB, Dufresne shared that over 6,500 posts were uploaded in two months (O'Flynn 2015). Dufresne's achievement was in crafting an online space for transnational debate between participants that went

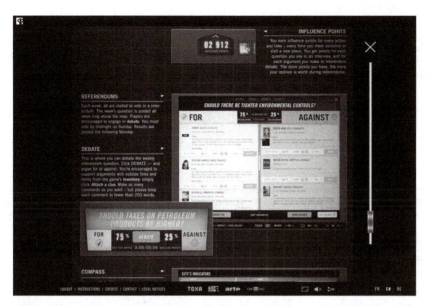

FIGURE 5.2 *Fort McMoney* (David Dufresne, 2013).

beyond what is now standard in webdocs. Many webdocs feature an explicit "Share Your Story" tab option that invites UGC, but does not necessarily support dialogue within an online community, which requires the active curatorial presence of community managers or what Dufresne terms "game masters."

In a variation of the "Share Your Story" prompt, Chris Milk and Aaron Koblin's interactive multimedia video *The Wilderness Downtown* (2010) played with the notion of the writerly text as created by audience engagement in a unique way. Produced in HTML5 for the Montreal band Arcade Fire, the Chrome experiment prompted viewers to write a letter to "your childhood self." The screen then presented a blank canvas for your text or visual message, which then appeared at a key moment, writing individuals into the narrative. The video's user experience design layered the lyrical, visual content with a personal documentary element that became emotionally effective owing to the video's late zoom in via Google Maps to a childhood address entered earlier, synced with the display of the message to one's childhood self.

Conclusion

In the context of most interactive digital works, we can map a series of axes that mark the range of forms that organize or express distinct elements that contribute to the whole. The first component is the story, narrative, or content architecture, where the axes function as:

1 linear/chronological/controlled to modular/fragmented/random
2 closed/finite databases to open/collaborative/crowdsourced/unfolding narratives

The second component manifests in the range of forms borrowed from existing genres and/or platforms (these do not map as a tidy spectrum): cinema, games, social media, installation and location-based experiences, podcasts, and so on. The third component is that of user experience design from HCI, which includes axes of:

1   degrees of responsiveness (e.g., of website or interface) from low to high
2   utility in function versus innovative, counterintuitive
3   utility in function versus expressive and/or artistic.

The challenge for analysis is that these schema do not correlate neatly, revealing again the limitations of discipline-specific theories or methodologies. For example, i-Docs that invite human creative participation or that create 3D physical immersive environments slip outside the disciplinary frame of user experience design. HCI and user experience design have developed in the context of human–computer interaction and as such fall short when critiquing human-to-human interaction. For these forms, experience design functions as a model for studying interaction as a qualitative experience across digital and physical media, with its attention to the possible multiplicities of human involvement. As i-Docs continue to grow in complexity, we will need agile combinations of theory and approach to elucidate fully their ambitions, successes, challenges, and impacts. Take, as one last example, an insight from Loc Dao, the NFB's current executive producer and creative technologist in digital content and strategy at NFB Vancouver, which he shared with me originally in 2010, referring to the design process behind the NFB's award-winning documentary *Waterlife Interactive*. As he explained, the NFB team partnered with the digital agency Jam3, and decided early in production that an evocation of the experience of water would be core to the design of the interactive website. "The experience and design goal," he said, "was to convey the liquidity and fluidity of water in the navigation and user experience. We wanted the user to feel like they were immersed and under water, diving in to explore the different angles of this issue" (Dao 2015). The sense of "liquidity" is integral to the website's designed experience, beginning with the load bar. If you have not played with this, go there now … And then think of how to account for your own participation and experience. http://waterlife.nfb.ca/#/

Bibliography

Aston, Judith, and Sandra Gaudenzi. 2012. "Interactive Documentary: Setting the Field." *Studies in Documentary Film* 6 (2): 125–39. doi:10.1386/sdf.6.2.125_1

Aziz, Plus. 2012. "Interactive Documentary Lets Users Experience the Forest Through Augmented Reality." *PSFK*, January. Available online at www.psfk.com/2012/01/interactive-ar-documentary-nfb.html.

Barthes, Roland. 1974. *S/Z: Essays*. Translated by Richard Miller. New York: Hill and Wang.

——. 1977. "Death of the Author." In *Image, Music, Text*. Translated by Stephen Heath. New York: Hill and Wang. 142–8.

Brachet, Alexandre. 2008. *Gaza/Sderot: Life in Spite of Everything*. ARTE. Available online at http://gaza-sderot.arte.tv/ (accessed January 18, 2015).

Dao, Loc. 2015. Email to author. January 19.

Dickerson, Joseph. 2013. "Walt Disney: The World's First UX Designer." *UX Magazine*, September 9. Available online at http://uxmag.com/articles/walt-disney-the-worlds-first-ux-designer.

Dovey, Jon. 2014. "Documentary Ecosystems." In *New Documentary Ecologies: Emerging Platforms, Practices and Discourses*, ed. Craig Hight, Kate Nash, and Catherine Summerhayes. New York: Palgrave. 11–32.

Droganes, Constance. 2007. "NFB at TIFF 2007: *Late Fragment* Creates a New Film Experience." CTV News. August 30. Available online at www.ctvnews.ca/nfb-at-tiff-2007-late-fragment-creates-a-new-film-experience-1.240821.

Dufresne, David. 2013. *Fort McMoney*. ONF/NFB. November 25. Available online at www.fortmcmoney.com/#/fortmcmoney (accessed November 28, 2013).

Frasca, Gonzalo. 2003. "Simulation Versus Narrative: Introduction to ludology." In *The Video Game Theory Reader*, ed. Mark J. P. Wolf and Bernard Perron. New York: Routledge. 221–35.

Gaudenzi, Sandra. 2013. "The Living Documentary: From Representing Reality to Co-creating Reality in Digital Interactive Documentary." PhD dissertation. Goldsmiths, University of London. Goldsmiths Research Online. Available online at http://research.gold.ac.uk/7997/ (accessed November 14, 2013).

Gifreu-Castells, Arnau. 2013. "El Documental Interactivo como Nuevo Género Audiovisual. Estudio de la aparición del nuevo género, aproximación a su definición y propuesta de taxonomía y de un modelo de análisis a efectos de evaluación, diseño y producción." PhD dissertation. Universitat Pompeu Fabra. Available online at www.academia.edu/6424020/El_documental_interactivo_como_nuevo_género_audiovisual._Estudio_de_la_aparición_del_nuevo_género_aproximación_a_su_definición_y_propuesta_de_taxonom%C3%ADa_y_de_un_modelo_de_análisis_a_efectos_de_evaluación_diseño_y_producción_PHD–Tesis_doctoral_ (accessed November 12, 2014).

Harris, Jonathan. 2007. *Whale Hunt*. Available online at http://thewhalehunt.org/ (accessed January 10, 2008).

Jenkins, Henry. 2009. "If It Doesn't Spread, It's Dead (Part One): Media Viruses and Memes." *Confessions of an Aca-Fan: The Official Weblog of Henry Jenkins*, February 11. Available online at http://henryjenkins.org/2009/02/if_it_doesnt_spread_its_dead_p.html (accessed February 11, 2009).

Juul, Jesper. 2003. "The Game, the Player, the World: Looking for a Heart of Gameness." In *Level Up: Digital Games Research Conference Proceedings*, ed. Marinka Copier and Joost Raessens. Utrecht: Utrecht University. 30–45.

Kelley, David. 2001. "David Kelley: Designing Products vs. Designing Experiences." August 28. Available online at www.youtube.com/watch?v=Rtk2Vp28Mcs (accessed September 9, 2013).

Koster, Ralph. 2010. *A Theory of Fun for Game Design*. 1st ed. Cambridge, MA: O'Reilly Media.

Lunenfeld, Peter. 2002. "The Myths of Interactive Cinema." In *The New Media Book*, ed. Dan Harries. London: BFI Publishing. 144–54.

McCloud, Scott. 1994. *Understanding Comics: The Invisible Art*. New York: William Morrow Paperbacks.

McMillion, Elaine. 2013. *Hollow: An Interactive Documentary*. Available online at http://hollowdocumentary.com/ (accessed February 26, 2014).

Mendez, Jeremy, and Leanne Allison. 2012. *Bear 71*. NFB. January 19. Available online at http://bear71.nfb.ca/#/bear71 (accessed January 21, 2012).

Milk, Chris, and Aaron Koblin. 2010. *The Wilderness Downtown*. August 30. Available online at www.thewildernessdowntown.com/ (accessed September 1, 2010).

Nash, Kate, 2012. "Modes of Interactivity: Analysing the Webdoc." *Media Culture Society* 34 (2). doi: 10.1177/0163443711430758

———. 2014. "Strategies of Interaction, Questions of Meaning: An Audience Study of the NFB's *Bear 71*." *Studies in Documentary Film* 8 (3): 221–34.

Nash, Kate, Craig Hight, and Catherine Summerhayes. 2014. "Introduction: New Documentary Ecologies—Emerging Platforms, Practices and Discourses." In *New Documentary Ecologies: Emerging Platforms, Practices and Discourses*, ed. Kate Nash, Craig Hight, and Catherine Summerhayes. New York: Palgrave. 1–7.

O'Flynn, Siobhan. 2006. "*Memento* and *Switching*: Modeling Narrativity Across Media." *Scope: An Online Journal of Film Studies* 4. Available online at www.scope.nottingham.ac.uk/filmreview.phpissue=4&id=122&section=film_rev&q=trap.

———. 2012. "Documentary's Metamorphic Form: Webdoc, Interactive, Transmedia, Participatory, and Beyond." *Studies in Documentary Film* 6 (2): 141–57.

———. 2014. "Hugues Sweeney: Experience Design Interview." *TMC Resource Kit*, June 26. Available online at www.tmcresourcekit.com/tmcrk-hugues-sweeney-experience-design-interview/.

———. 2015. "Fort McMoney & Strategies for International Co-Production: An Interview with David Dufresne." January 22. Available online at www.tmcresourcekit.com/fort-mcmoney-international-co-production-interview-with-david-dufresne/.

Saffer, Dan. 2009. *Designing for Interaction: Creating Smart Applications and Devices*. 2nd ed. Berkeley: New Riders Publishing.

Salen, Katie, and Eric Zimmerman. 2003. *Rules of Play: Game Design Fundamentals*. Cambridge, MA: MIT Press.

———. 2005. *The Game Design Reader: A Rules of Play Anthology*. Cambridge, MA: MIT Press.

Shedroff, Nathan. 2015. "Glossary." Available online at www.nathan.com/ed/glossary/ (accessed January 12, 2015).

Thalhofer, Florian, and Mahmoud Hamdy. 2004. *7 Sons*. Available online at www.7sons.com/ (accessed March 22, 2005).

Thalhofer, Florian, and Matt Soar. 2009. *Kosakow*. Available online at http://korsakow.org/ (accessed May 17, 2010).

Warsaw Rising Museum and the Topography of Terror Foundation. 2014. *Warsaw Rising 1944*. Available online at http://warsawrising.eu/ (accessed December 22, 2014).

Wohlberg, Meagan. 2013. "Ideas Battle Online for Control of Fort McMoney." *Northern Journal*, December 2. Available online at http://norj.ca/2013/12/ideas-battle-online-for-control-of-fort-mcmoney/ (accessed December 9, 2013).

6

INDIGENOUS DOCUMENTARY MEDIA

Pamela Wilson

Documentary film and video have been at the heart of indigenous media production for nearly a half-century. Following a long tradition of anthropological ethnographic films about indigenous cultures, the appropriation of media technology by indigenous peoples led to the emergence of indigenous self-representation on film. In some settler states, national institutions encouraged indigenous self-expression as early as 1968, when the National Film Board of Canada established an Indian Film Crew as part of its Challenge for Change project. This project created a new paradigm not only for indigenous filmmaking in Canada, but also for the social and political uses and circulation of documentary films as catalysts for the larger process of community development as well as struggle for self-representation and self-determination (Ginsburg 1999). Notable examples of other early projects generated by anthropologists and filmmakers include the Yirrkala Film Project,[1] Ian Dunlop's collaborative work with the Yolngu people of northeast Arnhem Land, Australia, beginning around 1970, which bridged the paradigms of ethnographic and indigenous film (see Deveson and Dunlop 2012), and Eric Michaels's pioneering work in the early 1980s regarding the first Australian Aboriginal broadcasting project, Warlpiri Media (Michaels 1994).[2] Through partnerships providing funding, technology, and training (such as those in South America like Video nas Aldeias[3] and the Kayapo Video Project), indigenous media producers began taking up cameras to present cultural realities in their own voices, often for cultural preservation or the telling of history from an indigenous perspective, or as activism against social, political, and environmental injustices. As Roy Marika, a Yolngu leader and participant in the Yirrkala Film Project, said in 1970:

> This is our chance to record our history for our children […] and our grandchildren. […] Before we die we should make a true picture, our own Yolngu picture, that will teach our children our dances and Law and everything—our singing—our own Yolngu culture.
>
> *(Deveson and Dunlop 2012: para. 36)*

Today, new generations of indigenous filmmakers around the world are continuing these traditional culture-based documentary forms and themes, as well as using new media technologies to reflect upon the multicultural subjectivities of globalized indigeneity.

The market for these productions has become vast: indigenous documentary and reality-based media (including journalism/news) provide much of the programming that today fills the schedules of the Aboriginal Peoples Television Network in Canada, National Indigenous Television in Australia, and Māori Television in Aotearoa (the Māori name for New Zealand),[4] as well as special programming slots in mainstream television. Much of the content has been produced and distributed by regional production companies and organizations such as CAAMA (Central Australian Aboriginal Media Association)[5] and Vision Maker Media (formerly Native American Public Telecommunications),[6] while other filmmakers have worked either independently, forming their own production companies, or under the auspices of state agencies (such as renowned documentarian Alanis Obomsawin's work with the National Film Board of Canada).[7] The Internet and social media have created digital outlets for indigenous media expression as well. IsumaTV,[8] a major online interactive, multimedia, and social networking platform, established in 2008 by Inuit filmmakers from Nunavut, Canada, encourages indigenous filmmakers to upload media productions for preservation, archiving, and global sharing; it features documentary-style projects of storytelling in over 50 indigenous languages. The result is an increasing visibility of indigenous media, allowing indigenous self-representation to become a powerful means of social activism and self-determination globally.

Defining the murky terrain

Writing about indigenous documentary media raises many questions. What does "indigenous" really mean? Who is able to claim to be an indigenous media producer? What, exactly, qualifies as an "indigenous documentary"? We soon find ourselves bogged in a mire of classificatory line-drawing where nothing is as certain as it seems, and semantic issues play a huge role not only in muddying our linguistic referents but also in delineating borders and boundaries of legitimacy fraught with cultural and identity politics.

We might begin by coming to some common understanding as to what "indigenous" signifies. At the heart of what makes indigenous media distinctive is the notion of *indigeneity*, reflecting the indigenous or Aboriginal experience. The current consensus about indigeneity in international law includes cultural groups that

1 can claim to have occupied and used the resources of a specific territory prior in time to other known occupants
2 self-identify as a distinct culture
3 voluntarily perpetuate cultural distinctiveness

4 have experienced "subjugation, marginalization, dispossession, exclusion, or discrimination, whether or not these conditions persist" (Wilson and Stewart 2008: 14).

Much of the developing international law surrounding indigenous issues has accompanied the international indigenous movement of the latter half of the twentieth century, shepherded by agencies of the United Nations, resulting in the passing in September 2007 of the Declaration on the Rights of Indigenous Peoples by the UN General Assembly.[9]

Next, we might consider the larger category within which we presume that we can locate indigenous documentary: *indigenous media*. Indigenous media studies has developed as an interdisciplinary academic field in the past few decades, bridging scholarship in anthropology, media studies, communication, cultural geography, and other related disciplines. One hallmark of this field has been the close working partnership between scholars and indigenous media producers. Within this context, one might define *indigenous media* as forms of media expression conceptualized, produced, and circulated by small-scale (usually locally rooted) indigenous cultural groups throughout the world for a variety of purposes, including cultural pre-servation, cultural and artistic expression, political self-determination, and cultural sovereignty. Today, most indigenous media producers, even in developing countries, have access to a broad range of media and communication technologies, limited primarily by geographical access, financial support, and geopolitical pressures and controls.

Is there something about seeing the world through indigenous eyes that privileges any work produced by an indigenous artist as "indigenous" media expression? Would a Native American producer's documentary about a mainstream American social or political issue be more "indigenous" than that of anyone else? On the other hand, when does a Native filmmaker's work cease to be considered "indigenous media"—or does it? Is an indigenous filmmaker obligated to only represent his or her own culture—or even another indigenous culture—in order for it to be con-sidered "indigenous film"? Whose vision needs to be conveyed in the film and its editing? Is it important that the camera operators and editors be indigenous? These are difficult questions, and no widely agreed-upon consensus exists, other than the expectation that the sovereignty of the film's ideas and images somehow be representative of a Native perspective and that the project be primarily shep-herded and carried out by following the vision of a person or collective considered to be indigenous. Moreover, the integral nature of cross-cultural partnerships in project development, training, and funding for indigenous media productions has often been overlooked. In fact, most of the appropriation of production technology by indigenous peoples has come through partnerships, either with institutions or with individual anthropologists, filmmakers, and activists, who help to form community-based projects and provide funding, technology, and training.

While this chapter focuses on film and video (as well as new innovations including documentary digital projects), the umbrella of indigenous media includes a much larger range of media forms, encompassing print, photography, art, electronic, radio, and other cultural channels of audio, visual, and written expression. The phenomenon of indigenous media has developed within the context of the globalization process as indigenous cultural groups have been introduced to the technical tools of modern communication and media technology. They have utilized these tools to achieve their own cultural and individual goals and visions.

Documentary film has often represented a "first wave" of indigenous media production. The urge *to document*—as in to provide a record of, to provide evidence for, to furnish proof of—has been and continues to be one of the most compelling motivations behind indigenous uses of film, video, and digital technology. The purposes of and targeted audiences for indigenous films have expanded over the decades as the intentions of the filmmakers in relation to these changing demands have shaped and reshaped the forms, the voices, and the messages of indigenous films. Indigenous filmmakers tell their stories, whether actual or mythical, using a variety of filming and editing techniques. The strong stylistic or generic delineation between documentary and feature films found in mainstream Western cinema is not as pronounced or important in indigenous filmmaking. Many of the pioneering indigenous feature filmmakers, such as Barry Barclay (Māori) and Zacharias Kunuk (Inuit), began their careers as documentary filmmakers and have moved back and forth between the two approaches with great fluidity. In fact, we might speculate that the entire question of "empirical truth versus fiction" regarding a film's subject matter is a construction imposed from a dominant Western cultural mindset; "truth" claims themselves are culturally specific.

While a number of recent indigenous filmmakers have become masters of the art of commercial feature filmmaking,[10] few of the early indigenous films were created for the primary purpose of entertainment. Rather, indigenous documentaries have most often served practical, generally collective, needs. These have included cultural knowledge preservation and documentation/archiving—for a culturally internal audience or to share with neighboring villages. Indigenous groups have frequently used visual and audio recording technologies to capture and freeze moments in time, which might then be replayed for later generations (in cases such as the archiving of rituals and oral traditions) or which can be shared externally to galvanize global political support in opposing settler states or corporations (in cases such as the abuses of indigenous rights by territory infringements, resource mining, or logging, as well as capturing verbal promises made by outside negotiators). Such films or videos have rarely been made for commercial gain, and they have generally been distributed externally, if at all, through not-for-profit institutional and educational channels.

Indigenizing the documentary paradigms

Indigenous media have challenged many dominant Western paradigms, including the one that reifies a documentary film as a single, bounded work, a piece complete within itself and containing a clear beginning, middle, and end, with all necessary information extant within it. However, indigenous "documentary" forms have clearly been heavily influenced by a variety of models of mainstream Western documentary film traditions, ranging from the voice-of-God, didactic documentary film paradigm to more visually poetic styles, as well as journalistic, observational, and first-person (auto-ethnographic) documentary styles. Nonetheless, these forms have been prone to innovating and "indigenizing" in terms of aesthetics, ranging from cinematic choices to narrative structures, and to broadening the concept to include more interactive and collaborative styles both of production and of textual presentation, especially in digital online formats.

Recent indigenous documentary films have moved away from the early ethnographic film model into fresh approaches that focus upon "unsilencing" silenced histories, exposing political and environmental issues that affect indigenous homelands and peoples, and offering individual explorations of cultural identity in a world of bi- or multicultural subjectivities. Digital projects and social media have also become significant conduits for new styles of indigenous expression through moving images. The development of interactive sites encouraging audience input—and blurring the line between producer and audience—resonates with and technically enables the philosophy among most indigenous cultures that values collaboration as well as collective authorship and input into a cultural production.

The technological innovations provided by digital and online media have enabled indigenous producers to embed and adapt more traditional styles of documentary film and video into broader interactive contexts that allow for nonlinear styles of creating, preserving, presenting, and consuming reality-based content and insights. These are often community-based digital archives and knowledge bases, interactive and participatory, available for contributions and consumption. Some have been created primarily for the community itself, as with the Ara Irititja Project,[11] a community-based and community-owned multimedia digital archive serving the Ngaanyatjarra, Pitjantjatjara, and Yankunytjatjara (Anangu) communities in Australia. On the other hand, some interpellate an outside audience, even at a personal level. For example, the interactive documentary *God's Lake Narrows*,[12] a project sponsored by the National Film Board of Canada, actually "reads" the location of the visitor's computer and personalizes the site by printing across the screen: "If you're in ___ [*your town*]___, you'd be ___ km away from God's Lake. All things considered I'm going to bet you've never visited. [...] The closest reserve to ___[*your town*]___ is ___ km. If you're not an Indian, you've probably never been there either."

Another major episodic documentary and multimedia project, *First Australians* (2008–), combines a more traditionally styled, linear broadcast documentary series (directed by renowned Aboriginal filmmaker Rachel Perkins)[13] with a parallel interactive, digital, nonlinear presentation form on the website. The online site[14] allows visitors/viewers to not only watch segments of the documentary in any sequence, through the use of an interactive site map and timeline, but also contribute to it. An invitation to participate in mid-2014 read: "The future is ours to create. We invite you to be a part of it and to share your story and contribute to the First Australians website." Interactive sites such as this, which invite participation and contribution, create an open-ended as well as collaborative cultural and artistic documentary product. While the infrastructure is developed by the creators/producers, the ultimate content of such products will not be determined or completed as long as the possibility exists for someone to add more stories.

Theoretical approaches to indigenous media

A number of significant theoretical approaches, all interwoven, have grown out of the first wave of indigenous media studies and provide relevant analytical tools not just for understanding indigenous documentary but maybe also for contributing to general documentary theory and scholarship as well. The major theoretical veins during the first two decades of indigenous media scholarship have been the acknowledgement and appreciation of indigenous, culture-specific aesthetics; the way that such aesthetics are embedded in local cultural politics; the concept of Fourth Cinema; the notion of visual sovereignty; a related focus on indigenous knowledge systems and their decolonization; and the use of indigenous media to counter the historical colonial gaze and to provide alternative accounts and perspectives that "talk back" to the dominant, hegemonic versions of history and cultural relations.

Embedded aesthetics

The leading theoretical voice to establish indigenous media as a field has been that of visual anthropologist Faye Ginsburg, whose influential essays and academic mentoring have inspired new generations of emerging indigenous media scholars across disciplines. Her germinal 1991 work articulated the "Faustian dilemma" of introducing technology to tribal peoples: Even as an argument could be made that the "invasion" of Western mass media technologies and media products might be disrupting Native cultures, new media tools have become extremely valuable in constructing indigenous identities and challenging outside cultural domination. Pointing out the complexity and diversity of Australian Aboriginal media productions, Ginsburg (1994) adapted Arjun Appadurai's concept of *mediascape* as a model for indigenous media, with special attention to how the aesthetic standards and values of indigenous media become negotiated in different arenas of production and reception, as well as how less visible cultural protocols, such as who participates and in what ways, become deeply embedded in media work.

Such indigenizing of styles includes the cultural practices of pre-production and planning as well as the way the text filmically tells its story or gets its message across. Aesthetic standards and values may be found in the processes of and decisions about selecting subjects that are "film-worthy" by cultural standards. They also concern the proprietorship and authority over indigenous cultural knowledge and self-representation of the group or community—that is, the determination of who has permission to share the information or tell the stories, and who must approve the way the stories are told and the conditions of the telling. Any analysis of indigenous filmmaking will also examine various degrees of individual or collaborative authorship at all levels: the degree of scripting or pre-planning; the negotiation of filming culturally sensitive material, locations, or persons; and any approval process needing the structure of authority or hierarchy and the division of labor (including division of roles based upon culturally significant categories such as gender, class, clans, status, or other classifications). As far as the creation of the filmic text is concerned, indigenous films may diverge from mainstream film in the formal and structural qualities of the film—such as cinematography, mise-en-scène, and editing—as well as the narrative or rhetorical structuring (the underlying cultural logic by which the story is told or an argument is structured, or whether a story or argument exists at all, as well as devices used for visual and aural storytelling).

Studies of indigenous media have primarily represented cultural and political approaches rather than formal ones adapted from cinema studies, though a few scholars, notably Steven Leuthold (1998, 2001), have taken a more formal analytical approach regarding aesthetics; the work of Hopi filmmaker Victor Masayesva, Jr., has particularly lent itself to this type of analysis. Leuthold (2001) described the rhetorical styles and motivations, usually for social and political change and indigenous self-representation, that structure many contemporary Native American documentaries. Aesthetic indigenization is not only apparent in the formal visual qualities of a film or video, however. Juan Salazar and Amalia Córdova (2008) discussed the poetics of indigenous media—the way that social and cultural practices, and especially notions of self-representation, become textually embedded into the process and the product of media production, especially in the political documentary genre (and sociopolitical movement) of *video indígena* in Latin America. Examining how indigenous knowledge systems shape the relational aspects of new media, Candice Hopkins (2006) focused on the primacy in indigenous film of the social and political role of the storyteller, who adapts and personalizes cultural content into narrative as part of a cultural circulation of knowledge.

Fourth Cinema

In Aotearoa (New Zealand), Māori filmmaker Barry Barclay emerged in the 1970s and 1980s as one of the most eloquent indigenous intellectuals and theorists regarding indigenous aesthetics and cinematic techniques, introducing the notion of Fourth Cinema in a 2002 speech in order to distinguish indigenous cinemas from the First, Second, and Third Cinema frameworks. The concept of Fourth Cinema developed from the notion of the Fourth World, a concept introduced by George Manuel and Michael Posluns (1974); building upon the three-world model, the Fourth World consists of those nations that are internally colonized and/or lacking in international recognition and power. These include indigenous groups as well as other stateless peoples. Barclay's eloquent 1990 treatise, *Our Own Image*, elaborates on how indigenous cinema, reflecting an indigenous cultural perspective and values, provides not only the foundation for what and whose stories are told through film, but also the techniques of telling those stories, through a culturally distinct language of cinematography, staging, and editing—which he calls Fourth Cinema.

Decolonizing indigenous knowledge: visual sovereignty and countering the colonial gaze

A major theoretical intervention in indigenous scholarship accompanied the 1999 publication of Linda Tuhiwai Smith's *Decolonizing Methodologies*, a critique of the re-colonization of indigenous knowledge by Western academics and a call for new types of indigenous methodologies operating from indigenous subjectivities. Michelle Raheja championed the concept of *visual sovereignty* from a Native American perspective in her 2007 analysis of the Inuit film *Atanarjuat: The Fast Runner* (Zacharias Kunuk, 2002, Igloolik Isuma Productions), examining the ways that indigenous filmmakers negotiate with existing paradigms and formulas for media production while also inserting their own cultural insights and adaptations to assert cultural self-definition and self-representation. Raheja contended that Native productions offer

> not only the possibility of engaging and deconstructing white-generated representations of indigenous people, but more broadly and importantly how it intervenes in larger discussions of Native American sovereignty by locating and advocating for indigenous cultural and political power both within and outside of Western legal jurisprudence.
>
> *(2007: para. 4)*

In her study of Andean media, Freya Schiwy (2009) argued that decolonization of knowledge, community networks, and pan-indigenous frameworks form key strategies for creating and sustaining indigenous knowledge.

Similarly, Kerstin Knopf (2010) applied the concept of "returning the gaze" to the works of indigenous visual artists and media producers to reveal how the "process of visual and sonic self-representation" metaphorically returns the neo/colonial gaze, since indigenous artists use the "formerly colonialist means of production" (i.e., media technologies) to create indigenous images and discourses "that look critically at colonialist images and discourse" (93). Exploring the increasingly integral role played by Aboriginal media in Canada's mediascape, Augie Fleras (2011) noted that these shifts in social power have been unsettling long-standing patterns of media and social hegemony, "unsilencing" Native voices. Arguing that Aboriginal use of digital and social media is making significant headway in overcoming marginalization, Fleras theorized that the indigenous film gaze has become empowered by challenging conventional gazes and correcting misrepresentations.

New theoretical directions

More recent scholarly works on indigenous media, representing a third generation of indigenous media scholars, draw attention to the practices and processes of both media-making and media consumption—particularly emphasizing the increasing centrality of their place in indigenous cultural practices. These scholars also note the increasing vitality of indigenous media in a globalized, transnational economy through which indigenous media practices and products become valuable elements of cultural and economic capital circulating in a global flow of funds, ideas, knowledge structures, and, ultimately, political and cultural power. This emerging generation of indigenous media scholarship raises important theoretical questions regarding the imbrication of indigenous media within the economic and cultural web of globalization, the centrality of indigenous negotiations of space—geographic, cultural, political, and cyber—by indigenous media, and the emergence of coun-terhegemonic styles and methods of production based upon indigenous ways of seeing, conceptualizing, structuring, and representing.

Indigenous media studies allows us access to the micro-processes of what Roland Robertson (1992) has famously called "glocalization"—in this case, the inter-penetration of global media technologies with hyper-local needs, creatively adapted to work within and to sustain the local culture rather than to replace it or homogenize it, as some globalization theorists have long feared. Sabra Thorner (2010, 2012) discusses the development for local uses in central Australia, and the subsequent global marketing, of Ara Irititja KMS (Knowledge Management System), a cultural heritage software tool that allows for the archiving, organization, and display of indigenous knowledge, representations, and cultural documents according to indigenous ontologies. She posits that one effect of transnational indigeneity has been to "destabilize conventional notions of globalization and indigenous participation in international flows of ideas and capital" (Thorner 2012: 2).

April Strickland (2012) provides insights about the way that Māori filmmaker Barry Barclay's incorporation of indigenous ideologies into the very practices of filmmaking has influenced indigenous media producers and theories transnationally. Strickland interrogates the possible ways that indigenous media-making—and parti-cularly the marketing of such indigenous media to a global audience—might be radically reconfiguring the traditional, colonial geopolitical relationships within which indigenous cultural groups have been both economically dependent upon and politically subservient to the nation-states in which they have resided. The global marketing of products created according to a locally meaningful structure of logic and cultural understanding begs for an analysis of the intricate complexities involved in such intercultural circulations and exchanges, from the trans-local to trans-national to trans-indigenous.

Toward geographic, political, and cultural sovereignty

Another recent issue raised by scholars, especially through the influence of the field of cultural geography, has been the centrality of indigenous negotiations of space— geographic, cultural, political, and cyber—by indigenous media. The significance of geographical space—with momentous local, cultural, and spiritual connections to specific features of the homeland or territory—has always been at the core of the indigenous or Aboriginal experience. Processes of dislocation and removal onto reserves have accompanied internal colonization in many parts of the world. That dispersal, as well as a later economically driven dispersal of many members of remote communities into diasporic urban areas and the subsequent development of urban indigenous communities (which frequently have consisted of ethnic mixes of indigenous individuals and families from multiple tribes or communities), has created new levels of indigenous identification, often labeled pan-indigenous, and indigenous diasporas. Indigenous diasporic space has required a reimagining of indigeneity in lived experience from the simpler notion of local, small-scale, traditional holistic and cohesive social groups that were the focus of early anthropological interest.

Diasporic indigeneity is a phenomenon related to complex contemporary identity formation and its accompanying social and cultural practices. Kristin Dowell (2012) addresses some of these issues in her study of the digital documentary art space, named *God's Lake Narrows* for a small Cree community in Manitoba, organized by the ITWÉ collective of indigenous Canadian film artists. Dowell suggests the significant role that digital media may play in facilitating and mediating those negotiations of connectiveness to the diasporic home locality, but also in creating various levels of trans-indigenous connectedness and identity as new social and political formations are forged. Dowell's focus on "how ITWÉ's media artists use digital technology to explore land, language, identity and shared Indigenous histories to redefine Indigeneity in the 21st century" provides an insightful case study (Kristin Dowell, personal correspondence, 2012).

Cory Mann's award-winning documentary *Smokin' Fish* (2011)[15] is a personal, autobiographical exploration of diasporic cultural identity. The film features the filmmaker as the main character in a story examining the complex interface between Mann's life as a capitalist entrepreneur living in Juneau but raised in San Diego (away from his culture's geographical homeland in Alaska)—making a living capitalizing, in fact, on mass-producing Tlingit artwork and selling it to a tourist market—and Mann's Tlingit roots, represented by his return to his family community and the circle of women who raised him in order to focus a few months on smoking salmon in the traditional cultural method. Through the film, he interweaves Tlingit cultural history with his own personal story, anchored by the process of preparing the fish.

Toward representational sovereignty

A continuing emphasis among contemporary scholars is upon the indigenizing of media structures and processes and the emergence of counterhegemonic styles and methods of production based upon indigenous ontologies. This indigenizing extends from the process of production to the style and shape of the product itself, as well as to the cultural logics of classifying (genres, for example) and of organizing cultural knowledge, such as the indigenous knowledge archiving and management systems developed in Australia. However, the most recent studies are bringing new types of examples to the analytical table and finding ways to broaden and refocus some of the earlier theoretical concepts, such as Raheja's notion of "visual sovereignty."

With regard to Barry Barclay's indigenization of filmmaking practices (as well as aesthetics and cultural sensibilities), Strickland notes that he "set an agenda for

Māori contemporary filmmakers to follow and created a template for other indigenous media practitioners to create similar models in their own communities to reclaim cultural and visual sovereignty" (April Strickland, personal correspondence, 2012). Kristin Dowell slightly recoded this concept of visual sovereignty to mean "the articulation of Aboriginal peoples' distinctive cultural traditions, political status, and collective identities through aesthetic and cinematic means, including a digital online presence" (Dowell 2012: 5). She emphasizes that this does not always happen just visually, however, noting the vital importance of soundscape to complement the visual images on the *God's Lake Narrows* site.

All of these examples illuminate the constraints of the concept of visual sovereignty; it is too limiting and one-dimensional, not broad enough to adequately theorize the various types of work that these new examples of indigenous documentary media embody. Beyond the visual "aesthetic and cinematic means" of articulating cultural sovereignty, we must consider the other dimensions of representation: the sound-scapes, the written or spoken word or language, the underlying structure of narrative or of organizing and mapping knowledge into categories or clusters or other forms of logical arrangement. Perhaps we would be better served with a term such as *indigenous representational sovereignty*—the use of a culture's own logic to structure the process and the product of representing cultural concepts through media forms—rather than *visual sovereignty* alone.

Constructing indigenous representational sovereignty: some case studies

Indigenous representational sovereignty has developed gradually, in different ways and to different degrees, over the past half-century. Indigenous peoples have been increasingly exposed to Western and global media within their own lives, and as such they have come to understand the potential power of media. In harnessing that power through the processes of self-representation, they have been able to "speak back" to the dominant hegemonic voices and also to participate discursively in larger intercultural conversations through media. This section presents a number of key case studies of the indigenous appropriation of media technologies; the reader should be aware that many more such cases exist than are represented here.

Navajo Film Themselves, rebooted

By most accounts, the earliest well-known experiment of "putting cameras in the hands of" indigenous artists to see what self-representation they might create with film technology occurred in the summer of 1966, when communication scholar Sol Worth and anthropologist John Adair introduced their Navajo Film Themselves project to tribal members in Pine Springs, Arizona. Their goal in what Leighton Peterson (2013) has called "one of the most revolutionary experiments in visual and cognitive ethnography yet completed" (29)—providing 16mm film technology to seven Navajos and training them technically—was to discover the degree to which any filmmaking through Navajo eyes might reflect a distinct cultural "grammar" or aesthetics. Findings included strong divergences from the dominant American film style in terms of visual narrative style, with a focus on walking (the journey, or the process of seeking) rather than on the destination activity, and a cultural reluctance to shoot facial close-ups, indicating some very significant differences in attitudes about the appropriateness of looking at or displaying someone else's face; the study also made noteworthy observations about the different cultural logics of narrative sequencing and visual storytelling (see Worth and Adair 1997). Yet, notes Peterson (2013), writing more than a generation later, "this question of which elements are Navajo and how participants' Navajoness affects the films may be the wrong questions to ask, reflecting outmoded anthropological frames" (35).

A new and interesting twist to the legendary story of the Navajo films has provided opportunities for new types of reflection, cultural work, and cultural resignification regarding the classic Navajo/Diné films. After restoration by the University of Pennsylvania and the Library of Congress beginning in 2007, the films returned home to the Navajo Nation through an initial screening in late 2011 and were then released as a DVD set in late 2012.[16] Peterson invokes Raheja's theoretical framework of visual sovereignty in describing this new, second life of the 1966 films:

> The recirculation of the films through the new DVD set, renewed community involvement, and a growing cadre of Diné filmmakers provides what Deloria (2004) calls a "moment of paradox and opportunity" for the emergence and actualization of visual sovereignty, defined as specific acts of self-representation by indigenous media producers in a variety of political, economic, and cultural contexts, where contemporary media practices are in dialogue with the past, leading, presumably, to indigenous cultural healing.
>
> *(Peterson 2013: 31)*

Future projects are growing out of the Navajo Film Themselves project, building upon the 1966 films and engaging with them through time across the generations, yet also resignifying them while doing so. In a distinct parallel to Arlene Bowman's thought-provoking and sometimes controversial *Navajo Talking Picture* (1985),[17] a documentary about the filmmaker's return to her ancestral Navajo community to try to film her traditional grandmother (against her grandmother's wishes), a recent short documentary by Navajo/Diné anthropologist and filmmaker Teresa Montoya, *Doing the Sheep Good* (2013), is also a self-reflexive account of homecomings, but of a very different nature. While studying and filming the return of the 1966 films to the Pine Springs community in early 2013, Montoya's film also showcases her own acceptance into the kinship network of the community by virtue of her family connections. Her film focuses upon the poignant display of cultural memory and recounting of familial relationships that "bringing the films home" kindled within the community. Montoya plans a longer documentary in the coming years as part of her doctoral work.

Another form of indigenization of documentary may be seen not so much in the formal style but in what Joanna Hearne (2006) has called the cultural politics of the reclaiming, repurposing, and recoding of film images originally produced in a colonialist context. Peterson noted that during the 2011 discussion a suggestion was made to encourage contemporary Navajo/Diné filmmakers to incorporate the 1966 footage into new works:

> In an idea that breaks with the project's history to date, and in conjunction with community involvement in [re]voicing the films, this collaborative effort will provide the next steps in visual sovereignty, with contemporary cultural producers directly engaging their mediated past, rearticulating the meanings and uses of once-colonized imagery. The potentials for new narrations and new films emerging from the footage were discussed with keen interest and would certainly take teaching and learning into new directions.
>
> *(2013: 36)*

A new generation of Navajo/Diné filmmakers has blossomed in recent years. Larry Blackhorse Lowe, Bennie Klain, Nanobah Becker, and others are described by Randolph Lewis (2010) as pioneers of a "Navajo national cinema" (including narrative, documentary, and experimental film) that expresses the particularities of Navajo cultural vision "in a way that may sustain the political sovereignty of the vast Navajo Nation" (50). Notable documentaries are Klain's *Weaving Worlds* (2007), a portrait of Navajo rugmakers, and the forthcoming *Lost Tribes*, covering the controversy about the annual Columbus Day parade in Denver.

Coniston, A Thick Dark Fog, *and the unsilencing of indigenous histories*

Francis Jupurrurla Kelly and David Batty's *Coniston* (2013) exposes the silenced history of a 1928 frontier massacre in Central Australia. Dozens of indigenous Warlpiri people, including women and children, were slaughtered at Coniston station by a white settler revenge party, led by Constable Murray, in retribution for the killing of white dingo-trapper, Fred Brooks, by a Warlpiri man, Bullfrog, whose wife Brooks had sexually appropriated. This tragic event marked the profound loss of the traditional indigenous lifestyle for many Aboriginal groups. The process of creating the film eight decades later involved gathering the voices and perspectives of as many survivors and descendants as possible and also included a meeting between the granddaughter of Constable Murray and families of the victims, at which time she issued an apology. The film's style is a hybrid documentary style including reenacted dramatic scenes of the historical event. As Kelly notes on the film's website,[18]

> This Coniston film is not only important for "now", but also for the future of Aboriginal people. They shot a lot of Aboriginal people a long time ago. Some people were shot for no reason in those days. I first heard a little bit about Coniston when I was about 16 or 18 years old. A lot of people in that time were not keen on talking about Coniston. They were, in that time, a little bit shy

because some of the people that were affected in those killing times were still around. Now that most of those people have gone, we want to talk about it. Us Aboriginal people have been hiding these proper stories about what really happened for all this time. It's now the right time to tell this story.

The significance of presenting the Aboriginal perspective about historical events cannot be overstated, and this trope has become quite important in indigenous documentary in many parts of the world. For example, quite a few documentaries have been produced in recent years in the United States and Canada to present Native perspectives about the distinctive Native American boarding school experiences of the early to mid-twentieth century, in which children were removed from their tribal communities and taken to white-run boarding schools to be de-acculturated of their Native cultures and assimilated into dominant society. A notable example is Randy Vasquez's *The Thick Dark Fog*, winner of Best Documentary at the 2011 American Indian Film Festival.[19]

The Thick Dark Fog, which raised over $17,000 via crowdfunding through Kickstarter, represents the kind of intercultural partnership that characterizes many contemporary indigenous films. The film team, including both non-Native members and executive producer Brian Wescott (Athabascan/Yup'ik), director of photography Kahlil Hudson (Tlingit), and assistant editor Sydney Freeland (Navajo), focuses on the life experiences of Lakota elder Walter Littlemoon. At age five, Littlemoon was removed from his family on the Pine Ridge reservation in South Dakota and placed in a federally run residential institution for Indian youth, where he was physically and psychologically abused (see Figure 6.1). Just as with many of his generation, Littlemoon's story is about his lifetime of regaining his culture and rebuilding his Lakota identity despite the traumas of his youth.

Children of the Jaguar

Another emphasis in recent indigenous documentary has been upon the local–global nexus, highlighting globally shared political and environmental indigenous issues by focusing upon local case studies. Eriberto Gualinga's *Children of the Jaguar*

FIGURE 6.1 Walter Littlemoon in *The Thick Dark Fog* (Randy Vasquez, 2011).

(2012, Selvas Productions)[20] focuses upon the lives of the 1,200 Kichwa people of Sarayaku, in the Ecuadorian Amazon, around whom an historic global coalition has been built to help resist the attempts of the Ecuadorian government and multinational corporations to exploit the oil reserves on their homelands. Filmed in 2011, it documents the visit by a delegation from Sarayaku to speak at a hearing of the InterAmerican Court of Human Rights in Costa Rica to protest against the nation of Ecuador for allowing exploitation of their natural resources without consultation with and approval by the community.

The film begins as the delegation enters the courtroom in Costa Rica, dressed in ceremonial garb and rhythmically beating drums. Through voiceover narration, the filmmaker says, "We're here, thousands of kilometers from home, in the hope that someone, finally, will give us justice. [...] We know our rights, and we're defending them."

The story then visually moves from the courtroom in Costa Rica to the ancestral village of Sarayaku, where the narrator introduces himself as a member of the Kichwa community of Sarayaku and visually shares the daily life of his culture and village with the viewer; interviews with community members add more voices to the tapestry. The conflict unfolds in a classic narrative structure: equilibrium was disrupted when an oil company intruded upon their lands, with government license, in 2002, turning the life of the village "upside down" (see Figure 6.2). Gualinga, at the time a student of communication and video, began recording the events with a handheld camera, capturing footage of villagers confronting the oil workers with frustration, and of military figures trying to block his filming.

The contemporary story is about the villagers' mobilizing both a public relations and a legal campaign against the Ecuadorian government and its complicity with the oil companies—and winning. An interesting aspect of Gualinga's storytelling is his juxtaposition of the Sarayaku villagers in the courtroom against those back in the village, all connected by digital technology so that the village is able to watch the court proceedings as they happen, projected onto a large screen in the village's meeting area.

According to the Pachamama Alliance, which legally represented the community, the court's ruling in the Kichwa's favor

FIGURE 6.2 Eriberto Gualinga's *Children of the Jaguar* (2012).

should dramatically affect Ecuadorian plans for development of the whole southern Amazon region of Ecuador. By upholding the community's rights to free, prior, and informed consultation, the ruling invites closer scrutiny of situations where the interests of extractive industry are superseding the rights of indigenous nations and Nature as outlined in Ecuador's constitution.

(Usner 2012: para. 4–5)

Conclusion

Questions as to how to represent, display, and teach indigenous cultural knowledge are deeply embedded in culturally specific ontologies and in contested histories of colonial misappropriation and disrespect of cultural knowledges and objects. The study of indigenous documentary filmmaking is a critical field for understanding these processes, not just in terms of technological adaptation but also regarding ideological issues, emphasizing the need for local cultural control over how, for whom, and under what conditions cultural knowledge may be captured, revealed, or displayed.

Indigenous or Aboriginal media are increasingly providing local and diasporic cultural groups and individuals with opportunities to open windows into economic sovereignty within a global economy, political sovereignty with regard to the surrounding nation-state, and representational sovereignty with regard to cultural control over structures and styles of representation. Ultimately, sovereignty of all types needs to belong to each of these culturally specific groups.

Notes

1 The Yirrkala Film Project is available as a DVD set. For more information, see http://sa-staging.com/search-programs/program/?sn=9214.
2 The home page for the Warlpiri Media Association, currently incorporated into PAW Media, is www.pawmedia.com.au/.
3 www.videonasaldeias.org.br/2009/index.php?
4 See Aboriginal Peoples Television Network (Canada) at http://aptn.ca/, National Indigenous Television (Australia) at www.nitv.org.au/, and Maori TV (New Zealand) at www.maoritelevision.com.
5 http://caama.com.au
6 www.nativetelecom.org/
7 www.nfb.ca/explore-all-directors/alanis-obomsawin
8 www.isuma.tv
9 For the full text of this declaration, see www.un.org/esa/socdev/unpfii/documents/DRIPS_en.pdf.
10 An increasing number of indigenous media producers have achieved respect as feature filmmakers and television writers/producers/directors, especially in those countries in which indigenous media have become more commercially institutionalized (such as Canada, Australia, and New Zealand).
11 www.irititja.com/
12 http://godslake.nfb.ca/#/godslake
13 Also available on DVD as well as online at http://topdocumentaryfilms.com/first-australians/.

14 www.programs.sbs.com.au/firstaustralians/content/
15 This film is available from Visionmaker Media at www.nativetelecom.org/films/smokin-fish or http://visionmaker.semkhor.com/product.asp?s=visionmaker&pf_id=FISH-11-H&dept_id=23265. A list of awards it has won is available at www.der.org/films/smokin-fish.html.
16 Distributed by Vision Maker Media: http://visionmaker.semkhor.com/product.asp?pf_id=NFTS-66-E&s=visionmaker.
17 Available from Women Make Movies at www.wmm.com/filmcatalog/pages/c277.shtml.
18 The film's website is http://coniston.pawmedia.com.au/.
19 The film's website is www.thickdarkfog.com/.
20 The film is distributed by Amnesty International and is available online at www.youtube.com/watch?v=Ma1QSmtuiLQ. It should not be confused with another film by the same name, also on YouTube, distributed by New Atlantis Documentaries, which is about another Ecuadorian indigenous group, the Huaorani people.

Bibliography

Barclay, Barry. 1990. *Our Own Image*. Auckland: Longman Paul.
Deveson, Philippa, with Ian Dunlop. 2012. "The Ethnographic Filmmaking of Ian Dunlop in a Decade of Change." *Humanities Research* 18 (1). Available online at http://press.anu.edu.au/apps/bookworm/view/Humanities+Research+Vol+XVIII.+No.+1.+2012/10401/ch02.html (accessed May 22, 2015).
Dowell, Kristin. 2012. "Expressions of Digital Indigeneity: Redefining Transnational Indigeneity Within and Between Borders in the Aboriginal Media Arts Collective Itwé." Unpublished paper presented at the 2012 American Anthropological Association, San Francisco, CA.
Fleras, Augie. 2011. "Unsilencing Aboriginal Voices: Toward an Indigenous Media Gaze." In Augie Fleras, *The Media Gaze: Representations of Diversities in Canada*. Vancouver: University of British Columbia Press. 215–28.
Ginsburg, Faye. 1991. "Indigenous Media: Faustian Contract or Global Village?" *Cultural Anthropology* 6: 92–112.
——. 1994. "Embedded Aesthetics: Creating a Discursive Space for Indigenous Media." *Cultural Anthropology* 9 (3): 365–82.
——. 1999. "The After-Life of Documentary: The Impact of *You Are on Indian Land*." *Wide Angle* 21 (2): 60–7.
Hearne, Joanna. 2006. "Telling and Retelling in the 'Ink of Light': Documentary Cinema, Oral Narratives, and Indigenous Identities." *Screen* 47 (3): 307–26.
Hopkins, Candice. 2006. "Making Things Our Own: The Indigenous Aesthetic in Digital Storytelling." *Leonardo* 39 (4): 341–4.
Knopf, Kerstin. 2010. "'Sharing Our Stories with All Canadians': Decolonizing Aboriginal Media and Aboriginal Media Politics in Canada." *American Indian Culture and Research Journal* 34 (1): 89–120.
Leuthold, Steven. 1998. *Indigenous Aesthetics: Native Art, Media, and Identity*. Austin: University of Texas Press.
——. 2001. "Rhetorical Dimensions of Native American Documentary." *Wicazo Sa Review* 16 (2): 55–73.
Lewis, Randolph. 2010. "The New Navajo Cinema: Cinema and Nation in the Indigenous Southwest." *The Velvet Light Trap* 66 (fall): 50–61.
Manuel, George, and Michael Posluns. 1974. *The Fourth World: An Indian Reality*. New York: Free Press.
Michaels, Eric. 1994. *Bad Aboriginal Art: Tradition, Media, and Technological Horizons*, ed. Paul Foss. Minneapolis: University of Minnesota Press.
Peterson, Leighton. 2013. "Reclaiming Diné Film: Visual Sovereignty and the Return of *Navajo Film Themselves*." *Visual Anthropology Review* 29 (1): 29–41.

Raheja, Michelle. 2007. "Reading Nanook's Smile: Visual Sovereignty, Indigenous Revisions of Ethnography, and *Atanarjuat* (*The Fast Runner*)." *American Quarterly* 59 (4): 1159–85.

Robertson, Roland. 1992. *Globalization: Social Theory and Global Culture*. London: Sage.

Salazar, Juan Francisco, and Amalia Córdova. 2008. "Imperfect Media and the Poetics of Indigenous Video in Latin America." In *Global Indigenous Media: Cultures, Poetics, and Politics*, ed. Pamela Wilson and Michelle Stewart. Durham, NC: Duke University Press Books. 39–57.

Schiwy, Freya. 2009. *Indianizing Film: Decolonization, the Andes, and the Question of Technology*. New Brunswick, NJ: Rutgers University Press.

Smith, Linda Tuhiwai. 1999. *Decolonizing Methodologies: Research and Indigenous Peoples*. London: Zed Books.

Strickland, April. 2012. "Local Roots, Global Citizenship, and National Self-Determination: Māori Media in the 21st Century." Unpublished paper presented at the 2012 American Anthropological Association, San Francisco, CA.

Thorner, Sabra. 2010. "Imagining an Indigital Interface: Ara Irititja Indigenizes the Technologies of Knowledge Management." *Collections: A Journal for Museum and Archives Professionals* 6 (3): 125–46.

———. 2012. "Links and Interfaces Bridging the 'Digital Divide': Interanimating Indigenous Ontologies and Internet Infrastructures in Australia and Beyond." Unpublished paper presented at the 2012 American Anthropological Association, San Francisco, CA.

Usner, Pat. 2012. "Sarayaku Ruling Upholds Indigenous Rights in Ecuador and Beyond." Press release, the Pachamama Alliance, July 27, 2012. Available online at www.pachamama.org/news/sarayaku-ruling-upholds-indigenous-rights-in-ecuador-and-beyond (accessed July 19, 2014).

Wilson, Pamela, and Michelle Stewart. 2008. "Introduction: Indigeneity and Indigenous Media on the Global Stage." In *Global Indigenous Media: Cultures, Poetics and Politics*, ed. Pamela Wilson and Michelle Stewart. Durham, NC: Duke University Press. 1–35.

Worth, Sol, and John Adair. 1997. *Through Navajo Eyes: An Exploration in Film Communication and Anthropology*. Albuquerque: University of New Mexico Press.

Documentary in New Contexts

7

TRUE LIFE

The Voice of Television Documentary

Laurie Ouellette

Since 1998, the weekly MTV series *True Life* has presented the "unique stories of young people, from the unusual and intense to the shocking and hilarious." Combining fly-on-the-wall observation with first-person storytelling and the fast-paced camera work, editing, and music that characterize the MTV style, each episode follows two or three subjects over the course of several weeks or months, with the purpose of revealing what it is like to experience their situation, identity, problem, or subculture. Intimate and subjective, these episodes take TV viewers inside the everyday lives of individuals who share something in common, and who narrate their biographies and reflect on the events being depicted on screen as they are happening. *True Life* values the raw authenticity and dramatic potential of immediate personal experience over broader forms of journalistic investigation or critique—as exemplified by the use of the singular "I" in the episode titles, for example, "I'm a Porn Star" (1998), "I'm a Pro-Wrestler" (1999), "I'm on Crystal Meth" (2000), "I'm Coming Out" (2002), "I'm Surviving High School" (2003), "I Live a Double Life" (2004), "I'm Dead Broke" (2005), "I Self-Injure" (2007), "I Have Acne" (2008), "I'm Changing My Sex" (2009), "I Have a Parent in Prison" (2010), "I'm Working My Way out of Poverty" (2012), and "I Have Social Anxiety" (2013). Trading on a seemingly inexhaustible supply of "extraordinarily ordinary" (Ouellette and Murray 2009) young people whose "true stories" are often difficult, non-normative, and/or traumatic, the series operates at the increasingly porous boundaries between conventional documentary and newer developments in first-person media and reality entertainment. This chapter situates *True Life* within the transformation of factual television in recent decades, and develops the concept of *voice* as a critical framework for evaluating these hybrid programs.

Within classic documentary film theory, voice refers to the manner in which non-fiction films "speak" through a combination of sounds and images, so as to present a coherent point of view or argument. The analysis focuses mainly on texts (films) and authors (directors), which limits its usefulness to industrial mediums like television. The rapid growth of first-person media in the 1990s across many genres and platforms, including video diaries and television talk shows, inspired new ways of thinking about the voice of ordinary people in the media. The question shifted from the organization of texts and the intentions of authors to the extent to which real people could authentically be themselves—and tell their stories—within these partly scripted and heavily edited formats. More recently, media scholars have turned to social theory to rethink voice as an ethical process of accounting for oneself and the conditions of one's life. Here, identity is understood to be performative, and questions of authenticity are less important than the extent to which diverse social experiences can be narrated as meaningful stories in media culture. At a time when neoliberal narratives of self-enterprising personhood tend to prevail on television and in social media as well, voicing alternative accounts of social life is considered especially important. *True Life* presents a compelling case study for thinking about the layers of voice in nonfiction television. As we shall see, the series provides a space where young people can have a voice—sometimes in opposition to dominant norms, but always on MTV's terms.

The voice of documentary

As Brian Winston contends, documentary theory has long been preoccupied with "claiming the real," an agenda that encompasses problems of mediation and transparency, the emergence of different documentary genres and styles, and the impact of new equipment such as portable cameras and microphones (Winston 2008: 35). Within this literature, the "voice" of documentary is generally attributed to the filmmaker and understood as a textual property—what Bill Nichols famously called "something narrower than style: that which conveys to us a sense of a text's social point of view, of how it is speaking to us and how it is organizing the materials presented to us" (1985: 260). In a widely cited 1983 essay (reprinted in 1985), Nichols described the voice of documentary as "that intangible, moiré-like pattern formed by the unique interaction of all a film's codes" (1985: 260–1). Here and in later writings, Nichols used the term "voice" to characterize both the "distinct characterization of individual films"—each film's style and manner of expressing its way of seeing the world—and the basis for grouping these "singular voices" into distinctive documentary modes or subgenres (FitzSimons 2009: 138; Nichols 1985: 2010). While subject to refinement and debate over the years, this conception of voice has played an enduring role in the theorization of documentary as a cultural form.

Within the framework developed by Nichols, which has tended to value experimentation with authorial voice over established documentary modes (Bruzzi 2006), *True Life* may seem like an unremarkable program. The opening features a proliferating array of small screens, each featuring an image of a real person who has been featured on the program. "True Life" appears in bold letters, while an offscreen voice-of-God narrator briefly describes the upcoming episode and the individuals whose stories will be told (as Nichols would describe it, in the *expository* mode). After this short explanation, the offscreen narration is dropped entirely and the program adopts a fly-on-the-wall approach. The actual people and events comprising the two or three linked segments are presented via the (unquestioned) presumption of "directness, immediacy, and the impression" of capturing reality in the raw (the *observational* mode) (Nichols 1985: 259–60; 2010). There is no attempt to unmask the ideological conventions of factual representation, and any attempt at artistic experimentation is discouraged by the weekly formula. The filmmaker does not participate in the situations being documented or engage directly or openly with the subjects, but remains hidden behind the scenes. Indeed, there is no singular "filmmaker" associated with *True Life*; the multiple individuals and production companies listed in the credits vary from episode to episode, overshadowed by the recurring stamp of the MTV logo. To understand why *True Life* merits attention in the larger sphere of contemporary documentary, we need a broader conception of *voice* as an industrial, social, and ethical process.

In a critical reassessment of the concept of voice in documentary theory, Trish FitzSimons (2009) points out some problems and limitations, especially when extending the concept of voice to television documentaries. By focusing on cinema, for example, theorists have neglected the industrial contexts of television production. This oversight is not surprising, as theorizing about documentary has developed within film studies. Michael Curtin speculates that television documentaries have received "only passing mention" within this oeuvre in large part because they lack an *auteur*—an identifiable individual to whom creative intention and meaning can be attributed (Curtin 1995: 4). The notion of the documentarian filmmaker as auteur is especially difficult to apply to commercial television, where the textual style and authority of a documentary (or any program for that matter) is negotiated among many different people (including employees and contractors) within large media corporations. *True Life* is co-created by MTV executives, audience researchers, casting agents, a rotating group of producers and directors, and production crews. The voice of any episode, and of the series as a whole, will reflect "multiple inputs" (FitzSimons 2009: 136), with the MTV network operating as the corporate author. These complex dynamics are not evident from the text alone: As FitzSimons contends, any attempt to understand a television documentary's "social point of view […] how it is speaking to us and how it is organizing the materials presented to us," must address wider institutional contexts and the associated "affordances and impedances that bring some individuals and groups to voice, and silence others" (2009: 141). In the case of American television, this would include the priorities and routines of networks such as MTV, as well as the impact of deregulatory policies, concentrated media ownership, advertising, and niche marketing on television production more broadly.

MTV appeared at the dawn of the 1980s, the decade that saw the concept of the public interest rewritten by free market telecommunication policies in the United States. Before then, television documentary had been tied to the expectation that broadcasters must inform and educate citizens, in addition to entertaining audiences and selling consumer goods, such as cars and toothpaste. As the deregulatory ethos took hold, this expectation diminished. While the major broadcast networks abandoned documentary for much more profitable forms of tabloid journalism (Raphael 2005) and public television was defunded, emerging commercial cable networks such as Lifetime and Discovery began experimenting with lighter documentary formats geared to specialized lifestyle clusters. MTV also embraced documentary as it moved away from 24/7 music videos and experimented with new forms of corporate social responsibility as a dimension of its brand identity.

Targeting the "fickle" 12-to-34-year-old demographic, the network's News and Docs division embarked on a mission to replace "boring" talking heads with more "interesting" youth-centric topics told in the snappy MTV style. News and Docs also declared an intention to "honor the voices of teenagers when depicting their experiences" (Cunningham 2014: 111). This mission differed from the waning public interest ideals rooted in the top-down dissemination of serious information, education, and enlightenment on a national scale. Promising to reflect the specialized tastes and real-life experiences of young people while also entertaining them for maximum profit, *True Life* exemplified a broader shift in the "civic function" of television documentary (Corner 2002). *True Life* did not entirely abandon the public interest as the historical rationale for television documentary as much as it reinvented the presumed civic purpose of documentary to facilitate MTV's niche marketing and branding practices.

Besides focusing on cinema and overlooking industrial processes, discussions of voice in documentary theory have also downplayed the roles of subjects and audiences, FitzSimons contends (2009). As cultural studies (and its uptake in television studies) has made clear, textual authority is never inherently stable or fixed; meaning is an interpretive process that involves viewer input. The role of audiences in establishing the voice of a documentary program or any other text has only intensified with the rise of social media, blogs, tweets, and other digital venues for viewer involvement and reflection. MTV makes extensive use of digital platforms to promote its programs, circulate video clips and full episodes, and solicit constant audience feedback. *True Life* has a designated place on the MTV website, a Facebook page, and a very active Twitter presence; the program is also discussed on MTV's corporate-social-responsibility-themed web forums (such as MTV Act) and on user-generated websites and blogs. These interactive platforms encourage MTV viewers to participate in the multifaceted voice of *True Life* episodes, even as they also function as clever marketing devices (Andrejevic 2004).

The people who appear in documentaries are also involved in determining the voice of the program or film. Nichols recognized this possibility in his 1983 essay, in which he noted the weakening of authorial voice that can result when subjects are allowed to speak for a film. For him, the role of the filmmaker was to organize these subjective voices into a coherent and hierarchical order so that the overall perspective of the documentary was foregrounded. In prioritizing the creative and social authority of the filmmaker, this hierarchical conception of voice limited the role of participants to illustrating and servicing an argument that is not of their own making—a tendency that Brian Winston sees operating especially acutely in the treatment of "victims" in documentary theory and practice (1991). There are important exceptions to this hierarchical approach to voice—most notably experiments with collective authorship involving marginalized communities and documentarians committed to overcoming the problem of "speaking for the other" (FitzSimons 2009; see also Ruby 1992).

Unlike these collaborative attempts to rethink the voice of documentary, *True Life* does not share decision-making power with its subjects, nor does it involve them in casting, scripting, editing, filming, or marketing practices. However, each segment of *True Life* does feature an extended first-person voiceover in which the person being documented introduces herself and explains her situation to the viewing audience. This first-person voice is heard throughout every episode, as the subjects reflect candidly on their life histories and describe their activities, thoughts, and feelings. Because the civic function of *True Life* is to present the experiences of the MTV demographic, this personal narration takes on high significance as a register of voice—not just as a textual convention, but as a social process that connects "real" people to the purpose of documentary, as well as to the MTV brand. *True Life* authorizes and enables young people to tell their own stories with regularity on television, even as MTV ultimately controls how these first-person narratives are constructed and circulated. In this sense, *True Life* exemplifies the broader explosion of "ordinary voices" across factual television formats in recent decades.

To analyze this development, we need an understanding of the documentary voice that is able to address the complexities of "giving an account of oneself" in a changing media culture (Couldry 2010; Butler 2005). When feminist documentary filmmakers of the 1960s and 70s developed extended interviews, personal monologues, and other techniques drawn from *cinéma vérité* to give voice to women as a marginalized group, they understood their work as a dimension of social change. For them, the expression of personal experience on camera was connected to a process of political empowerment that exceeded textual properties (Lesage 1984). "These films all had in common a concern for women and women's issues. Women and their environments were made visible in a new way. By eliminating the omniscient male narrator, women could speak in their own voices and validate their experiences" (Erens 1988: 556; see also Martineau 1984). Today, a diverse range of ordinary people can be found on television, clamoring for voice. The dramatic growth of first-person media, the proliferation of broadcast and cable channels, and the industry's search for cost-efficient factual programming to fill them have created a fertile climate for documentary-entertainment hybrids that enlist real people as subjects and quasi-performers. Indeed, as Graeme Turner (2009) and others point out, ordinary people are now essential to the business model of television, where they provide free labor as well as the raw material for the accelerated manufacture of disposable content. As an enduring example of this broader cultural shift, *True Life* raises the question: What does voice as a social process involve now?

First-person media and reality television

In *Freak Show: First Person Media and Factual Television*, Jon Dovey chronicles the "sea change in the nature of television documentary" since the 1990s (2000: 2). Observing the explosion of first-person factual formats in the United States and Europe, he notes "tidal waves of entertainment" flooding into "discursive zones previously reserved for education, information and enlightenment" as new factual genres staged claims on the real within a "theater of intimacy" (2000: 25). Subjective modes of expression proliferated across formats (talk shows, amateur video contests, video diaries, docusoaps) that encouraged ordinary people "to share their intimate fears and secrets" as they performed "the ordinariness of their own extraordinary subjectivity" (2000: 4). Even the single documentary was not immune to this tendency, as the documentary form "increasingly concerned itself with the subject's inner life, the individual feelings of ordinary folk in any everyday situation with dramatic potential" (2000: 105). According to Dovey, this change was connected to a shifting "regime of truth" to the extent that personal experience was beginning to surpass "general truth claims" as a guarantee of knowledge on television. In the new formats, he explained, "raw intimate experience" and the "self-spoken narratives of everyday life" were often foregrounded over objective knowledge and the "grand narratives" (such as patriarchy or class struggle) used to make sense of the social world in prior epochs (2000: 25–6, 109).

To be sure, there are precursors to the "subjective, autobiographical and confessional modes of expression" (Dovey 2000: 2) that have come to dominate television culture. For example, the magazine *True Story*, which inspired radio and television programs, circulated "first-hand" accounts of personal tragedy, deviance, and redemption as early as the 1930s (Mandziuk 2001). What Dovey points to is a rupture in documentary that was tied to a confluence of historical factors, from the "posting" of social movements such as civil rights and feminism as "already accomplished" and thus irrelevant, to the blurring of public and private, to deregulatory policies and new market pressures being placed on public service broadcasters. While he focuses on television, similar tendencies were apparent in independent film and video documentaries of the 1990s, which also embraced first-person conventions, from personal essay documentaries to collaborative ethnographic projects carried out with non-filmmakers. "First-person storytelling is beginning to emerge as its own genre […] marked not only by the first person voice testimonial, but also by the bringing of the viewer into the world of the storyteller's experience," said Patricia Aufderheide of this development. "Often socially engaged, it is rarely polemical. Indeed, it typically does not make a direct argument, but an implicit request for the viewer to recognize the reality of the speaker, and to incorporate that reality into his or her view of the world" (Aufderheide 1997: 16).

Unlike independent documentaries, which tended to showcase the personal experience of the filmmaker, first-person television unfolded in an industrial context that offered little control to its subjects. For Dovey, the problem was not the waning status of television documentary as a "discourse of sobriety" (Nichols

1994), but the constraints faced by the "speaking subject within the frame of somebody else's version of their biographical narrative" (Dovey 2000: 110). While it may seem as if television is bursting with ordinary people "speaking for themselves," they are in fact often following the "script" that the popular factual formats require of them, he explained. For example, the participants of daytime talk shows are strategically cast and coached by the show's producers to generate a spectacle of "trashiness" and interpersonal conflict (Grindstaff 2002). The relegation of real-life subjects to prescribed and often stereotypical roles is also evident in newer forms of reality-based entertainment, from competitions to dating shows. Yet, as Dovey cautions, it is important not to conflate the myriad factual television formats now on offer, as some present more meaningful opportunities for autobiographical expression than others.

Video diaries, which first developed in the United Kingdom in the 1990s, are a case in point. As Dovey points out, the BBC series *Video Nation*, which was created by its Community and Disability Programmes Unit, was intended to encourage a dialogue about the "socially situated nature" of specific lives. For the program, a wide range of people worked with producers to record scenes from their everyday lives. In the course of these short segments, difficult and painful experiences were often revealed. With no experts on hand to interpret the personal dialogues, and no therapeutic conventions to situate the audience as "judge, jury and therapist" (Dovey 2000: 126), the videos (which were shown between programs) could operate as points of viewer identification and recognition. Rejecting the connection between confessional discourse, othering, and the enforcement of social norms, the subjects of *Video Nation* used strategies of "speaking the self" such as coming out and testimony of "feeling, sentiment and subjectivity" to "declare their identity and frame it within a social context" (Dovey 2000: 127). While in a traditional documentary this personal testimony would be used to support an expositional argument, here the articulation of experience was open-ended. At the same time, these highly subjective moments retained a relevance to the "social body," Dovey contends, in that they often expressed personal experiences of broader issues (poverty, single motherhood, racism, sexual discrimination, health care) and referenced a community of citizen subjects who could understand and "care about each other" across their commonalities and differences (2000: 127).

Whereas *Video Nation* was created under the auspices of noncommercial public broadcasting (and was an attempt to update its paternalistic mission), *True Life* was developed by a for-profit cable network with minimal public interest obligations. As a consequence, *True Life* is chock full of advertising and geared to a specialized consumer demographic (the youthful MTV audience) rather than members of a national public. However, there are also commonalities. There are no experts or hosts on *True Life*, and the first-person narration evidences many of the "self-speaking" strategies noted by Dovey, including coming out as non-normative, witnessing the "realities" of everyday life, and testifying about feelings, emotions, and sensibilities. To be sure, there is a commercially motivated shock value in the ongoing pre-sentation of individuals who embody exoticized subcultural identities (from chub chasers to professional wrestlers), face challenging circumstances (from being bipolar to having a "hot" mom), or possess unusual habits (from foot fetishes to eating sand). Yet, the articulation of private experience is also connected to "issues of the day," and the series consistently profiles young people experiencing drug addiction, eating disorders, relationship turmoil, financial difficulties, health problems, and other issues that impact young people. As with *Video Nation*, the confessional nature of the program is open-ended. The disclosure of intimate experience through the first-person narration is not tied to broader forms of journalistic inquiry or social critique, but nor is the viewer stitched into the practices of judging and shaming that characterize so many contemporary reality programs. The performance of "ordinariness" (however exotic, unusual, traumatic, or different) is offered as a point of identification and understanding among the MTV audience, which is encouraged to see itself in the infinity of expanding *True Life* screens, each depicting a different and unique experience of youthful personhood. In that sense, the liberal humanism that undergirds *Video Nation* is at work here too, reconfigured within the logic of niche marketing and cable branding.

While *True Life* was an early example of first-person television, it is now a rare entity, in that it draws from the conventions of observational documentary without adding the gaming elements and artificial environments that have become standard fare in reality television. For John Corner, productions like *True Life*, which exemplified the turn to "intimate stories" and the changed "tonality of documentary voice" that resulted, were the launching pad for reality programs like *Big Brother* that stage the conditions of intimate experience for pure entertainment value and make no attempt to connect the personal to the wider dynamics of social life. These programs have been accompanied by a heightened degree of "self-consciousness" on the part of ordinary subjects, so that appearing on television is less about ordinary people's voices than it is a performance in its own right (Corner 2002: 53). While the premise of *True Life* hinges on claims of authenticity, and the episodes are always shot in "natural" settings, entertainment-oriented storytelling techniques and elements of self-display are in evidence as well. *True Life* operates within the broader commercial television culture, and it is not immune from the pressures and expectations associated with other forms of factual programming.

MTV News and Docs executive Lauren Lavin (who graduated from the MA program in Documentary Film Production at Stanford and is the producer of several feature documentaries, including the 2003 film *Tupac: Resurrection*) contends that by allowing subjects to tell their stories, *True Life* maintains a higher purpose than the newer reality forms. She highlights episodes that have had "big effects," including "True Life: I'm Coming Out" (2002), which followed several young people coming out of the closet to their parents: "A lot of young people come out to their parents and the parents can't accept it. It's a very troubling, difficult thing. So we don't whitewash it. We try to show what really happens. I know that's had a huge effect on our viewers. Still, now, there will be gay kids working here at MTV who'll say, I saw that show, and that's what made me decide to come out. Because I saw someone else do it," Lavin explains (Cunningham 2014: 117). The episode

"Driving While Black" (1999), which won a NAACP award, is also cited for presenting everyday life "from the point of view of being black, and being pulled over for no reason other than the color of your skin" (Cunningham 2014: 119). Yet, Lavin also acknowledges that reality programs like MTV's *The Real World* series (1992–present) has "set the bar very, very high for things to 'happen' on *True Life*. Audiences want some drama. They want exciting things to happen. They're used to that now. They're waiting for that. And it's tough to get that, and stay honest to your characters." Every *True Life* character must go through a "story arc" involving a beginning, middle, and end. "There's something they want that they can't get, or there's something that they want that they do get. They're not profiles, they're storytelling [...] and it's tough to do that if you're not going to live with the character for three years," says Lavin (Cunningham 2014: 129).

Lavin concedes that *True Life* has a script—"every single thing we do has a script" (Cunningham 2014: 131)—but she does not reveal the extent to which the first-person narration—the principal register of voice in *True Life*—is part of this scripting process. Regardless, the authenticity of the speaking subjects is far from self-evident. Long before filming, MTV executives brainstorm the topics to be covered each season and the best way to "cast" them. These ideas are run through the Research Department at MTV, which amasses extensive data on the MTV audience, and on young people more broadly. Once a topic is approved, casting agents set about finding the "right" people to appear in the episode (Hooper 2000). Working from the social types identified in the brainstorming and research process, they post "casting calls" on MTV.com and sites like Craigslist. "Do you want to tell your story on *True Life*? We're adding new episode ideas all the time. So keep checking back to find out if your story is coming up. See below for new episodes in development," states a recent announcement on the MTV website (http://remotecontrol.mtv.com/casting-calls/true-life-casting-calls/).

These casting calls sometimes reference MTV's attempt to address a timely issue, as with the announcement for "True Life: I'm Being Slut Shamed." "Slut shaming is when women are unfairly and harshly attacked for being sexually active, or for seeming to be sexually active, or for expressing their sexuality," the call explains. Exemplifying the search for social actors to represent forms of personal experience of interest to MTV, the call asks: "Are you being insulted, mocked or bullied for expressing your sexuality? [...] Is anyone spreading explicit videos or photos of you in an attempt to hurt you? Is your sexuality a topic of conversation online, in school, at work, or in your town? [...] If you appear to be between the ages of 16 and 29 and you've answered yes to any of these questions, you could be in a new episode of *True Life*."

Once an episode is cast, small, on-location crews arrive to collect footage in close consultation with MTV News and Docs executives. The presence of the television cameras, coupled with conventions of camera work, editing, music, and storytelling, further compromise any assumption of reality in the raw. The "true stories" that result are carefully crafted and packaged in the service of entertaining audiences. Yet, *True Life* is billed as a documentary (one of the longest-running documentary series on American television), and its claim to realism works differently from the stage-managed conventions of reality entertainment (including MTV's reality programs). The absence of hosts, experts, contrived settings, and prizes, the singularity of *True Life* episodes, and the premise of pluralism and understanding (as opposed to judgment) allow for some of the open-endedness and potential recognition and understanding that Dovey ascribes to *Video Nation* and other diary programs.

The extended first-person narration that overlays all episodes distinguishes *True Life* from conventional television documentaries as well as programs like *The Real World* and *Big Brother*, where confessionals refer only to the insular world created by television itself. The question remains: To what extent are these first-person accounts shaped by MTV? Are subjects "speaking themselves," or are they following a scripted formula? To what extent do they perform for the camera? In the remainder of this chapter, I want to present these questions in a slightly different way, focusing less on degrees of authenticity and more on the social and political importance of voice as a process that is always both embodied and mediated. At an historical moment when social identity is increasingly theorized as a performance rather than an essential or fixed essence, authenticity may not be a necessary condition for the expression of voice as a social process. What are the possibilities for giving an account of oneself within the hybrid conventions and "story arcs" that constitute *True Life*? To consider this question, we need to bring television documentary into conversation with social theory.

Giving an account of oneself

In *Why Voice Matters: Culture and Politics after Neoliberalism*, Nick Couldry describes a "crisis" of voice in contemporary times. While social media, reality television, and other places for ordinary people to speak have proliferated, these forums are dominated by the logics associated with neoliberalism—self-enterprise, self-improvement, privatization, competition, and consumption. YouTube videos, as an "expanded zone of self-display," epitomize neoliberalism's impetus to commodify the human, to the extent that "page views and positive commentary on people's postings of themselves performing or simply 'being themselves' can literally be counted and monetized as part of the process of self-branding" (Couldry 2010: 82). While there is no formal or mandatory "script," YouTubers often write themselves into a narrative that is "not theirs to adapt or control," and that represents a "deep denial of voice, a deep form of oppression," Couldry contends (2010: 9). Similar processes prevail across reality television, as ordinary people perform marketable versions of themselves in the hopes of monetizing their personas and brands (Hearn 2008).

Couldry advocates an expansion of voice—particularly "voice that matters"—as an alternative to a neoliberal narrative of personhood. While documentary theorists conceive of voice as the "perspective that a particular text constructs through various devices" (Couldry 2010: 10), his approach is different. Voice is more than an expression of opinion or the claim of representation (in the media or the political system). Rather, voice is the "process of giving an account of one's life and its conditions." This entails an open-ended engagement with oneself, a process of reflecting "back and forth" between one's actions and experiences, and it also relies on narrative, a "basic feature of human action" (2010: 7, 9). Giving an account of oneself involves telling a story about oneself and the social world in which one acts. Couldry attributes the crisis of voice to the unequal distribution of resources for having a voice that is recognized and validated, and the widening "gap between people's lives and the narratives available" in neoliberal societies, where individuals are increasingly called upon to adopt norms and behaviors drawn from the logic of the free market, such as competition, self-branding, and self-enterprise. The gap between dominant templates for selfhood and the articulation of lived experience matters, for to "deny value to another's capacity for narrative—deny her potential for voice—is to deny a basic dimension of human life," he contends (2010: 7).

This conception of voice is helpful for making sense of first-person media and its spillage into reality television. It moves us beyond questions about narrative style and organization of documentary texts and the accuracy (or not) of representations of the real, to a more complex understanding of how subjective experience is communicated, and the implications of this process. Voice is not guaranteed by references to intimacy, interiority, or ordinariness. Placing a camera on an ordinary person, setting up a confessional booth, or authorizing someone to "be themselves" on television do not in themselves constitute voice. Nor for that matter does interviewing or filming a subject for a documentary. Drawing from Judith Butler (2005), Couldry theorizes voice as an "embodied process" of articulating the world that will draw from a history of reflection and self-interpretation. Voice can be expressed in personal or collective ways, but it never arises from individuals in isolation, because "having a voice" is a social process, requiring the shared resources integral to recognition, interpretation, and validation. Voice is not a "true" expression of a pre-constituted or authentic self, but is part of the ongoing project of selfhood.

Indeed, voice is not expressed as much as it is always performed. Butler's view of "authenticity" as a process of performance provokes new questions about the heightened self-consciousness attributed to first-person and reality television. "The 'I' has no story of its own that is not also the story of a relation—or set of relations—to a set of norms," Butler points out (2005: 8). There is no authentic personhood outside the norms and conventions of society—"self-making" outside the norms that "orchestrate the possible forms that a subject may take" is impossible. This does not mean that voice is impossible, Butler contends, but the use of voice as a critical social process must expose the limits of what is taken for granted. To narrate the self and its conditions in this way is to maintain a "critical relation" to existing norms, Butler contends. This self-reflexivity is always relational, in that it is incited by an "other" and may lead someone else into self-reflection as well: "The account is an act—situated within a larger practice of acts—that one performs for, to, even on an other [...] sometimes by virtue of the language provided by the other" (130). When subjects tell their stories, to what extent do they expose, and/or do they position themselves in relation to, social norms? How is the act giving an account of oneself performed—and for whom? What does voicing one's story on television—with its imagined audience—contribute to this process?

With these conceptual resources in mind, I want to take a closer look at the possibilities and limitations of voice in "True Life: I'm Homeless" (2009), an episode featuring young people whose personal experiences are connected to the economic consequences of neoliberalism, or what Lisa Duggan calls the upward redistribution of wealth (2004). Drawing from Couldry (2010), I consider how the subjects account for themselves and the conditions of their lives, and the extent to which they explain their homelessness in "non-social ways, for example in terms of individual failings or initiatives" that reiterate neoliberal logics. I am also interested in Couldry's criteria for evaluating the value placed on voice as a social process: What narratives are possible (or not) within the structure of the episode? To what extent is private experience linked to other (possibly collective) sites, conditions, stories, or practices? (Couldry 2010: 127). Finally, following Butler, I consider the performative possibilities of voice, and the episode's engagement with normative ideas about homelessness and homeless people.

"True Life: I'm Homeless"

Between 2007 and 2009, *True Life* presented a number of episodes clustering around subjective experiences of economic hardship, including "I Live in the Projects" (2007), "I'm Supporting My Family" (2007), "I'm in Debt" (2007), "I Have Broke Parents" (2009), "I Can No Longer Afford My Lifestyle" (2009), and "I'm Homeless" (2009). In the context of rising housing costs, the financial crisis, and the recession that followed, MTV News and Docs decided that topics related to unemployment, poverty, debt, and other issues covered in the news were relevant. In "I'm Homeless," an offscreen male narrator asks the audience, "What's it like to have virtually no money for food and a place to lay your head? In this episode you'll meet three young people led by their dire circumstances toward the treacherous path to homelessness." Footage of these three individuals flashes on the screen—a teenage girl surrounded by boxes, a young man begging for food, and a young woman on the streets of New York.

We first meet Katie, a white teenager whose mother is out of work. Unable to pay their rent, they have been evicted from their apartment, and are now preparing to live in their car. The camera focuses on Katie's face, and she explains, "I'm just so, so angry, it's so hard doing this. The situation is becoming unbearable." Katie's candid expression of her feelings echoes the self-speaking strategies (coming out, witnessing, testimony) discussed by Dovey in the context of *Video Nation* (see Figure 7.1). The audience understands Katie's situation as an aberration of norms enforcing middle-class home ownership, but is not encouraged to judge her. The omniscient narrator states: "Katie desperately wants to find a place to live. Will she and her mom ever be able to afford housing of any kind?" establishing the beginning, middle, and end of her story arc. Katie's first-person account of herself and her conditions will unfold within these parameters. Kenyatta, who is African American,

FIGURE 7.1 Katie brushes her teeth in the bathroom of a chain restaurant, but cannot afford to eat breakfast there.

is a "young transsexual who moved to New York with nothing to her name," the narrator explains. She has been living in a network of youth shelters, but is turning 25, which means she's "aging out of youth services." Soon she will have to leave the homeless shelter where she is living. Kenyatta's story is also framed as a suspense-filled enigma: "With no job and no family, can Kenyatta find a place to live before she's forced to the street?" Ronnie, the final subject featured, "has been addicted to drugs and alcohol for years." He is a white man who appears to be in his mid-twenties, sleeps outside, and survives by begging for food and spare change. Ronnie believes that his life could be better in sunny California. His story arc: "Can Ronnie make it across the country to his promised land? Or will those California dreams be extinguished along the way?"

Following this set-up, the program adopts a more observational style. The male narrator is dropped, and the subjects themselves take over the role of explaining their stories, actions, and situations. Katie begins: "My name is Katie, I'm a junior in high school and I live with my mom and my dogs," she states, while the camera shows her shopping with her mom at the Dollar Store. She explains that her dad died of colon cancer, and she and her mom (who has chronic health problems) had been living on survivors' Social Security. When she turned 16, their payments were cut; unable to pay rent, they were kicked out of their apartment. The camera shows them packing their belongings to be placed in storage. Katie's disheveled mom sobs uncontrollably. Katie speaks to her confusion: "I still can't make sense of it all … I have no idea what's going to happen next." The camera follows Katie and her mother as they drive around in their car, looking for parking lots to spend the night in. She and her mother figure out that they are living a paradox: "You need a job to get a place to live, and you need a place to live to get a job." They have 12 dollars to last until the next Social Security check arrives in two weeks.

Katie's narration bears witness to the stress of uncertainty and the increasingly harsh conditions of her material existence. "The last two weeks have been incredibly difficult. We have a loaf of bread and we've been able to get a box of Pop Tarts ... We have no money for food or gas, and no job prospects." Eventually, the pastor from church calls; someone has offered them a room in their house for a few months. Katie knows it is a temporary fix, but she and her mother rejoice at the prospect of sleeping in a bed.

Next, Kenyatta tells her story: "My name is Kenyatta and I'm 25 years old. I would never have thought in a million years that I would become a homeless person." Having grown up in the South, a difficult place for a transsexual woman, she boarded a bus to New York when her single mother died of cancer. With nowhere to go upon arrival, she eventually learned about a homeless shelter for queer youth. On her recent birthday, she was deemed ineligible for youth social services; the camera cuts to her packing up her belongings at the shelter, dressed in a long white designer gown. "I may be homeless but I refuse to let myself look that way ... There are good looking, clean homeless people out there." Kenyatta performs her gender identity, and she also performs her voice as a homeless person. Her narration is an act that references and disrupts norms and expectations. Later, she gives a going away speech to her friends at the shelter. "I've gained a family, we are a community and we have to look out for each other because nobody else will," she states (see Figure 7.2). Later, Kenyatta meets with a social worker and tries to rent a cheap room, but is rejected. She worries out loud about what will happen when she has to leave the temporary place she is staying in just a few days.

Next up is Ronnie: "My name is Ronnie, and New York City is a rough place to be homeless," he states, while the camera shows him panhandling and begging for food. "I was homeless on and off since 14," he explains, blaming himself for

FIGURE 7.2 Kenyatta, who has aged out of youth social services, says goodbye to her friends at the homeless shelter.

drug use, fighting with his parents, and ending up in and out of rehab and jail. Ronnie and his girlfriend are camping out at a public park, reflecting on the conditions of their existence: "Freedom's all you got, especially when you're homeless ... The only thing I got is the power to do whatever I want whenever I want," Ronnie explains. They decide to head west—hopping freight trains and then hitchhiking until Ronnie is arrested for unknown reasons. The camera cuts to an image of him in jail. He remains optimistic that he will be released and on his way to California soon.

None of these first-person stories provides a critical explanation for youth homelessness, let alone the structural inequalities of wealth associated with neoliberalism. At times, the subjects rely on neoliberal narratives and blame themselves for their situations: Ronnie cites his juvenile delinquency, while Kenyatta worries that she spent too much of her money on designer clothes and "fabulousity." However, she also notes the oppression she experienced as a transsexual in the South as the reason she "can't go home." Katie models the ideal self-enterprising citizen when she starts a blog from the family's car to generate private donations for a motel room. Yet, she also witnesses the spiral into homelessness from an embodied position, and testifies about the anger, fear, and confusion she experiences as a result. Kenyatta reflects on her personal history and her current situation; she refuses to recognize herself in the stereotypes of homelessness and negotiates her own social norms. Ronnie is the least reflexive, and his narration rarely goes beyond a description of his activities. He also embraces homelessness as a form of "freedom." In this statement, he both internalizes neoliberal discourse (freedom of choice, autonomy) and rejects the enterprising behavior and consumption associated with those ideals. Ronnie has no alternative explanation for his situation, but he claims an identity outside middle-class expectations and norms.

Fulfilling the story arc, the viewer is presented with a final update on each of the three characters. Titles appear on a black screen, informing us that Katie is looking for work, but will lose her survivors' Social Security if she finds a job. Her mother has not found work. Kenyatta found summer employment as a peer counselor for queer youth, and is sharing a low-rent apartment with a friend. Ronnie was released from jail—his current whereabouts are unknown. These "resolutions" may provide a form of artificial closure, but the words and images that linger are the occasions when Katie, Kenyatta, and Ronnie give an account of themselves and the conditions of their lives. These accounts ask for recognition and understanding, and sometimes dislodge expectations as well. *True Life* makes no attempt to explore its own formal conventions or priorities, nor does it attempt to ameliorate homelessness. Those aims do not fall within the civic function of new television documentary. However carefully scripted, cast, edited, and packaged, the episode does encourage an understanding of homelessness as an embodied social position that cannot be reduced to stereotypical assumptions and expectations of "others."

As reality entertainment and documentary continue to blur, and personhood is filtered through the neoliberal logic of competition and self-enterprise, *True Life* presents one place on commercial television where we might encounter voice as a social process. To be sure, this process of self-accounting is partial, contradictory, and medi-ated through MTV's own profit-making goals and conventions. Indeed, as we have seen, with its lack of an author and reliance on tightly controlled topics and scripts, the series is hardly progressive according to earlier conceptions of voice. However, if we rethink voice as a broader ethical process, the ongoing expression of diverse social narratives by a range of sometimes non-normative and underprivileged subjects is notable. It may not be "true life" exactly, but *True Life* does offer a range of testimony about the increasingly harsh social conditions in which subjects are made, and live.

Bibliography

Andrejevic, Mark. 2004. *Reality TV: The Work of Being Watched*. New York: Rowman and Littlefield.

Aufderheide, Patricia. 1997. "Public Intimacy: The Development of First-Person Documentary." *Afterimage* 25 (1): 16–32.

Bruzzi, Stella. 2006. *New Documentary*. 2nd ed. London: Routledge.

Butler, Judith. 2005. *Giving an Account of Oneself*. New York: Fordham University Press.

Corner, John. 2002. "Performing the Real: Documentary Diversions." *Television and New Media* 3 (3): 255–69.

Couldry, Nick. 2010. *Why Voice Matters: Culture and Politics after Neoliberalism*. London: Sage.

Cunningham, Megan. 2014. "Lauren Lazin: Pitching and Television Co-production." In *The Art of Documentary: Fifteen Conversations with Leading Directors, Cinematographers, Editors and Producers*, ed. Megan Cunningham. New York: New Riders. 342–7.

Curtin, Michael. 1995. *Redeeming the Wasteland: Television Documentary and Cold War Politics*. New Brunswick, NJ: Rutgers University Press.

Dovey, Jon. 2000. *First Person Media and Factual Television*. London: Pluto Press.

Duggan, Lisa. 2004. *The Twilight of Equality: Neoliberalism, Cultural Politics and the Attack on Democracy*. Boston: Beacon Press.

Erens, Patricia. 1988. "Women's Documentary Filmmaking: The Personal Is Political." In *New Challenges for Documentary*, ed. Alan Rosenthal. Berkeley: University of California Press. 554–65.

FitzSimons, Trish. 2009. "Braided Channels: A Genealogy of the Voice of Documentary." *Studies in Documentary Film* 3 (2): 131–46.

Grindstaff, Laura. 2002. *The Money Shot: Trash, Class, and the Making of TV Talk Shows*. Chicago: University of Chicago Press.

Hearn, Alison. 2008. "Meat, Mask, Burden: Probing the Contours of the Branded Self." *Journal of Consumer Culture* 8 (2): 197–217.

Hooper, Joseph. 2000. "It's Not All Dazzle: MTV Has a Conscience Too." *New York Times*, May 14. AR36.

Lesage, Julia. 1984. "Feminist Documentary: Aesthetics and Politics." In *Show Us Life: Toward a History and Aesthetics of the Committed Documentary*, ed. Thomas Waugh. Metuchen, NJ: Scarecrow Press. 223–51.

Mandziuk, Roseann M. 2001. "Confessional Discourse and Modern Desires: Power and Please in True Story Magazine." *Critical Studies in Media Communication* 18 (2): 174–93.

Martineau, Barbara Halpern. 1984. "Talking about Our Lives and Experiences: Some Thoughts about Feminism, Documentary and Talking Heads." In *Show Us Life: Toward a History and Aesthetics of the Committed Documentary*, ed. Thomas Waugh. Metuchen, NJ: Scarecrow Press. 252–73.

Nichols, Bill. 1985. "The Voice of Documentary." In *Movies and Methods, Volume II*, ed. Bill Nichols. Berkeley: University of California Press. 259–73.

——. 1994. *Blurred Boundaries: Questions of Meaning in Contemporary Culture*. Bloomington: Indiana University Press.

——. 2010. *Introduction to Documentary*. 2nd ed. Bloomington and Indianapolis: Indiana University Press.

Ouellette, Laurie, and Susan Murray. 2009. "Introduction." In *Reality TV: Remaking Television Culture*, ed. Susan Murray and Laurie Ouellette. New York: NYU Press. 1–15.

Raphael, Chad. 2005. *Investigated Reporting: Muckrakers, Regulators, and the Struggle over Television Documentary*. Urbana, IL: University of Illinois Press.

Ruby, Jay. 1992. "Speaking For, Speaking About, Speaking With, or Speaking Alongside: An Anthropological and Documentary Dilemma." *Journal of Film and Video* 44 (1–2): 42–66.

Turner, Graeme. 2009. *Ordinary People and the Media: The Demotic Turn*. London: Sage.

Winston, Brian. 1991. "The Tradition of the Victim in Griersonian Documentary." In *Image Ethics: The Moral Rights of Subjects in Photographs, Film and Television*, ed. Larry Gross, John Stuart Katz, and Jay Ruby. Cambridge: Oxford University Press. 34–55.

——. 2008. *Claiming the Real: Documentary, Grierson and Beyond*. London: British Film Institute.

8

INTERROGATING THE MEDIA

Errol Morris in the Information Age[1]

Kris Fallon

One of the more haunting moments in documentary cinema, and certainly one of the most discussed, must surely be the final scene in Errol Morris's haunting whodunit, *The Thin Blue Line*. The film investigates the murder of Dallas Police Officer Robert Wood and the subsequent trial and conviction of Randall Adams. After digging through the evidence and hearing the testimony of the figures involved, the film closes on a tape-recorded interview with one of the case's suspects, David Harris, who all but confesses to the crime. Harris's casual, almost playful admission that he killed one man and sent another to prison sent chills down my spine the first time I saw the film, and is certainly the "smoking gun" moment that cements the film's status as one of the more famous documentary films.

If the confession settled the question of who killed Robert Wood, it also ignited competing claims by film scholars about the nature of Errol Morris as a filmmaker, and what, if anything, his films can tell us about the world. For Linda Williams, the moment serves as a type of *vérité* counterpoint to the slippery, postmodern hall of mirrors established by the film's conflicting reenactments of the event in question. As she writes, the film approaches historical truth as something "strategic and contingent" rather than something guaranteed by the camera's "mirror with a memory" (Williams 1993: 10). For Carl Plantinga, on the other hand, the confession, and its related impact on Randall Adams's freedom, cements Morris's status not as a postmodernist but rather as a realist, a firm believer in the possibility of truth's representability (Plantinga 2009: 54). Morris himself, in typically playful form, calls himself the "ultimate anti-postmodern postmodernist" (Bloom 2010: 125).

Regardless of where one comes down on Morris's status as a postmodernist, the *Rashomon*-like nature of the film's various perspectives in contrast to its final moment of certainty makes for a jarring juxtaposition, and contributes in no small part to his reputation as a filmmaker willing to take on the weighty issues of truth and representation. What further marks the scene as exceptional is not what we hear on the tape, but rather what we see on the screen. That is, while we hear David Harris's confession, what we see is a series of shots of the tape recorder itself. Though artfully shot, the 90 seconds of footage stands out as strange, appearing almost like a Sony commercial rather than the "gotcha" moment of the entire story. Throughout the rest of the film, the testimony of the experts and eyewitnesses and their onscreen interviews are offset with various documents, newspaper clippings, and reenactments. At this most critical of moments, why focus on something so arbitrary?

This emphasis on the medium of the message is indicative of a larger emphasis in Morris's work on interrogating and exploring various forms of media and what access, if any, they can offer us to reality. These media interrogations, appearing alongside his more widely discussed interviews, make Morris's work particularly significant for the question of documentary film and technology for two reasons. First, throughout his career Morris has been among the more experimental documentary filmmakers in pushing visual aesthetics past straightforward, sober representation, utilizing CGI and other techniques as they become available. Second, Morris is among those directors directly engaged in reflexively questioning the ground on which any representational medium can claim to offer a version of events, or truth. As film has shifted from analogue celluloid to digital media, this strain in his work has become more explicit. Morris has always pushed the boundary of what an image track is capable of revealing, utilizing reenactments, found footage, and other techniques to illustrate and complicate a particular speaker's observations, much as the famous flying milkshake in *The Thin Blue Line* signified the conflicting accounts about that fateful night in Dallas. I will argue here that his later work demonstrates that photographic images and other media forms might be just as mistaken as an eyewitness testifying in court. As a filmmaker, Morris still hunts down truth with the doggedness of a detective on the case, chasing down interviews and turning over the evidence. As his career has progressed, his cases have gotten more complex, taking on issues of history, war, and even torture, a complexity that is mirrored in the media evidence he considers.

Technology and the documentary tradition

Morris is not alone in pushing the boundaries of documentary aesthetics through technological innovation. There is of course a prominent strand within documentary's history of utilizing technology in the service of representing reality, a tendency that remains quite active. Early on it appears in Dziga Vertov's reflexive celebration of the kino-eye's capacity for capturing the world in *Man with a Movie Camera* (1929) and Leni Riefenstahl's technological innovation in both *Triumph of the Will* (1935) and *Olympia* (1938) (Müller 1994; Sontag 2002: 79–80). In the postwar years, documentary's technophilia manifested itself in the American direct cinema movement's embrace of 16mm equipped with sync sound as a tool for capturing events on the fly (or as a fly on the wall) with minimal intrusion. In our current moment, a similar thread can be seen in films such as *The Cove* (2009) and *Leviathan*

(2012) that utilize novel technologies, including night vision cameras, thermal imaging, or multiple GoPros in order to deliver rich, multi-sensory experiences to viewers (Howell 2013; Heise and Tudor 2014).

It might be claimed that all of these films treat novel technology as means toward more accurate versions of what Brian Winston refers to, in a more limited context, as a mode of "scientific inscription" (Winston 1993). While all documentary, by definition, utilizes the camera as a technology to record the world, certain films and filmmakers turn to technologically innovative expansions of documentary aesthetics in order to explore and capture previously unseen facets of the world, be it the scale of a Nazi rally or the grim monotony of commercial fishing. What makes Morris an important part of this tradition is his embrace of technology to investigate the general knowability of reality, what I referred to earlier as the postmodern strain within his work. Like all documentary filmmakers, Morris turns to the medium to explore reality, even if the reality he wants to explore is the increasingly mediated nature of the world around us.

The Fog of War: animating archival media

This tendency to simultaneously experiment with and interrogate different forms of media is perhaps most apparent in Morris's Oscar-winning 2003 film *The Fog of War.* The documentary is structured loosely around 11 lessons drawn from the life of former Secretary of Defense Robert McNamara, who played a crucial role in leading the United States into the Vietnam War. The film draws extensively on archival material and a long interview with McNamara himself.[2] But *The Fog of War* is more than a biography of McNamara's life using archival material. That is, in the process of translating the material to the screen, Morris reinterprets these events, and ultimately offers a critique of McNamara himself. The film presents this critique through a dense layering of archival media, what Morris has called the "residue of history" (Grundmann and Rockwell 2000: 7).

At the center of the aforementioned 11 lessons lies the film's primary critique: "Lesson 7: Belief and Seeing."[3] The chapter illustrates the double function of archival media, which is a broader issue explored throughout the film, at once depicting McNamara's recollections on screen and simultaneously drawing larger conclusions about the fallibility of our own quantitative and photographic approaches to the past, and to reality itself.[4] The lesson drawn from this double function echoes throughout the film from its opening moments to its epilogue. Using it as a critical lens, the film interrogates the relationship between images and the events they document and communicate, and comes to offer a multifaceted view of the controversial subject of the film itself.[5]

To get a sense of how the film achieves this, we need look no further than its opening. The first footage we see is a grainy, black-and-white television recording of a young McNamara standing behind a podium adjusting the height of a chart and asking his audience if this is "a reasonable height for people to see." The camera then cuts to McNamara at the podium, where he states: "Earlier tonight … let me first ask the TV, are you ready? … all set?" Just as he is about to begin again the film cuts to the opening credits. Taken together, these brief moments hint at the primary themes in the film. We are introduced, via the news footage, to McNamara not just as the film's main subject and sole interviewee, but further as someone who is sufficiently media savvy to control the message he is about to send. He delivers this message, moreover with the aid of charts and graphs in a manner that is reasonable to the audience. His impact on those immediately present matters less than making sure that the "TV" is ready. The film's opening, an ironic behind-the-scenes beginning from the past, immediately reveals the manipulated nature of the media, which carry such messages. Lest we miss this, the closing of the opening credits gives way to the following exchange between McNamara and Morris:

MCNAMARA: Let me hear your voice level so I can know if it's the same.
MORRIS (OFF SCREEN): How's my voice level?
MCNAMARA: Fine. Now I remember exactly the sentence that I left off on. I
    remember how it started, and I was cut off in the middle, but you can go back
    and fix it up somehow. I don't want to go back and introduce the sentence
    because I know exactly what I want to say.
MORRIS: Go ahead.
MCNAMARA: Okay. Any military commander [.]

(*The Fog of War*, 2:55–3:10)

As in his archival appearance before the cameras, McNamara maintains full control of his message, to the extent that he suggests how Morris should eventually edit the film by "fixing it up somehow." Ignoring the advice and leaving the outtake in, Morris reminds us once again that such messages are shaped and framed not just by the speaker but also by the sender.[6]

The footage in between these two clips is no less significant. Grainy, archival shots are intercut with the credits and set to Phillip Glass's score. These depict soldiers on a ship looking out at the horizon using various optical devices (binoculars, sonar equipment, maps and charts), apparently preparing for battle of some sort. Although they are presented in brief segments lasting no more than a few seconds each, the situation is made clear: They are ready to respond with force to any threat they perceive. If one is observed via the optical, infrared, and topographic means (binoculars, sonar, and maps respectively) at their disposal, the information is communicated and a course of action is set. Bookended by reminders of the manipulated nature of media, these shots offer a stern warning about the mediated nature of the information used to wage war. All together, the opening sequence suggests that what follows will be very much about the nature of this mediated world, both in the present moment and also in the historical records it leaves behind.

As the opening demonstrates, archival materials are included not simply to illustrate the content of McNamara's narration, but to offer a counterpoint that challenges, amplifies, and expands upon the claims of its subject. Their formal presentation also simultaneously undermines any straightforward or objective access to past events through these media. Even as Morris depends on the archive to create the film, he questions the obvious legibility of the truth it might contain.

Positioning itself at a distance from the archival unity present in something like the work of Ken Burns, *The Fog of War* argues that these representations are not only fallible, but also fallible in a manner that evinces the historical misperceptions at the time.[7] Morris's inclusion of archival material seeks to critique its pretensions and misperceptions of the hidden truths that may lie beneath. This skepticism regarding access to the past is, of course, the thrust of the film. As McNamara states at the outset, "In my life I've made mistakes, but my rule has always been to try and learn, and pass these lessons on to the future." The film expands the scope of McNamara's project beyond events and decisions to include the material residue they leave in their wake. One technique Morris uses for questioning the believability of archival imagery is re-contextualization, a common strategy in the works of other archival filmmakers such as Bruce Conner. Whatever its original purpose, it seems unlikely that the footage of battle preparation from the opening credits was intended to question the ability of the military to gather proper intelligence, as I have been suggesting here. The film's inclusion of the outtakes from the press conference that open the film suggest a similar, subversive rereading of the footage's original meaning. Thus, the industrial and propaganda materials which form the backdrop for the film all play unwitting roles in testifying to their own limitations and reveal their latent potentiality for remediation and reinterpretation. Unlike other found footage films, however, here the material is combined by Morris with the testimony of an eyewitness observer. While Morris's work clearly shares political sympathies and formal methodologies with Conner's biting, ironic media satire, he differs from Conner in his utilization and juxtaposition of archival material with the first-person interviews of his subjects.[8] *The Fog of War* thus seeks a middle ground between the earnest archival unity of Ken Burns's work and the ironic self-reflexivity of Conner's assemblages.

Neither entirely redemptive nor dismissive of the archive, Morris also takes a unique approach to these materials by digitally altering them at key moments to punctuate and critique McNamara's thoughts. Digital alteration—usually associated with undermining or faking the truth—here suggests that such transformations can reveal it. In one of the film's more notorious segments, McNamara relates how he and General Curtis LeMay arrived at the means and methods for firebombing Japan during World War II. As Morris claims, this is the first place that McNamara has discussed his participation in these events, events which many consider to be tantamount to the eventual choice to drop the atomic bombs on Hiroshima and Nagasaki. After stating an operation had burned to death "100,000 civilians, men, women, and children, in a single night," Morris asks McNamara if he knew this was going to happen. The latter replies, "In a sense, I was part of a mechanism that recommended it." At this moment, after having chaotically flipped through

FIGURE 8.1 AND 8.2 Above: Digits cascading from the bomb bay doors imply that Robert McNamara's weapon of choice was statistical data. Below: Locations and percentages of destruction superimposed on historical photographs give each element a depth that it lacks on its own.

documents, photographs, and images that document the missions, the film cuts to an image of animated blue numbers and statistics falling from the bomb-bay doors of an aircraft down onto a city below (see Figures 8.1 and 8.2). The original source material, a black-and-white, sepia-toned photo, is identical to countless others that feature bombs falling out of airplanes, but this one overtly implies that the use of statistical rationality was as damaging as heavy explosives. Again, whatever its original purpose, through the use of CG animation the photograph becomes the film's most direct indictment of its subject.

Shortly after the "falling statistics" shot, McNamara describes a report he wrote for LeMay that argued for flying the B-29s at a lower altitude during their bombing missions. While this decision increased the risk of a plane being shot down, it dramatically increased its effectiveness in "target destruction." Utilizing a technique that Morris has described as "3-D photography,"[9] the film cuts to a black-and-white image of bombs dropping from a plane. The camera appears to zoom in to the image, but rather than simply enlarging the elements equally as a typical zoom would, elements in the foreground appear to expand and move more rapidly out of the frame than those in the background. The visual effect not only yields the impression of three-dimensionality that Morris describes but also gives us the feeling of dropping out of the plane alongside the bombs themselves. In a sense, this is exactly what the men who piloted the planes were doing, given that, under McNamara's direction, they lowered their flight altitude to the extent that they became targets themselves for Japanese anti-aircraft fire. While the shot lasts only approximately eight seconds on screen, the 3-D effect is startling enough to mark it out among the dozens of similar images that the film contains and emphasizes the significance of this portion of McNamara's testimony. As the image digitally "comes to life" relative to the others, we gain the sense that McNamara has gone from being a witness of history to one of its actors, directing its outcome rather than passively observing its course.

One final instance of digital manipulation further illustrates Morris's critical approach to his archival material. Although less technically innovative than the previous two, its effect is no less powerful. This moment comes as McNamara discusses the result of the firebombing that LeMay carried out on Tokyo and the devastating impact the bombs had on what he calls "a wooden city." Morris's voice is heard off screen asking McNamara: "The choice of incendiary bombs, where did that come from?" McNamara replies to the effect that the problem was not the method of destruction but its extent. He goes on to list the other cities that were similarly destroyed, comparing each target to a similarly sized American city. He states: "He went on from Tokyo to firebomb other cities. Fifty-eight percent of Yokohama; Yokohama's roughly the size of Cleveland. Fifty-eight percent of Cleveland destroyed […] Ninety-nine percent of Chattanooga destroyed, which was Toyama. Forty-one percent of the equivalent of Los Angeles, which was Nagoya." As he lists the cities destroyed, a black-and-white photograph of ruins appears superimposed with the name of the Japanese city and the percentage destroyed in red text. This red text fades, giving way to the name of the American city in black text over the same photo. At first, the technique simply illustrates McNamara's examples, but once he stops with the list above, the image track goes on, listing dozens of other cities at an accelerating pace in time with the music. McNamara's point is certainly powerful enough on its own. Combined with the effect of the extended list and its chaotic, accelerated pace, it becomes ample evidence of McNamara's admission at the end of the sequence "that [LeMay], and I believe I, were behaving as war criminals."

Graphic superimpositions of this sort are nothing new, but their use here nonetheless stands out for the ambivalent position they occupy between McNamara's message about the past and the film's message about him. They pose a contrast between two forms of evidence and representation: the statistical and the photographic. The images of devastation are sufficiently generic that they signify the general concept rather than describe specific events. Their historical specificity and their emotional connection to the audience derive entirely from the quantitative information affixed to them and the direct comparison this enables. The film, however, simultaneously calls this type of statistical information into question, or at least aligns it with the rational worldview that brought about this devastation in the first place. Thus, this statistical information also lacks a level of historical sufficiency without an eye toward the physical devastation to which it corresponds, a dimension provided by the images that form its backdrop.

At once distrustful of the archive but reliant upon it, dismissive of logical rationality but earnest in pursuing some level of historical truth, the film sits evenly between an abstract meditation on media and an exploration of the past that it has captured—a divided attention which would carry over to Morris's next cinematic project, *Standard Operating Procedure* (2008).

Standard Operating Procedure: digital photography and database aesthetics

If *The Fog of War* works as a meditation on the archive writ large, drawing in many forms of media from many different sources, then the focus of the archive in Morris's next film, *Standard Operating Procedure*, is far more closely circumscribed. Rather than explore charts, graphs, reconnaissance photos, news footage, audio tapes, newspapers, and any number of other media as *The Fog of War* does, *Standard Operating Procedure* turns its attention to one specific form of media—the digital photograph—as it is instantiated in one specific collection: the images that emerged from the Abu Ghraib prison complex in Iraq in April of 2004. In spite of this shift in scale, however, *Standard Operating Procedure* continues *The Fog of War*'s exploration of the relationship between historical events, the social actors they involve, and the media artifacts they produce. Like *The Fog of War*, the film is as much about the media presentation of an event as it is about the event itself.

The shift from *The Fog of War* to *Standard Operating Procedure* is thus not a clear thematic break but rather a shift in focus and scope. Rather than focus on the life of a single individual who had a hand in several of the bloodiest and most technologically mediated wars of the twentieth century, *Standard Operating Procedure* meditates on the role of a specific media technology in relation to a specific event. If Morris tightens the focus of *Standard Operating Procedure* to a single technology and event, the problem he explores, namely the role of photography in our understanding of an event, is approached on a number of fronts at once. In addition to the film, Morris writing a blog for the *New York Times* and formulating his thoughts there alongside the film expands our understanding of both.

Tellingly, Morris's first post to his blog appeared nearly a year before the film premiered, but its content clearly reflected what must have been a major preoccupation at the time, given the film that he was in the midst of making. Entitled "Liar,

Liar, Pants on Fire," it discusses the potential for photographic manipulation and the role of context in photographs' reception and interpretation—an issue that returned front and center once the film came out. It begins: "Pictures are supposed to be worth a thousand words. But a picture unaccompanied by words may not mean anything at all. Do pictures provide evidence? And if so, evidence of what? And, of course, the underlying question: do they tell the truth?" (Morris 2007). This post offers a fitting preamble to the blog itself, and subsequent posts deal further with photography and reenactment, perception, memory, and any number of other issues central to the investigation in *Standard Operating Procedure*.

Unlike the film, the blog only occasionally considers the Abu Ghraib photographs. It focuses instead on the larger issue of truth and photographic representations, exploring the work of Roger Fenton, Matthew Brady, Walker Evans, and others to do so. In typical Morris style, his posts often begin with a series of older, archival images and pose a series of questions relating to the circumstances surrounding their creation and the extent to which they reflect the truth of the scenes they capture. The discussion is part detective mystery and part reflection on the fraught relationship between reality and representation, or between history and memory, all common elements in his films. Thus, in spite of their absence, the blog is almost haunted by the issues that the Abu Ghraib images pose.

One post, for example, takes Roger Fenton's two nineteenth-century images from the Crimean war entitled "Valley of the Shadow of Death," which have been discussed by Susan Sontag and others, and proposes that one of the nearly identical images must have been staged (Sontag 2004). Calling them "ON" and "OFF" in reference to the placement of a series of cannonballs in the middle of a road, Morris investigates a number of different techniques to determine whether Fenton or another party moved the cannonballs into the road, or into the ditch for the second image.

I raise the issues presented in the blog because how we read Morris's blog in relation to *Standard Operating Procedure* affects how we interpret the aim of the film, and its subsequent success or failure. That is, if we see *Standard Operating Procedure* as an investigation into the Abu Ghraib prison scandal and the question of American policy on torture, then we are inclined to place it alongside other films dealing with similar issues, such as Michael Winterbottom's *The Road to Guantanamo* (2006), Alex Gibney's *Taxi to the Dark Side* (2007), or Rory Kennedy's *Ghosts of Abu Ghraib* (2007).[10] This is perfectly appropriate given the subject matter and thrust of the companion text. If, however, we place the film in the context of Morris's previous film on war, *The Fog of War*, and his other activities on his blog and elsewhere, then the subject matter takes on a different valence entirely. Seen as part of an ongoing meditation on the relationship between representation and reality, photography and the external world, the film is less about specific policies and events or individual culpability and more about the nature of perception, representation, and human behavior. As the content on the blog indicates, the role of photography in warfare and the nature of that particular technology in documenting and interpreting such momentous events is a topic that occupies Morris far beyond any one particular instance or set of photos. We might conclude, then, that *Standard Operating Procedure* is not so much about Abu Ghraib the profilmic event as it is about the Abu Ghraib images, and their role in establishing Abu Ghraib as primarily a media event.

Almost without exception, discussions of the film point out that the Abu Ghraib images are digital rather than analogue photographs, and that this fact has something to do with the mutability and transportability of their contents. Had they not been, so the logic goes, they would have been far easier to contain and perhaps less likely to have been created in the first place. Lacking the need for a third party to develop the images, digital photos have the ability to reveal their contents while remaining the exclusive property of their creators to a greater extent than analogue photos. As digital files, however, they are also readily open to copying and sharing, lending them an instantaneous ubiquity that analogue photos lack. Digital photos, moreover, are far more open to manipulation via programs like Adobe's Photoshop. All of this is surely accurate and would seem to lend itself to consideration of the types of issues I have been claiming to most interest Morris. The film does not emphasize either of these points. Rather, *Standard Operating Procedure* highlights and questions another aspect of the digital nature of the Abu Ghraib images: their status as a collection of files, or, more accurately, as an open database. When interrogating the database-like availability of these images for public use, Morris most deeply engages the larger themes of representation, mediation, and truth that became so evident in his blog posts.

As with *The Fog of War*, the first moments of the film are revealing. While the opening credit sequence rolls, or rather floats, the viewer is immersed in a cloud of spatially diffuse images floating back and away, a double movement which yields the impression that as we drift steadily forward, our attention is directed stubbornly backward at images fading slowly into the distance. Many are immediately legible as the more iconic images from the Abu Ghraib scandal, but they appear here robbed of any framing context but the frame itself. The film instead places them in a blank, nonrepresentational space that is rather overtly rendered as "no place." In order to understand the film's approach to the Abu Ghraib scandal, we need to focus not on the images but rather on this blank space and the role that it plays here and throughout the film. While this will at first seem counterintuitive and perhaps the epitome of uninterested spectatorship (how could one *not* look at these images?), this space allows the film to cinematically illustrate the less tangible database to which these images belong. Instead of offering a blank slate or empty canvas, the film is instead attempting to create a form of database aesthetic.[11]

In his influential *The Language of New Media*, Lev Manovich describes the database as the dominant symbolic form of the computer age, our new interface to the cultural field and one that replaces the centuries-long dominance of the narrative form as sustained by older media such as the novel and film (Manovich 2001). While he points out that the two forms, the database and narrative, have always existed alongside each other, he argues that at different points either form rises to prominence, an exchange currently taking place thanks in part to the widespread adoption of the computer as the Universal Media Machine.[12] For Manovich, the database as a cultural form comprises a collection of discrete entities with an infinite number of possible *arrangements* but lacking in any single narrative that orders or prioritizes these items. Unlike the narrative, which imposes specific cause/effect, beginning/middle/end relationships on its constituent elements, the database leaves the relationship between its content less defined.[13] In these terms, we might say that *Standard Operating Procedure* is a narrative about a database, and the historical and political implications of approaching media as such.

Returning to the opening credit sequence, the cloud of images that float there before the viewer present themselves, in this reading, as a collection of discrete digital records, which, as products of various digital imaging technologies, they undoubtedly are. Presenting them as a random cluster with no immediate logic to their arrangement or spatial distribution foregrounds the material status these records have had at various points in their existence, from the nonlinear editing software that rendered this shot, to the hard drives of the computers to which they were downloaded, and to the memory cards of the cameras with which they were originally recorded. As digital files, they can be ordered according to any number of different principles, selected or skipped depending upon various preferences.

We can see this same aesthetic principle at work at several other points in the film. The discrete nature of the image as individual record, for instance, is emphasized most explicitly in the description given by Army Investigator Brent Pack of "metadata." He defines the term as a "fancy two dollar word for information about information" that allows him to order the images according to various factors including the date they were taken or the camera was used. As he describes organizing the photographs according to various interpretations, the screen image responds by arranging and rearranging images into various timelines (see Figures 8.3 and 8.4). Indeed, Pack's investigation as it is presented in the film is this migration from one form, the database, into another, the linear narrative. As he puts it, "The pictures spoke a thousand words, but unless you know what day and time they were talking, you wouldn't know what the story was."

Again and again the various social actors in the film highlight this same tension between the extreme legibility of what the images depict and their collective inability to, as Pack says, narrate the story adequately. In essence, this is the tradeoff inherent in the database/narrative distinction that Manovich makes. For example, a recording of an opera or the soundtrack of a musical can be experienced as a linear narrative that tells a story from beginning to end, but these individual tracks can also be added into a music database like iTunes where the order can be shuffled and the contents mixed and matched with songs into ever-changing playlists. Causality and narrative determination are replaced with flexibility and freedom. The same distinction holds true for the individual image versus the collection of

FIGURE 8.3 AND 8.4 In *Standard Operating Procedure*'s "metadata" sequence, images are arranged and rearranged, isolated and compared, according to the embedded data about their date and time of capture. The sequence foregrounds the size of the original data set (below) and renders visible the otherwise invisible data that underpins it (above).

images within a database. Each individual image may offer a mediated, representational glimpse of what existed before the camera at a given moment in time. A database of images such as Flickr allows for multiple and even contradictory groupings and interpretations to coexist.

The extended CGI sequences that I am describing as a form of database aesthetic seek to demonstrate this flexibility. By emphasizing the database nature of the Abu

Ghraib images and the consequent lack of fixed narrative causality, the film is fore-grounding the freedom of interpretation they enable. Once the images surfaced in the media, any number of individuals and institutions began selecting specific ones and placing them into various discursive contexts, from the army investigation that Pack started in early 2004 to the *60 Minutes* broadcast that eventually introduced the scandal to the public. As Morris, echoing Susan Sontag, claimed in his first blog post, "a picture unaccompanied by words may not mean anything at all." The Abu Ghraib images entered this vacuum of meaning, and as they circulated through the mediascape, any number of commentators stepped in to fill the void by adding terms and categories that would fix their interpretation. Pack eventually classified them into the two distinct categories of "criminal act" and "standard operating procedure," offering one organization and interpretation. But others emerged as well. The same "hooded man" image appeared on Fox News with the caption "Detainee 'Abuse'" and on the cover of *The Economist* with the headline "Resign, Rumsfeld."

The film itself is an attempt to understand "what the story was" that produced these images, in essence transforming a database of images into a narrative about a specific historical event. Though the film foregrounds the plasticity of its source material, it does not, however, evacuate it of meaning entirely. Quite the opposite. By translating the database into a linear narrative, the film utilizes any number of techniques to account for the structure the database lacks. Interestingly, however, the film lacks entirely those elements so omnipresent in *The Fog of War*. Rather than focus on a collage of external visual media sources and archival documents, the film focuses exclusively on the Abu Ghraib images themselves and supplements them with other non-visual material: interviews, Sabrina Harmon's letters, entries from the log books, and, notoriously, the reenactments. Instead of animating the archive by digitally manipulating its contents as he did in *The Fog of War*, Morris aestheticizes it in order to foreground the immaterial, mutable nature of the digital archive itself.

The Unknown Known: truth in the information age

After the success of *The Fog of War* and the failure (at least commercially and critically) of *Standard Operating Procedure*, Morris's output became simultaneously smaller in scale and more widely varied in the number of venues and platforms in and on which it appeared. In addition to his blog for the *New York Times*, Morris also published several books, avidly adopted the short-form microblog Twitter, and produced a series of short films that range from long commercials to short documentaries. Alongside all of this, he also released two feature-length films, *Tabloid* in 2010 and *The Unknown Known* in 2014. While neither of these films evince the formal or thematic audacity of his prior two films, both nonetheless fit within the larger thread that I am claiming becomes increasingly apparent in Morris's work and are hence worth considering briefly in this context.

Tabloid offers a portrait of Joyce McKinney, a onetime pageant queen whose romance with her high-school sweetheart Kirk Anderson took a bizarre, tabloid-worthy turn in the late 1970s. Fearing Kirk had been brainwashed by the Mormon Church, McKinney decided to abduct him and spirit him off to the English countryside to deprogram the indoctrination against premarital sex. The story became a sensation in the British press, and the film draws on interviews with the journalists who covered it, sampling liberally from the extensive media archives that McKinney and her admirers amassed.

The focus of *Tabloid* becomes more apparent when considered alongside Morris's next project, 2014's *The Unknown Known*. Like *The Fog of War*, the film is a portrait of a former secretary of defense, Donald Rumsfeld, a key proponent of the 2003 American invasion of Iraq. In spite of numerous parallels between the two films and their subjects (both were the architects of unpopular, unsuccessful wars), Rumsfeld's charisma and obvious desire to engage the press make him far more like McKinney than McNamara. Both clearly love the attention of an audience, and both succeed in the end at remaining a mystery.

McKinney's mysteries, and the interest of the media in exploring them, however, are of a different order of magnitude than Rumsfeld's. *The Unknown Known* delves into American history dating back to the Nixon presidency, and focuses on the more infamous events of the last decade, including the invasion of Iraq and allegations of government-sanctioned torture. In archival footage, journalists spar with Rumsfeld in press conferences, but unlike the episodes of McKinney's life, which inspired Paparazzi-esque coverage, the events in question are of clear public importance. The outcome, however, is hardly any different. In this sense, both films are about the failure of information to provide meaning.

The entry point for Morris's investigation is the vast trove of memos that Rumsfeld was famous for dictating throughout his career, which his staff came to refer to as "snowflakes." Rumsfeld estimates these snowflakes must number in the millions. Like the other films discussed here, *The Unknown Known* foregrounds this archival material throughout the film. The main visual trope, what we might think of as its signature technique, is a mode of digitally compositing text and image together and then pulling focus between the two. Throughout the film, text from newspapers, the dictionary, and Rumsfeld's memos appears over, under, and around the interviews and other images (see Figures 8.5 and 8.6). At other points, the words appear to come off the page, and begin tumbling down a black hole of language. As in Morris's other films, this form of layering and animation is less technologically innovative than the best cutting-edge special effects available, and yet more visually complex than most other work done in documentary. As with *Standard Operating Procedure*, the technique brings the material to life, lit-erally animating it, but the focus is on language and information, not visual records of an event.

Layering text and image together in this way forces the two forms of information to appear in depth, recalling Morris's observation that meaning arises through a combination of the two together. Here, they present a wealth of information but

FIGURE 8.5 AND 8.6 In *The Unknown Known*, animating and enlarging the dictionary definitions of the terms Donald Rumsfeld uses demonstrates the extent to which language and the print medium of the office memo allow him to remain shrouded in a sea of language.

very little satisfying explanation or meaning. The film ponders how it might be possible, in the face of a million plus recorded memos that would seem to include every thought Rumsfeld has ever had, for him to remain such a mystery. Like an individual snowflake, each of the memos has a unique, aphoristic crystal of meaning which Rumsfeld clearly enjoys parsing. Taken together, however, the sheer volume of memos hampers visibility and blankets entire landscapes of rugged detail in bland uniformity, like a blizzard of snowflakes. Rather than using language to explain himself and his actions, Rumsfeld wields it as a tool of obfuscation, a means of changing the subject.

In this way the film pushes the metaphor of the snowflake out to the broader universe of visual documents it animates and the world of information they inhabit. At first glance, *The Unknown Known* appears to be about documents, memos, and print culture, old if not outdated forms of media. But as media historian Lisa Gitelman points out, digital formats like the PDF demonstrate the persistent power and influence of the printed document to shape what form information should take (Gitelman 2014: 111–36). Rather than dying out, the document, and print culture more broadly, has evolved and multiplied, like Rumsfeld's snowflakes, into an overwhelming avalanche of information. How is it, in an age of ubiquitous media coverage, social and otherwise, that anything remains unknown?

Conclusion

Interestingly, the recording device on which Rumsfeld captured his many memos, or at least the film's representation of it, bears a striking resemblance to the one that appears at the conclusion of *The Thin Blue Line*. Where one device managed to capture a level of truth and set a man free, the other allowed a man to remain veiled behind the words it recorded. Morris's famous claim that "truth isn't guaranteed by a camera" apparently applies to Sony micro-cassettes as well, and as I hope I have shown, to an even wider array of media forms in between. This does not mean that truth is unattainable (as evidenced by the ending of *The Thin Blue Line*), but it is rather simultaneously possible and fragile. Morris's work, particularly since *The Fog of War*, demonstrates that the emergence of digital information and technology neither necessitates nor guarantees any level of truth. Pronouncements about the power of information to facilitate decision-making and human understanding of the world drive a desire for and faith in the records these media provide, but Morris reminds us that they should be treated with the same scrutiny as the eyewitness accounts which wrongly convicted Randall Adams. In an era of ubiquitous cameras and increasingly ubiquitous computing technologies that allow for the ever more detailed documentation of broader facets of reality, this is an important warning to heed.

Notes

1 Portions of this essay were first published as "Several Sides of Errol Morris" in *Film Quarterly* and "Archives Analog and Digital" in *Screen*. I would like to thank University of California Press and Oxford University Press for the permission to use them here. See Fallon 2012; Fallon 2013.

2 *The Fog of War* was the first Morris film to be accompanied by a companion text. See Blight and Lang 2005.

3 This lesson's title would eventually lend itself to the title of Morris's 2011 book on photography, *Believing Is Seeing: Observations on the Mysteries of Photography*, further evidence of its centrality for his thoughts in this film and beyond.

4 As Stella Bruzzi argues in her excellent discussion of the film, the operant conflicts in the film are dialectically structured around themes like past/present, intention/outcome, etc., a point I largely agree with. In this spirit I would add the belief/seeing pair to the list. See Bruzzi 2006: 230–8.

5 On a side note, "Lesson 1: Empathize with Your Enemy," which draws on McNamara's experiences with both Fidel Castro and Nikita Khrushchev, also seems to double as an enjoinder to the audience, many of whom might vilify McNamara for his role in Vietnam, to check any prejudices against McNamara at least long enough to hear him out.

6 As John Corner puts it, McNamara is here revealed as "a seasoned media performer, still concerned with the technicalities of his portrayal" (Corner 2009: 120).

7 Similarly laden with archival material, Burns's films earnestly attempt to collect and coordinate a wealth of historical material by pairing elements that will expand upon and reinforce one another. Archival photographs, panned and scanned in what has famously become the "Ken Burns effect," are accompanied by period music and the narration of letters, diaries, speeches, and newspaper articles from the time. This archival unity implies that a variety of media perspectives provide a sufficient representation of the past to comprehend its enormousness, a concept antithetical to Morris's approach.

8 Consider, for example, Bruce Conner's use of found footage and media coverage in *Report* (1963–67). Conner's juxtaposition of the footage from John F. Kennedy's funeral

procession with battle footage and a bullfight offers a startling, subtle critique of a society that thrives on the media-driven spectacle of violence. Indeed, David Mosen's analysis of the film in *Film Quarterly* sounds eerily reminiscent of *The Fog of War*. He states: "In Conner's eyes society thrives on violence, destruction, and death no matter how hard we try to hide it with immaculately clean offices, the worship of modern science, or the creation of instant martyrs. From the bullfight arena to the nuclear arena we clamor for the spectacle of destruction" (Mosen 1966: 55). For an extended analysis of the film, which expands upon the connection between the film and its media roots (what he calls the "complicity of the moving image media in the rise and fall of John F. Kennedy" [250]), see Bruce Jenkins's "Bruce Conner's *Report*: Contesting Camelot" in Perry 2006: 236–51.

9 In the interview with arts blogger Greg Allen, Morris actually claims "dozens" of such stills were created for the film, but that this is the only one which survived into the final cut (Allen 2010).

10 These three films obviously place *Standard Operating Procedure* in a constellation of films on torture and detainee abuse. Read alternatively as a film about the direction of the war in Iraq, the film might be seen alongside others such as *Gunner Palace* (Petra Epperlain and Michael Tucker, 2004), *Uncovered: The War in Iraq* (Robert Greenwald, 2004), *Iraq in Fragments* (James Longley, 2006), and *No End in Sight* (Charles Ferguson, 2007).

11 The term "database aesthetic" is taken from Victoria Vesna's collection of the same name. In it, Vesna collects discussions from several prominent new media artists as well as theorists like Warren Sack and Lev Manovich, and curators of digital art like Christiane Paul. See Vesna 2007.

12 The term "Universal Media Machine" is Manovich's, one he uses to describe the rise to prominence of the computer as an essential tool in the creation, distribution, and consumption of various forms of media.

13 It should be noted that this does not mean that the database itself is unstructured, but simply that interacting with a database from an end user perspective is open to many different structures and interpretations.

Bibliography

Allen, Greg. 2010. "Learning at Errol Morris's Knee." Greg.org: The Making Of. Available online at http://greg.org/archive/2004/02/20/learning_at_errol_morriss_knee.html (accessed September 19, 2010).

Blight, James G., and Janet M. Lang. 2005. *The Fog of War: Lessons from the Life of Robert S. McNamara*. Lanham, MD: Rowman & Littlefield.

Bloom, Livia. 2010. *Errol Morris: Interviews*. Jackson: University Press of Mississippi.

Bruzzi, Stella. 2006. *New Documentary: A Critical Introduction*. 2nd ed. London: Routledge.

Carlyle, Thomas. 1869. *Heroes and Hero-Worship*. London: Chapman and Hall.

Corner, John. 2009. "Documenting the Political: Some Issues." *Studies in Documentary Film* 3 (2): 113–29. doi:10.1386/sdf.3.2.113/1

Fallon, Kris. 2012. "Several Sides of Errol Morris." *Film Quarterly* 65 (4): 48–52. doi:10.1525/FQ.2012.65.4.48

——. 2013. "Archives Analog and Digital: Errol Morris and Documentary Film in the Digital Age." *Screen* 54 (1): 20–43.

Gitelman, Lisa. 2014. *Paper Knowledge: Toward a Media History of Documents*. Durham: Duke University Press Books.

Grundmann, Roy, and Cynthia Rockwell. 2000. "Truth Is Not Subjective: An Interview with Errol Morris." *Cineaste* 25 (3): 4.

Heise, Tatiana Signorelli, and Andrew Tudor. 2014. "Shooting for a Cause: Cyberactivism and Genre Hybridisation in *The Cove*." In *Impure Cinema: Intermedial and Intercultural Approaches to Film*, ed. Lúcia Nagib and Anne Jerslev. London: I.B. Tauris. 268–81.

Howell, Peter. 2013. "Experiential Documentary Leviathan Immerses You in the Gruesome Sights and Sounds of Commercial Fishing." *Toronto Star*, March 14. Available online at www.thestar.com/entertainment/movies/2013/03/14/leviathan_a_fisheye_view_aboard_a_commercial_trawler_review.html.

Manovich, Lev. 2001. *The Language of New Media*. Cambridge: MIT Press.

Morris, Errol. 2007. "Liar, Liar, Pants on Fire." NYTimes.com, July 10. Available online at http://opinionator.blogs.nytimes.com/2007/07/10/pictures-are-supposed-to-be-worth-a-thousand-words/.

Mosen, David. 1966. "Review: 'Report' by Bruce Conner." *Film Quarterly* 19 (3): 54–6. Available online at www.jstor.org/stable/1210246.

Müller, Ray. 1994. *The Wonderful, Horrible Life of Leni Riefenstahl*. FRG: ARTE.

Perry, Ted. 2006. *Masterpieces of Modernist Cinema*. Bloomington: Indiana University Press.

Plantinga, Carl. 2009. "The Philosophy of Errol Morris." In *Three Documentary Filmmakers: Errol Morris, Ross McElwee, Jean Rouch*, ed. William Rothman. SUNY Press. 43–60.

Sontag, Susan. 2002. *Under the Sign of Saturn: Essays*. New York: Picador.

——. 2004. *Regarding the Pain of Others*. New York: Picador.

Thussu, Daya Kishan. 2008. *News as Entertainment: The Rise of Global Infotainment*. Thousand Oaks, CA: Sage.

Vesna, Victoria, ed. 2007. *Database Aesthetics: Art in the Age of Information Overflow*. Minneapolis: University of Minnesota Press.

Williams, Linda. 1993. "Mirrors Without Memories: Truth, History, and the New Documentary." *Film Quarterly* 46 (3): 9–21. doi:10.2307/1212899

Winston, Brian. 1993. "The Documentary Film as Scientific Inscription." In *Theorizing Documentary*, ed. Michael Renov. New York: Routledge/American Film Institute. 37–57.

9

DOCUMENTARY AND THE SURVIVAL OF THE FILM AUTEUR

Agnès Varda, Werner Herzog, and Spike Lee

Helen Hughes

Introduction: the creative spirit of the independent auteur

This chapter looks at the careers of three established independent filmmakers who have had considerable success at the beginning of the twenty-first century with documentary films. Toward the end of her career Agnès Varda won great acclaim with *The Gleaners and I* (*Les glaneurs et la glaneuse*) (2000) and *Two Years Later* (*Deux ans après*) (2002), as well as with *The Beaches of Agnès* (*Les plages d'Agnès*) (2008) and *Agnes Here and There* (*Agnès de ci de là Varda*) (2011). Werner Herzog established himself as a documentary filmmaker working from an American base with *Grizzly Man* (2005), *Encounters at the End of the World* (2007), *Cave of Forgotten Dreams* (2010), *Into the Abyss* (2011), and *On Death Row* (2012–13). Spike Lee extended his work and the reach of his production company with *4 Little Girls* (1997), the TV miniseries *When the Levees Broke: A Requiem in Four Acts* (2006), and *If God Is Willing and Da Creek Don't Rise* (2010). He has also been part of the accelerating growth of the corporate documentary with short online films such as *Mo'ne Davis: I Throw Like a Girl* (2014). These films are all squarely in the documentary tradition, presenting stories about recent and historical events, and they are all distinctly authored, with stylistic characteristics that mark them as the work of a named director, or auteur known for their feature films.

When the idea of the auteur was formulated in France in the 1950s, its promulgators argued for giving creative control to a new generation of directors who wished to see the feature film become a more serious art form, equating it to painting or classical music but with its own medium-specific expressivity (Truffaut 1954). The figure of the "auteur," usually a director, was seen as creating a specific personal vision through ongoing treatments of themes across films, and the development of a signature style. In the United States, critic Andrew Sarris took up auteur theory to evaluate films, to judge them as expressive works of art within a director's body of work (Sarris 1968).

In the 1950s and 60s, when filmmaking was supported as an art form in Europe with small state-funded budgets, the *cinéma vérité* style of documentary filmmaking in Europe contributed to the independent art house film scene, which strongly featured the works of acclaimed auteurs such as Ingmar Bergman, Federico Fellini, and Jean-Luc Godard. More recently, the auteur concept has been applied more widely to include documentary filmmakers representing various styles, particularly as budgets have increased for production and documentary films have been distributed through theatrical release. This chapter will discuss the developing role of auteur documentary in contemporary independent filmmaking, through the study of Varda, Herzog, and Lee, as they have expanded beyond their feature films to produce important nonfictional work.

The documentaries of Varda, Herzog, and Lee might be termed auteur documentaries, as they are the expression of the established cultural voices of their directors and have received notice partly because of their recognizability. However, the three filmmakers display their contemporary authorship not just by occasionally hopping over the boundary between feature filmmaking and documentary. There are a number of strategies in their arsenal that mark them as independent vibrant artists who can express their vision in many different forms as a way of life. These strategies include building their own production and distribution infrastructures and developing central themes or sets of concerns that power their art and cement their reputation. Characteristic of their contemporary work is a sense of fearlessness in traversing media. They have moved successfully from analogue to digital technologies and, trading on their status as established celebrities or icons with a track record, have been able to use developing digitalized environments to branch out in many directions.

What role, then, has documentary filmmaking played in the work of these three directors? It is worth considering the way in which their documentary work relates to their artistic practice, as they provide possible models for maintaining creative control and constitute perhaps the future of auteur filmmaking. In her features and documentaries, Varda expresses her perspective as a female filmmaker, her role as a part of a family surrounded by other artists and filmmakers, and her interest in grassroots creativity. Herzog continually refers back to his roots in the Bavarian Alps in Germany and his early sense of a vocation as a filmmaker to reconnect with a Romantic tradition, searching for ecstatic images that are nevertheless commensurate with the world of the late twentieth and early twenty-first centuries. Spike Lee describes his mission as to bring to the screen aspects of African American culture and experience of life that have been excluded from mainstream representations of American society. His work includes both celebration and anger, showcasing comic genius, a live and deep musical heritage, and a street language that is imitated all over the world. It also registers the sense of persecution of a community that feels excluded and alienated, but that is also developing means to become more strongly present, not least through filmmaking. These directors' works are themselves an expression of and an argument for the diversity of creative perspectives.

Agnès Varda

The concept of the film auteur was born just as Agnès Varda (1928–) became active as a filmmaker. Varda's debut film, *La Pointe Courte* (1954), came out shortly after François Truffaut's article "A Certain Tendency in the French Cinema" was published in *Cahiers du cinéma* (1954). Truffaut's article attacked the industry values of French filmmaking and advocated the promotion of a cinema of *auteurs* who would film stories conceived for the screen. Perhaps because Varda's filmmaking had come from a different visual context—that of fine art and photography—she came to be understood as the first filmmaker of the French New Wave, particularly after the film historian Georges Sedoul claimed her as such in his *Dictionnaire du cinéma* in 1965.[1]

Varda studied art history and photography at the Académie des Beaux Arts in Paris and was working as a still photographer when a friend asked her to shoot some moving images for a project. Having tried out the medium, she went on to make *La Pointe Courte*, a feature film about the breakup of a marriage that is distinctive for the way in which it incorporates documentary footage of the fishing town where it was shot as well as of the people living and working there. The cinematography emphasizes the textures of the rocks and fishing vessels, using them as a means to express the connections between character and place and the intransigence of the characters' emotions. Varda is an auteur in the ways advocated by the *Cahiers du cinéma* cinephiles. Her work, like that of other French filmmakers grouped under the name of the Rive Gauche or Left Bank such as Alain Resnais, Chris Marker, and Marguerite Duras, has remained throughout her career spread across different media. She continually engages with still photography, short film, documentary, the essay film, and installation art.

Many of Varda's best-known feature films, such as *Cléo de 5 à 7* (*Cléo from 5 to 7*) (1961) and *Sans toit ni loi* (*Vagabond*) (1985), engage specifically with the representation of women's lives. *Cléo* in particular became the subject of an extended debate among feminist critics about its representation of a female perspective exploring and challenging the objectification of women through photographic media (Flitterman-Lewis 1996). *Vagabond* focuses on a homeless young woman who moves through the countryside and seems to merge with it, becoming unapproachable in the process. Varda has spoken about the way in which she sought to film the story using the "texture" of documentary (Glicksman 2002). *Jacquot de Nantes* (1990) takes this subjectivity further, in being a wife's film about her husband Jacques Demy, expressing her vision of his childlike fantasy world of filmmaking in a fictional form, complementing the much sadder and rawer documentary she made later about his life and death (*L'Universe de Jacques Demy*, 1993/95).

The success in the new millennium of the documentary films *The Gleaners and I* and its follow-up *Two Years Later* brings out the significance of nonfiction and art cinema for Varda's career. *The Gleaners* starts out as an investigation into the concept of gleaning, searching first of all for a definition in a wonderfully tactile old leather-bound volume of an encyclopedia which Varda typically finds at home,

FIGURE 9.1 Varda continuing with her heart-shaped potatoes, in *Two Years Later* (2002).

revealing herself as a collector of such things. The investigation goes on to accumulate into an incisive grassroots account of the myriad ways in which French society is pervaded from rich to poor by the ancient spirit of gleaning, including most significantly the practice among the poor of retrieving discarded food from refuse bins and at the end of market days. As a result of the film, Varda became a central figure for the campaign against food waste, with an image of her with a heart-shaped potato—discarded because of its non-standard shape—becoming an icon for campaigners.

Varda's work on *The Gleaners* was particularly innovative on the cusp of the new millennium for the ways in which she shows herself experimenting with new ways of shooting films using a DV camera. One important aspect of this new practice, however, was in the way it linked up with the past. As Varda put it in an interview with Melissa Anderson for *Cineaste*, the Sony DV CAMDSR 300 took her back to the freedom of her early career in the 1950s (Kline 2014: 174). Later in the interview, Varda discusses the relationship between documentary and fiction throughout her career:

> What I'm trying to do […] is to bridge the border of these two genres, documentary and fiction. […] I've been trying all my life to put into fiction films the *texture* of documentary. […] In documentaries […] the subjects […] almost become fictional characters. So I've always been working on the border.
>
> *(Kline 2014: 181)*

The innovations of *The Gleaners* are not only about linking the past to the present. They are also to be found in Varda's use of the DVD as a means to link the present and the future and distribute the optimistic spirit of her filmmaking practice in yet another way. The DVD distributed by Ciné-Tamaris has a wealth of information about the history of the relationship between the subject of gleaning and practice of painting; it also includes both *The Gleaners and I* and *Two Years Later*, dividing each film up into discrete episodes focused on the individuals participating. While watching the first film the viewer is invited to jump to the second film via a link to find out what happened later in the life of the interviewee. In this way Varda uses the interactivity of the digital medium to work with a shortcoming of documentary film, its tendency to abandon participants *in medias res*, leaving both the viewers and the participants in the lurch.

Varda distributes her films largely through her own production company, Ciné-Tamaris, which she first founded in 1954 as Tamaris Films in order to produce *La Pointe Courte*. She reestablished the company with Demy as Ciné-Tamaris in 1975 to produce the documentary *Daguerréotypes*. *Daguerréotypes* typifies Varda's quirky moves from fiction to documentary and back again, in that it focuses on the street where she lives. The street name's reference to photography inspired her to make a film about it, but its subject is nevertheless a small and local street with shops and houses, and the film is simply one that could be made from home, where she was bringing up her family. In time, cinema distribution and video production and distribution were added to the company, and the website now proudly asserts: "We can boast of being one of only two or three independent production companies that have survived since the 60s" (Ciné-Tamaris n.d.).

Varda's later projects continue to use developments in media production and distribution to explore how the episodic nature of filming and memory can be integrated into the concept of continuity or continuous time. *The Beaches of Agnès* plays with the space that, perhaps more than any other, symbolizes the washing away of old traces and the creation of new memories. Varda describes it as a playful auto-biographical film, and it can be seen as a visualization of life guided by the art of salvage and reintegration. As a film that tends toward the still image, it nevertheless works on the line between the medium of memory (photography) and the medium of anticipation (film). The television series *Agnès Here and There* builds on the persona that Varda has established, by now built up as the "grandmother" or "mother" of the New Wave, the exemplar of filmmaking true to the experience of women, and an insightful commentator on the quality of contemporary French life. In the series, Varda goes about visiting her wide range of artistic friends, famous and obscure, as she shows her films around the world. Ironically and playfully, she uses the electronic medium of the here and now (television/video) to show life as it is lived during the period when, as Varda puts it, you get old and are given lots of awards (2011). This convergence through one of the pioneer channels of convergence, the French television channel Arte, is a demonstration of how one kind of artist-led auteur filmmaking is surviving quite well in the new world of digital transformations.

Werner Herzog

The German New Wave, which started out as Young German Cinema, developed slightly later than the French New Wave and picked up many of its debates as part of the struggle to establish a viable German film industry through state support for new directors. The German signatories of the Oberhausen manifesto published in 1962 declared that the industry was moribund and in need of a new impetus, which would be provided by the young auteurs who had already started winning prizes for their short films (Hake 2008: 153).

Werner Herzog (1942–) was a young director who benefited from the limited support that was available. At the beginning of his career, he won prizes for *Last Words* (1967) at Oberhausen and for *Signs of Life* (1968) at the Berlin International Film Festival. Speaking about the developments in a documentary film in 1968, Herzog commented on a possible future for a liberated independent cinema:

> I could imagine that there are much better and more sensible possibilities of exploiting a film and reaching audiences with it. […] [T]echnological advances could facilitate the development of 8mm film so that an entire feature film can be purchased, like a record, and projected onto the wall at home, and you can watch it as often as you want, at any given time.
>
> *(Roth 1968)*

Werner Herzog appears to fit the German Romantic model of the inspired, possibly slightly mad, and oftentimes highly ironizing visionary (Prager 2007: 11–15). If auteur theory were no more than a strategy to bring filmmaking into the mold of the arts, then it would fit Herzog neatly in many ways. And yet, like the true Romantic artist, Herzog has also appeared to be somehow at odds with his own image throughout his career, a factor that has been analyzed as a "performance" of authenticity by Brigitte Peucker (Peucker 2012). In the course of the 1970s, Herzog established himself as the maker of a series of feature films set in striking environments, eliciting remarkably intense performances from actors such as the volatile and slightly sinister Klaus Kinski (*Aguirre, Wrath of God*, 1972; *Nosferatu*, 1979; *Fitzcarraldo*, 1982) and the tragic but ultimately heroic Bruno Schleinstein (*Every Man for Himself and God Against All*, 1974; *Stroszek*, 1977). Herzog himself became part of the performance of his films first through his appearances on television in the promotion of German filmmaking. His public profile increased during the public debates that arose with respect to the preparations for and filming of *Fitzcarraldo* (Herzog, 1982), in which Herzog was accused of exploiting indigenous peoples in South America. Herzog himself contributed to the elaboration of the history of his career through his 1999 documentary *My Best Fiend* (*Mein liebster Feind*), an account of the career of Klaus Kinski. In this film Herzog presents himself as the equal of Kinski in terms of his capacity for dramatic gesture.

My Best Fiend marks a point at which Herzog's career began to shift from that of the New German auteur toward a different identity within a largely American context, and it can be read as a film that advertises his achievements and capacity for more exploits. The second half of the 1980s and the 1990s were a difficult period for filmmaking in Germany. Funding for the arts was significantly reduced under the conservative government of Helmut Kohl. Film funding had always in any case been a contested issue, and the negotiations over the deregulation of media markets as part of the GATT talks in 1992 swung the debate toward commerce, bringing in a different consciousness of the role of film as part of national culture. Peucker points out that Herzog's style of promotion of himself and his work was already being understood as a marketing strategy from the middle of the 1980s (Peucker 2012: 39). With filmmakers more dependent on market success, Herzog's celebrity status extended his filmmaking career far beyond that of his German and art cinema contemporaries.

Documentary has played a significant role in that extension. If the first part of Herzog's career is defined by his success in feature filmmaking, the second part has been about the discovery of his documentary talents. Like Varda, Herzog has made documentary films throughout his career, and like Varda he has experimented with the relationships between documentary, fiction, and experimental film. *Last Words* is often mistakenly called a documentary, but it is in fact a short fiction film that experiments with narrative conventions. Herzog comments:

> Today *Last Words* has such a boldness for me in its narrative form and an utter disregard for the narrative "laws" that cinema traditionally uses to tell stories. Compared to *Last Words, Signs of Life* is very conventional. And without *Last Words* I do not think that *Fata Morgana* or *Little Dieter Needs to Fly* would have happened, nor would certain narrative stylizations that I went on to develop subsequently.
>
> *(Cronin 2002: 14)*

Herzog's approach to documentary is notoriously creative. Objections to his methods reached a peak with the film *Lessons in Darkness* (*Lektionen in Finsternis*) (Herzog, 1992), in which he faked a quotation from the philosopher Blaise Pascale for the opening intertitle. Unlike Varda, who makes a distinction between scripted and unscripted films, Herzog puts words into his participants' mouths, asks them to act out gestures, and most controversially of all adds voiceover commentaries and intertitles which mythologize what is seen on screen. All of these effects heighten the drama of the image in ways that can recall propaganda techniques from the early twentieth century. The audience response at the Berlin Film Festival to *Lessons in Darkness*—which put spectacular helicopter footage of the burning oil wells after the Gulf War in Kuwait to a dramatic soundtrack containing music by classical composers Edvard Grieg, Gustav Mahler, Arvo Pärt, Sergei Prokofiev, Franz Schubert, Giuseppe Verdi, and Richard Wagner (*Das Rheingold, Parsifal*, and *Götterdämmerung*)—was of outright rejection (Cronin 2014: 293).

While *My Best Fiend* looks back on and dramatizes a combative career within the context of German cinema, *Grizzly Man* (Herzog, 2005) looks toward a different relationship, not so much with the ill-fated wildlife campaigner Timothy Treadwell as with the citizens of the United States in the new millennium. Before this film, Herzog had already made several television documentaries on American subjects in his "first U.S.-American period," as John E. Davidson puts it in his analysis of films from 1976 to 1984 (2012: 417). While those films were made for the German television channel Süddeutscher Rundfunk, and are hence representations of Americans to German audiences, and subsequent films up to *Grizzly Man* were European co-productions, *Grizzly Man*, *Encounters*, and *Into the Abyss* are all American productions, with the 3-D film for Arte *Cave of Forgotten Dreams* also having a significant US input. These films and their success establish Herzog as a resident commentator on American life, albeit with a German accent, with the capacity to create a domestic debate about behavior and social norms.

Treadwell had a sizable personal following before *Grizzly Man* was made, and Herzog's selection of footage for the film, his account of Treadwell's life and motivation for protecting Grizzly bears, as well as his commentary on the meaning of nature provoked a response from the environmental activist community. The documentary *Encounters at the End of the World*, like *Grizzly Man*, keys into twenty-first-century environmental debates. The Antarctic provides significant evidence for the progress of global warming and is often used by activists as a site that provides evidence of an urgent need for action. Herzog does not engage in this kind of reflection, however, and in focusing on the people conducting science on the continent, he overtly dismisses attitudes connected to the environmental movement, expostulating about "tree huggers," ironizing the use of the emperor penguins as the icon for all things Antarctic, and celebrating the often tragic as well as destructive spirit of human investigation.

This opinionated, slightly grumpy-old-man stance on contemporary issues is carried over into the film *Into the Abyss*, which makes a case against capital punishment by demonstrating its profoundly negative effects on the people engaged by society to carry it out. This documentary, which also spawned a miniseries, *On Death Row*, represents a return to Herzog's more conventional documentary style, still focusing on individual experiences of extreme situations but in a more restrained way, allowing participants space to tell their stories and audiences space to interpret them.

The transition that Herzog has undergone from the late 1960s to the second decade of the new millennium is thus threefold. First, the transition is from 35mm film (for features) and 16mm film (for documentary) to HDCAM, with the usual period of transition integrating both film and digital video for *Grizzly Man* and *The Wild Blue Yonder* (2005). The shared picture quality among documentary, fiction film, and television has an interesting effect on the balance between the forms, with *Encounters at the End of the World* representing the landscape above and below the water just as spectacularly as *The Wild Blue Yonder*, the science fiction feature that Herzog concurrently directed during his stay in Antarctica.

Second, it is a transition from a context in which young filmmakers fought for state intervention to create a free, artistically (rather than commercially) defined cinema to a world in which funding for independent filmmaking comes from both state and private sources, spreading risk and introducing commercial considerations at the stage of concept development. Like Varda, Herzog expresses pride in the longevity of his production company; he is also creative with his DVD production and distribution, often including documentaries on the music of participating artists in the home viewing packages. As with Varda, the production company is more than a financial vehicle. It is the central expression of independence. As Herzog has put it rather abrasively:

> Fifty years ago, when I walked out of the office of those pompous producers and established my own production company, I knew I would never shoot a single frame of film if I continued wasting my time with such people. [...] If your project has real substance, ultimately the money will follow you like a common cur in the street with its tail between its legs.
>
> *(Cronin 2014: 244–5)*

Despite the bravado of this statement, Herzog, like other independents, engages in many more activities than directing. His career as an actor, with roles in films as diverse as Harmony Korine's *Julien Donkey-Boy* and Christopher McQuarrie's *Jack Reacher*, flows from and feeds back into his persona as a director of features and documentaries. His role in the mockumentary *Incident at Loch Ness* (2004) directed by Zak Penn, in which he plays a director wishing to debunk the idea of the Loch Ness monster even as it appears behind him, is an ironic treatment of his ironic persona, sending up the mockumentary strategy as much as the Hollywood tendency to create new hybrid words to characterize the absurdities of pitching a film. Herzog has now even voiced an animated version of himself in *Penguins of Madagascar* (Darnell and Smith, 2014) (see Figure 9.2). These additional activities have been part of the third and final transition from a German to a European to an American base in production.

While his recent feature films have been less successful commercially, his diversification in the field of documentary has been remarkable, building on a long history of engagement with the form that has in part been about denying the

FIGURE 9.2 *Penguins of Madagascar* (Darnell and Smith, 2014), with voicework by Herzog.

distinctions between documentary and fiction, creating a mythology of the everyday not only in terms of the stories told but also in terms of the way he has told them. Herzog has thus continued a pattern established at the start of his career, when he recognized his future as an independent filmmaker as a way of life rather than a career. Even in his early days, he produced his own films, raised his own financing, published his own books and scripts, and sold them at screenings of his films. The digital world appears to be a natural destination for his essentially anthropological understanding of his métier. Ever the mythologist, he declares:

> I see the role of the film director as being that of the storyteller in a busy, noisy market in Marrakech, surrounded by an excited crowd. He knows he has to hold his audience's attention at all times. Eventually, when he is finished, if the people are satisfied, he walks away with coins in his hand.
>
> *(Cronin 2014: 250)*

Spike Lee

Spike Lee (1957–) is the final director to be discussed in this exploration of auteur documentary filmmaking into the digital age. In the case of Lee, survival is not only about the financial viability of his work, but perhaps more about the maintenance of a role as a filmmaker whose vision goes beyond making films. In 2006, Lee directed two films: *Inside Man*, a feature film about a moral siege at a bank that had been founded on corrupt wealth, and *When the Levees Broke*, a documentary about the failure of the government to deal with the devastating effects of Hurricane Katrina on communities in New Orleans, and in the Gulf States of Louisiana, Mississippi, Alabama, and Florida. *Inside Man* was, as Colin Tait explains, Lee's highest-grossing film up to 2006 ($183,960,186), reaching a large, international audience, and interpretable as "a success based on what seems to be Lee's abandonment of racial politics in order to cater to a larger, more mainstream audience" (Tait 2009: 41). Although Tait interprets the film as a political critique of corporate finance, it is notable that *When the Levees Broke*, a film about the inadequate response to Hurricane Katrina and the racially charged debate that followed, provoked much more engagement with the director's vision. Comparing the reception of the two films in the popular press, Paula Massood comments:

> Lee's fiction films upset the compact between Hollywood and spectators because they ask uncomfortable questions of their audiences (both black and white) rather than entertain them; in this sense they are difficult. His non-fiction films, by contrast, are expected to be historical and informative, and therefore visibility is a virtue rather than a limitation.
>
> *(Massood 2008: xxvi)*

Like Varda, Lee first made his name as a filmmaker making feature films with strong documentary characteristics, a distinct cinematographic style, and a perceptive eye for social observation. Like Herzog, he pinpoints his own personal breakthrough as the moment he rejected the chase after the big budget and started to make a realizable low-budget film without enough money to shoot it—he started out with a grant of $18,000 from the NY State Council on the Arts and raised the rest through family and friends as he went along. The resulting film, *She's Gotta Have It* (Lee, 1986), the first film through which he came to prominence, was shot on a total budget of $175,000, on 16mm film in a stylishly grainy black and white, and in a "confessional, documentary style," as Karen Hoffman (2011: 106) describes it. The film features a purported, possible, but ultimately non-feminist portrayal (as Lee himself has said) of a woman who, by desiring and pursuing sex with three men, is "living her life as a man" (Glicksman 2002: 9).

She's Gotta Have It was a critical and commercial success, grossing more than $8.5 million (Hoffman 2011: 120) and establishing Lee as a central force in the creation of a new, programmatically black voice in American cinema. Just as Varda's exploration of camera perspective in *Cléo de 5 à 7* can be connected with contemporary work on the female perspective, Lee's formal innovation related to the invisibility of the black community and negativity toward black men on the cinema screen. At the time of the release of *She's Gotta Have It*, there was already a debate about Steven Spielberg's film adaptation of Alice Walker's novel, *The Color Purple*. In an interview Lee commented, "Whoopi Goldberg says that Steven Spielberg is the only director in the world who could have directed this film. Does she realize what she is saying? Is she saying that a white person is the only person who can define our existence?" (Glicksman 2002: 10). Lee continued to create films with extraordinary and continuing cultural resonance, such as *Do the Right Thing* (1989), about the triggers for interracial unrest and rioting; *Jungle Fever* (1991), about an Italian–black sexual fling; and a biopic of the controversial Malcolm X (*Malcolm X*, 1992).

As with Varda and Herzog, Lee has backed his vision by setting up his own production company, Forty Acres and a Mule Filmworks, in 1986, and remaining active as an independent filmmaker throughout his career. The name of the company, based on what was promised to newly freed slaves, also reflects his role "to hold his cinematic mirror up to reflect African-American reality as experienced by his genera- tion" (Mosier Richolson 2002: 25). He declares himself to be a "forerunner in the 'Do It Yourself' school of independent film" on the website for the company, which in addition to producing his own films has also created a context for the growth of black American cinema. Continuing his entrepreneurial spirit, Lee expanded Forty Acres and a Mule into music and book publishing. The 1990s was also the decade in which Lee became known for his Nike commercials, in which he continued the character Mars from *She's Gotta Have It*. Although it was not a decade for big independent films (Khoury 2002), the commercial work made him into a bigger public figure. The documentary *4 Little Girls* extended his style of articulate framing and considered but swift editing into the telling of historically significant stories through interviews and archival documentation. As with Varda and Herzog, there is the sense that the feature films, theatrical documentary, and nonfiction television productions come from the same creative pool and process. There is also no clear separation with the commercial work, which also brings African American heroes, particularly athletes, more into the public sphere.

From 2000 Spike Lee's works as a director have reflected the changes in the industry and the increasing diversity of forms. He has directed fiction and documentary, short and long pieces, for theaters and television screens, in addition to advertisements and online branded content. The funding for these projects is hence also diverse, coming from the studios, television networks, and corporate sponsors. Speaking about his decision to raise funds for an independent film through the website Kickstarter, he has commented on the way the industry has changed since he started out:

> I have been doing kickstarting before there was Kickstarter. That's how I raised the money for my first film. [...] Crowdfunding is the new wave to get financing. Crowdfunding is where you go directly to your base, directly to the people who love a body of work that's been amassed over three decades.
>
> *(Lee 2013)*

While he has continued to fight to make independent feature films, documentary has not only increased in frequency as a form within his oeuvre as a whole, it has also increased in its significance for the recognition of his work and role as a commentator on contemporary American life. *When the Levees Broke* is, like *The Gleaners and I* and *Encounters at the End of the World*, about environmental and social justice. Just as Varda describes her process in her film, Lee turns the participants in his documentary into characters, so that the film is not only a compilation of evidence about the economic and social context of the disaster, but also a document of the individuals and communities who went through it. The miniseries is striking in its respect for the participants and its sense of pace, using the space of the television series to introduce, develop, and return to many different points of view. As the participants name themselves at the end of the film, they are asked to put up a picture frame that demonstrates how they have contributed as performers to this film (see Figure 9.3).

FIGURE 9.3 Framing participation in *When the Levees Broke* (Spike Lee, 2006).

As such the production is not just a mass of complaints but a strong collection of portraits, the sounds and images of a time, a place, and a people.

When the Levees Broke can be seen as a film that expresses Spike Lee's perspective on the world, as do his feature films. A significant aspect of all his films is the use of a varied palette of musical expression to refer to the connections between emotions, faces, places, and events. The music in *When the Levees Broke* brings the considered but improvisatory rhythm of jazz to Lee's slightly quizzical, ironic stance, helping to turn treatment of place-specific events into a larger social vision.

Documentary and the survival of the independent filmmaker

All three directors discussed here make films as a way of life. Like Herzog, Spike Lee has told of how he has worked with his family and his "base," putting his profits into each of his succeeding films and into his students' projects, too. The documentaries of Varda, Herzog, and Lee in the new millennium have played an integral role not only in expanding the definition of film but also in creating an understanding of who independent filmmakers are today and what lies in their emerging horizon. More importantly, they highlight that documentary filmmaking is about more than profit or box-office success. Varda, Herzog, and Lee are entrepreneurs, and celebrities if not icons, with a strong belief in art as capital. When it comes to their documentary productions, the voice of the auteur is integral to the presentation of places and people. Not only is documentary a significant part of the survival of auteur filmmaking, but the auteur also continues to be an innovative force in documentary in the digital age.

Note

1 All authors on Agnès Varda's career have interesting things to say about the relationship between her work and the *Nouvelle Vague*, each with a slightly different emphasis. See Flitterman-Lewis 1996: 248–9, Smith 1998: 1–11, Kline 2014: ix, and Bénézet 2014: 3.

Bibliography

Ames, Eric. 2012. "The Case of Herzog: Re-opened." In *A Companion to Werner Herzog*, ed. Brad Prager. Oxford: Blackwell. 393–415.

ARTE G.E.I.E. 2011. *Agnès de ci de là Varda, une série documentaire réalisée et commentée par Agnès Varda*. Available online at www.arte.tv/fr/Agnes-de-ci-de-la-Varda-15/4304968. html (accessed January 6, 2014).

Bénézet, Delphine. 2014. *The Cinema of Agnès Varda*. London and New York: Wallflower Press.

Ciné-Tamaris. n.d. "Ciné-Tamaris Production." Available online at www.cine-tamaris.com/ cinetamaris/cine-tamaris-production (accessed December 31, 2014).

Cronin, Paul, ed. 2002. *Herzog on Herzog*. London: Faber and Faber.

——. 2014. *Werner Herzog: A Guide for the Perplexed*. London: Faber and Faber.

Curtin, Michael, Jennifer Holt, and Kevin Sanson, eds. 2014. *Distribution Revolution: Conversations about the Digital Future of Film and Television*. Oakland, CA: University of California Press.

Davidson, John E. 2012. "The Veil Between: Werner Herzog's American TV Documentaries." In *A Companion to Werner Herzog*, ed. Brad Prager. Oxford: Blackwell.

Flitterman-Lewis, Sandy. 1996. *To Desire Differently: Feminism and the French Cinema*. New York: Columbia University Press.

Glicksman, Marlaine. 2002. "Lee Way: Interview with Marlaine Glicksman in 1986." In *Spike Lee: Interviews*, ed. Cynthia Fuchs. Jackson: University Press of Mississippi. 3–12.

Goldstein, Steve. 2002. "By Any Means Necessary: Spike Lee on Video's Viability." In *Spike Lee: Interviews*, ed. Cynthia Fuchs. Jackson: University Press of Mississippi. 184–6.

Hake, Sabine. 2008. *German National Cinema*. 2nd ed. Abingdon, New York: Routledge.

Hoffman, Karen D. 2011. "Feminists and 'Freaks': *She's Gotta Have It* and *Girl 6*." In *The Philosophy of Spike Lee*, ed. Mark T. Conard. Lexington, Kentucky: University Press of Kentucky. 106–22.

Khoury, George. 2002. "Big Words: An Interview with Spike Lee." In *Spike Lee: Interviews*, ed. Cynthia Fuchs. Jackson: University Press of Mississippi. 146–54.

Kline, T. Jefferson, ed. 2014. *Agnès Varda: Interviews*. Jackson: University of Mississippi Press.

Lee, Spike, interview by Trish Regan. 2013. "Spike Lee Gets Very Heated at Kickstarter Criticism." *Street Smart* (Bloomberg Television). July 31. Available online at www.bloomberg.com/news/videos/b/9a00bb87-b9f2-4201-b4b2-9a6615866048.

Massood, Paula J., ed. 2008. *The Spike Lee Reader*. Philadelphia: Temple University Press.

Meigh-Andrews, Chris. 2014. *A History of Video Art*. 2nd ed. New York and London: Bloomsbury.

Mosier Richolson, Janice. 2002. "He's Gotta Have It: An Interview with Spike Lee." In *Spike Lee: Interviews*, ed. Cynthia Fuchs. Jackson: University Press of Mississippi. 25–34.

Peucker, Brigitte. 2012. "Herzog and Auteurism: Performing Authenticity." In *A Companion to Werner Herzog*, ed. Brad Prager. Oxford: Blackwell. 35–57.

Prager, Brad. 2007. *The Cinema of Werner Herzog*. London and New York: Wallflower Press.

Roth, Wilhelm. 1968. *Die Erben von Papa's Kino: Notizen zum jungen Film in der Deutschen Bundesrepublik*. Film. FRG: Constantin.

Sarris, Andrew. 1968. *The American Cinema: Directors and Directions 1929–1968*. New York: Dutton.

Smith, Alison. 1998. *Agnès Varda*. Manchester and New York: Manchester University Press.

Tait, Colin R. 2009. "Class and Allegory in Spike Lee's *Inside Man*." In *Fight the Power! The Spike Lee Reader*, ed. Janice D. Hamlet and Robin R. Means Coleman. New York: Peter Lang. 41–60.

Truffaut, François. 1954. "Une Certaine Tendance du Cinéma Français." *Cahiers du cinéma* 31: 15–28.

10

THE ETHICS OF APPROPRIATION

"Misusing" the Found Document in *Suitcase of Love and Shame* and *A Film Unfinished*

Jaimie Baron

Since nearly the beginning of cinema, documentary filmmakers have been reusing pre-existing footage in new films in order to produce new narratives and arguments. From the compilation films of Soviet filmmaker Esfir Shub to the political polemics of Emile De Antonio to the critical comedies of Michael Moore, documentary films have mined found footage for new—and often subversive—meanings. In recent years, however, documentary filmmakers have increasingly been appropriating audiovisual documents not only from official government and commercial archives but also from a variety of other sources, including home movie collections and online digital databases such as YouTube. These alternative "archives" contain almost any kind of audiovisual material, from the most banal to the most sensational, and their wide availability broadens the question of what constitutes the ethical appropriation and reuse of a found document in documentary film. On some level, any appropriation of any document is fundamentally a "misuse." That is, as any document is appropriated, it is also repurposed and made to say something that was not intended—or, at least, not anticipated—by whoever produced it for their own purposes. However, this does not mean that all appropriations are inherently unethical. Indeed, the act of appropriation of found documents may be accompanied by a range of effects, from the ethically suspect to the ethically ambiguous to the profoundly ethical.

The work of Bill Nichols and Vivian Sobchack has contributed greatly to our understanding of documentary ethics, and their ideas can be productively extended to a consideration of the ethics of appropriation. Nichols has argued that, in addition to recording the objects in front of the camera, the camera also inscribes the ethical stance of the documentary filmmaker vis-à-vis her subject. He writes: "An indexical bond exists between the image and the ethics that produced it. The image provides evidence not only on behalf of an argument but also gives evidence of the politics and ethics of its maker" (Nichols 1991: 77). In other words, as viewers, we read an ethics of the documentary filmmaker in the images she has filmed. I would argue that we similarly read an ethics of the filmmaker in the documentary images—and sounds—she has *appropriated*. That is, appropriation compounds and complicates the ethics inscribed through the direct act of recording "reality." Appropriation of previously recorded material creates a double-layered structure for our perception of the ethical stance of the film: on the first layer, the stance of the original film-maker toward her material, and, on the second, that of the filmmaker who has appropriated this material, editing and reframing its images and sounds to a new end. It is the relation between these perceived stances that determines whether we read the reuse as ethical or not.

What are the criteria by which we evaluate the relation between these stances? In her "phenomenology of the ethical gaze," Sobchack delineates a series of doc-umentary "gazes" entailed in the filming of an actual death which seem to justify this filming, an act that might otherwise be regarded as unethical. The gazes that she identifies as ethical include the "accidental gaze," the "helpless gaze," the "endangered gaze," the "interventional gaze," and the "humane gaze" (Sobchack 2004: 249). In other words, the filmmaker may accidentally record the death, may be helpless to prevent the death, may herself be endangered in the situation, may attempt to intervene to prevent the death, or may record an image of death out of compassion for the dying, all of which seem to justify the filming of indexical, documentary death. The act of appropriation, however, always occurs at a remove. The filmmaker appropriating the recording does not share the situation with her filmed subject; therefore she is not in the same danger. Being in a different space and time, she is helpless in that she cannot intervene, but this does not in itself justify the appro-priation, because she can choose whether or not to appropriate these images and sounds. Indeed, her appropriation is deliberate and cannot be excused as accidental. In fact, it is only the humane gaze—or a version of it—that may persist in the act of appropriation. Sobchack writes:

> Marked by its extended duration, the humane gaze resembles a "stare"—a fixed look that tends to objectify that at which it gazes—except for the fact that it *visibly and significantly encodes in the image its own subjective responsiveness to what it sees.*
>
> *(253)*

Likewise, the appropriation filmmaker's framing and editing of the image of death must convey a sense of "subjective responsiveness" and compassion for the dead for her reuse of the image to appear ethical. Otherwise, the appropriation will likely seem unethical, a violation of the rights of the dead.

While images of death bring questions of ethics into intense focus, this required sense of "subjective responsiveness" also applies to the appropriation of images—and sounds—that generate a feeling of ethical violation or transgression for other reasons. For instance, the feeling of transgression may arise when a found document we read as having been intended strictly for a private or limited audience is used in a public documentary. This is particularly the case when it involves recordings of romantic and/or sexual activities. Even if recordings of these activities exist, if we understand that they were addressed only to a particular audience—a lover, for instance—it may seem like an ethical violation for a filmmaker to appropriate them for widespread display. However, as with an image of death, this understanding will depend, at least in part, on our sense of the subjective responsiveness of the appropriation filmmaker, how she chooses to reframe these private recordings and to what end. In addition, rather than exclusively through the duration Sobchack describes in relation to the act of direct filming, this sense of subjective responsiveness in the act of appropriation may emerge through editorial and other formal strategies—particularly anonymization and occlusion, discussed below—which may reduce the feeling of ethical transgression.

Our sense of the appropriation filmmaker's subjective responsiveness is even more important when we read the gaze of the original image as unethical, such as may be the case with found documents originally produced by those we perceive as perpetrators of a crime—prime examples include the Nazis who filmed and photographed their Jewish victims, the Khmer Rouge who photographed their prisoners before executing them, and the American soldiers who photographed and videotaped their atrocities against Iraqi prisoners at Abu Ghraib prison. Images originally created in unethical circumstances, often with the clear intention of dehumanizing the photographed, may be ethically repurposed only if their original purpose is actively interrogated or undermined. To reuse such images in a "straight" way may be read as complicit with the perpetrators, and the appropriation may therefore seem unethical. In order to ethically reuse an already ethically compromised image, a "countergaze"—aligned with the humane gaze and its subjective responsiveness—must deconstruct the original purpose of the image and present an opposing one.

Ultimately, however, the sense of what constitutes an ethical appropriation depends on the individual viewer, who must perform a complex (if not explicitly thought out) evaluation of multiple ethical layers. She must assess not only the ethical stance inscribed in the original image but also the ethical stance inscribed in the act of appropriation and reframing. Through this multilayered act of viewing, she must decide for herself if the strategies and ends justify the "misuse" of the found documents.

Document(ary) eavesdropping

The soundtrack of Jane Gillooly's *Suitcase of Love and Shame* (2013) is composed of selections from 60 reels of audiotape recorded over three years in the 1960s and found in a suitcase Gillooly purchased on eBay in 2009. These audiotapes were recordings of the love "letters" of two people, Tom and Jeannie, who were having an affair. Most of the time, each recorded the audiotapes alone and then sent them to the other. At other times, they made tapes together. As a whole, these recordings—along with other documents and souvenirs—constituted what Jeannie refers to on one tape as their "memory library." In *Love and Shame*, the sounds of Tom and Jeannie speaking to each other on these recordings are accompanied by partially visible found images of Tom and Jeannie, images of the suitcase and tape reels themselves, Gillooly's own evocative images, and sometimes a black screen. While Gillooly's film actively "misuses" documents we understand as having been intended only for private use in a public documentary, it simultaneously deploys several key strategies that work to justify their "misuse" and to imbue the appropriation with a sense of subjective responsiveness that diminishes the sense of ethical transgression.

One of the primary attractions of Tom and Jeannie's recordings is their sense of being private. Gillooly has noted that

> the recordings were made in a uniquely unselfconscious state with the goal of reaching out to another human being—the lover—so much so that we listeners, a half-century later, can feel as though they are speaking directly to us, that we are in the room with them. Yet we know that Tom and Jeannie never expected these tapes to be heard by anyone [else].
>
> *(MacDonald 2013: 40)*

In fact, this couple's lack of self-consciousness is precisely what makes these recordings seem so "authentic." In the digital era, most of us are aware that private recordings can be made public with a single click, but this was not the case in the 1960s. Tom and Jeannie seem completely unaware that anyone other than them might ever listen to their recordings, so there is almost no sense of inhibition. Yet, since they were recording themselves, there is no feeling of ethical transgression inscribed in the recordings themselves. Indeed, if we are to read the aural equivalent of a "gaze" associated with these recordings, it might be termed a "hermetic gaze," looks enclosed within an intimate realm.[1]

However, along with this sense of unselfconscious authenticity, there is also a sense that we should not be listening to the details of these strangers' intimate lives. Sometimes, these details are sexual. At one point we can hear Tom and Jeannie having sex, breathing hard and moaning. Later, during one of the funniest parts of the film, Tom describes the process of casting his penis in wax to send Jeannie for Valentine's Day. On a later tape, we then hear Jeannie talking about, and then masturbating with, the wax dildo. Although this may seem rather funny, after Jeannie climaxes, she begins to cry, saying, "I'm sorry darling but I cry when it's not you there and I just have to make out. Oh darling, oh how I love, how I miss you." In fact, while the sexual moments seem intensely private, the emotional displays seem perhaps even more so. This is particularly the case on another tape Jeannie recorded, on which we hear her crying and talking about her longing for Tom and her sense of worthlessness without him. She says:

> I love you, I just worship you Tom. I think you know that I love you so much. It—it's terribly hard being away from you so long at a time. You have so many, many things to fill your days, and your mind overflows with the

preparations that you make for your classes and your article. And sometimes I feel as though I—I'm not contributing anything anywhere to anybody. With the exception of my deep love that I have for you, try to express to you, that's about really all I accomplish in the way of relations with other humans, Tom.

During this poignant confession—clearly meant only for Tom's ears—Jeannie's vulnerability heightens the sense that we were not meant to hear these recordings. The hermetic and intimate space that Tom and Jeannie created and inhabited together is violently torn asunder by our presence.

"No one has ever told me I shouldn't have used the recordings," Gillooly says of the response to her film, but she notes that a few audience members have reacted negatively—an older man angrily shouting "we don't need this" during a screening, a woman leaving the screening room during a Q&A with the filmmaker after belatedly realizing that Tom and Jeannie were real people rather than actors.[2] These reactions suggest that some viewers may see Gillooly's appropriation as encouraging the aural equivalent of a "voyeuristic gaze," which we generally understand as unethical.[3] However, the generally positive response to the film suggests that most viewers perceive something akin to the humane gaze in Gillooly's appropriation, a sense that she is sympathetic to Tom and Jeannie and tells their story not to exploit them but to try to understand and empathize with their experience.[4]

Suitcase of Love and Shame uses several strategies to avoid ethical transgression and to give viewers the sense that Gillooly's is a humane—or at least a respectful—gaze. First, except for their first names, Tom and Jeannie remain anonymous; we never learn any details from the soundtrack that would allow us to identify them. As Gillooly has stated,

> I don't use their names and [...] I avoided certain narrative threads that would more closely reveal who they were. I edited passages to deliberately mislead the audience to think something happened in a different geographic location. As much as possible I try to discourage the audience's impulse to figure out who they are.
>
> *(Durant 2014)*

Second, visual representation of Tom and Jeannie is almost entirely absent. Gillooly did have access to some images of Tom or Jeannie, mainly in the form of photographic slides that were also found in the suitcase. However, the film includes only fragments of these images so that we never actually see what Tom and Jeannie look like. Instead, we see a shoulder, an ankle, the top of a head revealing a swath of red hair, a hand holding a glass, and so on. Thus, although we hear a great deal, our voyeuristic desire to see—or at least to see clearly—is thwarted (see Figures 10.1 and 10.2). This suggests a certain ethics on the part of Gillooly, who protects her subjects to some degree.

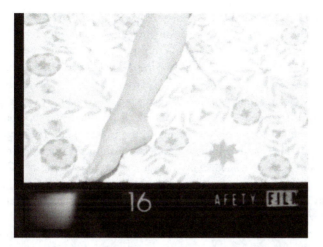

FIGURE 10.1 *Suitcase of Love and Shame*: A fragment of an image showing Jeannie's ankle, maintaining her anonymity.

FIGURE 10.2 *Suitcase of Love and Shame*: A partial image of Tom, occluding his face.

Moreover, these strategies of anonymization and visual occlusion serve not only to shield Tom's and Jeannie's identity (if not their privacy), but also to transform their story into a metonym for a wider historical and cultural narrative. Gillooly has suggested that Tom and Jeannie's story is not unique but represents many other liaisons that occurred behind closed doors during the 1960s. She notes:

> I want to protect their anonymity, but I also don't feel that knowing the details of where they were from is important. I believe the film is much stronger for your not knowing—*Suitcase of Love and Shame* represents a way of life that was hardly exclusive to Tom and Jeannie or to any particular American location.
>
> *(MacDonald 2013: 38)*

Thus, Tom and Jeannie become metonymic representatives of similar hidden experiences during a particular era of American history. Indeed, the indexicality of their recordings also generates a sense of the particular space and time in which Tom and Jeannie lived. We hear the sound of the Miss America Pageant on television, which Jeannie included on one of her tapes. We catch the sounds of dogs barking and secretaries querying in the background of a few of Tom's tapes, some of which were recorded at his veterinary practice. Often, we can hear someone speaking on the radio or a record playing in the background. The larger historical space beyond Tom and Jeannie's hermetic relationship emerges through the ambient sounds captured incidentally or intentionally. Furthermore, Gillooly does not reenact Tom and Jeannie's story in any literal sort of way on the image track. Instead—in addition to the occluded images of Tom and Jeannie, and the images of the suitcase, the audio cases, and the turning audio reels themselves—Gillooly inserts evocative images of the façades of typical middle-class American homes, a lighted window on a dark night, an empty street corner from above, a dark room with light coming through a door that is open just a crack, the lights of a passing car. These images produce an affective substitution that further suggests that Tom and Jeannie's situation was not exceptional. What we are seeing is the evocation of a context. The façades of multiple homes suggest the complex relationships that continue to occur behind those walls, the unrecorded secrets of which we will never know.

Suitcase of Love and Shame also reflexively foregrounds questions of its own ethical status, inviting the viewer to actively reflect on the filmmaker's act of documentary eavesdropping. On the film's website, Gillooly describes the effects she attempted to achieve:

> the listener/viewer is variously located within and outside of the events— complicit and voyeuristic. The "eavesdropping viewer" [is] compelled despite feeling embarrassed and uncomfortable with the knowledge and access they have been given and the transgressions they imagine they see.
>
> *(Gillooly n.d.)*

The film confronts viewers with their own experience of listening in on a conversation not meant for their ears. By presenting us with audio but not images of what we are hearing, the film opens a space within which we cannot help but picture what we are hearing. Thus, we are actively and ethically complicit in constructing the image of the relationship between Tom and Jeannie, visualizing the intimate moments of which they speak in our own minds. When we hear Tom describing his penis in Jeannie's mouth, it is quite difficult not to imagine the scene, even though we are not presented with an image of it. This act of imagination emphasizes not only the filmmaker's but also the viewer's role in the violation of Tom and Jeannie's private space.

As *Suitcase of Love and Shame* demonstrates, when private documents and their "hermetic gaze" are appropriated and made public in a documentary film, our experience of voyeurism and/or eavesdropping may produce a sense of ethical transgression. However, the strategies of anonymization and visual occlusion may ameliorate this sense to some degree. Moreover, the film's metonymic representation of an otherwise undocumented aspect of a particular kind of experience at a particular moment in American life acts as at least partial justification for the ethical transgression, producing from it a sense of a broader historical significance. Tom and Jeannie's experience may even hold a universal resonance that transcends their historical moment, offering us an insight into the complexity of human relationships that cuts across time and space. Thus, although we are certainly trespassing on a private space, these ends may—at least for some viewers—warrant the incorporation of these found private documents into a public documentary.

Document(ary) rectification

A different set of ethical issues based on appropriating and "misusing" found documents arises when the documents themselves have been produced by makers whom we know or perceive as perpetrators of crimes, and so are already inscribed with an unethical gaze. Indeed, in contrast to a film like *Love and Shame*, which raises questions of whether certain found documents *should* be reused, in other cases there seems to be an ethical imperative to reuse them to expose and critique their original purpose. One such case is Yael Hersonski's *A Film Unfinished* (2010). This film concerns an unfinished film shot by the Nazis in the Warsaw Ghetto in 1942 and rediscovered in 1954 in an East German film archive, in a series of film canisters labeled "Das Ghetto." These are some of the few existing filmic images of the Warsaw Ghetto. These silent black-and-white images depict, among other scenes, busy streets full of carts and people, elegantly dressed Jews shopping or eating a lavish meal in a restaurant, a meeting of the Jewish Council, a circumcision ceremony, Jewish men and women separately taking a ritual bath, lingering portrait shots of individual Jewish men and women, emaciated Jewish corpses lying in the street, and bodies of dead Jews being pushed down a chute into a mass grave.

Hersonski's film indicates that, although these images were understood to have been propaganda when they were first found, in the intervening years their status as such was forgotten and the footage came to be regarded as a reliable source depicting ghetto life. The voiceover narration explains: "Ironically, after the war, this film commissioned by the Nazis turned into a trustworthy document for any filmmaker seeking to show what really happened, to tell the untellable. The cinematic deception was forgotten and the black-and-white images were engraved in memory as historical truth." Indeed, Stuart Liebman notes that Frédéric Rossif's *Le Temps du ghetto* (1961) and Alexander Bernfes's 1968 BBC documentary about the ghetto "rather naively exploited the images as such" (2011: 15). He further argues that, through their reuse, these images became fundamental to our vision of the ghetto: "Almost without exception, the conceptual foundation for their continual recycling [...] was and still is the same: This, the filmed images imply, is the way the Warsaw Ghetto looked; this was the way it was [...] [while] in fact, there is a profound gap between the way the ghetto appeared to the German cameramen's lenses and the way it was" (2011: 15). Hersonski's film thus sets out to rectify this case of mistaken reception. Other documents—both written and visual—are summoned in order to reframe the images of "Das Ghetto."

In order to understand the images properly, the film argues, we need to understand *why* they were produced. "In the absence of a final version of the film," the narrator says, "the intentions of the propagandists can never be determined. One can only surmise." Nevertheless, *A Film Unfinished* carefully attempts to piece together the Nazis' intentions in producing this footage. As Ursula Böser notes in her analysis of the film, the "process of audio-visual quotation raises questions about the historicity and origin of the archival footage, about what it was once meant to mean" (Böser 2013: 38). The question of what this particular footage "was once meant to mean" is crucial because it determines whether we read the footage as a reliable document of the Warsaw Ghetto or not. It is precisely the Nazis' intentions—which cannot be precisely known but are inevitably imagined by the viewer and can be determined to some degree by other evidence—that are at stake in Hersonski's appropriation and re-reading of the images.

Böser also notes the status of "Das Ghetto's" images as an instance of "perpetrator images," theorized by Marianne Hirsch (2008: 39). Hirsch suggests that certain images may inscribe the "gaze of the perpetrator" and, in the case of the Nazis, also their "genocidal intentions" (122). But this inscription is not immediately obvious from the "Das Ghetto" images themselves. Some of the images do read as unstaged actuality, particularly images of the starving begging for food and corpses lying in the street. As the camera lingers on starving children and dead bodies, the gaze looking at them might be mistaken for a "humane gaze" in that they are marked by duration, which could lead us to see them as compassionate. However, our extra-textual knowledge of the Nazis' campaign to murder all of Europe's Jews belies this interpretation. A "gaze" that more likely describes these images is another gaze identified by Sobchack: the "professional gaze." Sobchack writes that this gaze is "marked by ethical ambiguity, by technical and *machinelike competence* in the face of an event that seems to call for further and more humane response" (2004: 255). These horrifying unstaged scenes suggest this sense of a dispassionate, machinelike recording of a situation that seems to demand compassionate intervention.

Meanwhile, the degree of staging in other images is initially unclear. Many of the scenes from "Das Ghetto" emphasize a disparity between impoverished and starving Jewish residents of the ghetto and those who are better off. Böser asserts that

> Even in its unfinished and silent state the rhetorical structure and propagandistic thrust that underlies the Warsaw footage is readily evident. It is predominantly conveyed through the constant juxtaposition of extremes between or within shots: the film is structured around the contrast between the well-clad and well-fed who live a life of "luxury," and the destitute and emaciated whose bodies are discarded as waste.
>
> *(2013: 42)*

Yet, even if these images are read as unstaged, the repetition of this juxtaposition could still suggest a professional gaze, purporting to simply "document" the uncaring attitudes of rich Jews toward their poorer fellows. However, as Hersonski's film reveals, reading the Nazi camera's gaze in terms of the ethically ambiguous professional gaze is, in fact, far too generous. *A Film Unfinished* reveals the gaze of "Das Ghetto" to be a "propagandistic" and "dehumanizing" gaze, and a fundamentally unethical form of filmmaking.

In *A Film Unfinished*, voice frequently acts as counterpoint to the "Das Ghetto" images. As we watch the silent "Das Ghetto" footage, voiceover narration provides post hoc historical context, explaining the origins of the footage and the history of its (mis)use. The status of the footage as documentary evidence then begins to be further undercut as diary entries of Adam Czerniakov, the head of the Warsaw Ghetto Jewish Council, about the Nazi film crew's activities are read on the soundtrack. Czerniakov notes the various ways in which the Nazi filmmakers coerced Jewish actors into participating in the film through payment or fear. He further describes the ways in which some of the scenes were staged. For instance, over corresponding images, we hear a voice reading Czerniakov's diary entry for May 3, 1942:

> At 10 a.m. the propaganda crew arrived. They started to take pictures in my office. First, they staged a scene of rabbis and petitioners entering my office, etc. Then they removed all the paintings and charts and brought in a nine-armed candlestick with all the candles lit.

As we watch the images overlaid with this narration, their staged and stilted nature becomes glaringly evident. Later, during the circumcision scene, we also hear Czerniakov's entry about the event. He states that the Germans insisted that the procedure be performed in a home rather than a hospital, which would have been customary and, presumably, safer. He also notes that the scene was in jeopardy since it was uncertain if the main "actor," the baby, would live long enough to complete it. Yet the Nazis were determined to film the scene. Czerniakov's diary entries juxtaposed against the "Das Ghetto" footage undermine any claim that the images might represent "typical" Jewish life in the ghetto; rather, these images are revealed as fictional and—in the case of the circumcision scene—utterly inhumane.

Like Czerniakov's diary entries, the transcript of postwar testimony by German cameraman Willy Wist, read aloud on the soundtrack over a stylized reenactment of his deposition, serves to undermine any sense that the scenes were objective representations of the ghetto. Wist claims he was just filming what he was told to film, stating that he had little direct contact with the Jews but that SS officers chose Jews for him to film whom they "deemed appropriate for filming." Wist also notes that the Jews were "frightened of the SS [so] there were no incidents during filming." These statements emphasize the fact that the film subjects were carefully chosen by the SS for particular reasons and coerced into participating. Wist also admits his own sense that the very choice of film subjects revealed a propagandistic intent. "I never knew what the purpose of the films we shot was," he says.

"However, it was absolutely clear to me that they were intended for propaganda, particularly because we were focusing on the extreme differences between the rich and the poor Jews." Wist repeatedly attempts to disown the dehumanizing, propagandistic gaze, even complaining at one point that "we didn't have a chance to express ourselves," but he nevertheless acknowledges his participation in constructing a false representation.

In addition to the narrated voices of Czerniakov and Wist, a third historical voice—or set of voices—is summoned to act as counterpoint to the "Das Ghetto" imagery. Emanuel Ringelblum, a Jewish historian who was forcibly resettled in the Warsaw Ghetto, organized a group of Jewish writers, artists, scientists, workers, and even children to document in writing their experiences in the ghetto, thereby creating an archive of Jewish experience known as *Oneg Shabbat*. Excerpts from some of these documents are also read on the soundtrack, some directly addressing the German filmmakers' activities. "They continue filming everything inside the ghetto," one voice says. "All the scenes are being staged. On Smocza Street, they assembled a crowd of Jews and ordered the Jewish policemen to disperse them." Another voice adds, "In order to achieve a more 'natural' effect, guns were fired in the air to induce people to flee in panic." As we watch these scenes, which might have been read as documentary crowd footage, the narration transforms the footage into a massive performance, albeit one in which the Jewish actors are genuinely frightened. This scene in *A Film Unfinished* ends with a freeze frame in which Hersonski zooms into the background of the image to focus on a German cameraman recording—another blow to the ostensible spontaneity of the event (see Figure 10.3). Clearly, multiple German cameras were in position to film this scene. The archival statements, combined with Hersonski's editing, serve to further weaken the "Das Ghetto" images' claim to be straightforward documentation, unmasking the professional gaze as a propagandistic gaze.

FIGURE 10.3 *A Film Unfinished*: A German cameraman visible in the background of a riot staged by the Nazis for the unfinished film *Das Ghetto*.

Hersonski's own documentary images also work as counterpoint to the images from "Das Ghetto." For instance, the Nazi footage is frequently interspersed with recent interviews with elderly survivors of the ghetto, who were children or young adults when the "Das Ghetto" footage was produced. As these survivors watch the footage—the light from the screen reflected on their faces—they comment on it, reframing our reading with their personal recollections. The survivors remember the specific locations and some of the people seen in the footage: a street performer named Rubenstein, a woman who frequently stood in the street holding her baby and begging for a piece of bread. They also remember the presence of the film crew, the fear that the Jewish residents experienced when the crew appeared, and the crew's overt interest in filming corpses lying in the street. These reminiscences undermine any pretense to a humane or even professional gaze by further exposing the unequal power relations between the filmmakers and their subjects. Other observations challenge certain images' claim to documentary status. Over scenes of a market, one survivor notes that the Germans "brought geese to the market to prove that Jews were living in reasonable conditions," changing the food we see for sale into props. Over footage from "Das Ghetto" showing a well-dressed Jewish woman setting a table with flowers and a teapot in a well-appointed apartment, another survivor comments, "Where did one ever see a flower? We would have eaten the flower. Who could stay in their private apartment with their furniture and their teapot? Who? Only the privileged like Czerniakov." This commentary overtly contradicts any pretense to typicality in the footage staged in Czerniakov's apartment. Moreover, a third survivor comments explicitly on the filmmakers' tendency to film the starving beside those who were better off. She says:

> There were many contrasts in the ghetto. Many people kept clean and pre-
> served their dignity. We used to shower and brush our teeth every day. Our
> mother took good care of us, even though the conditions were impossible.
> People who are not starving to death don't surrender their humanity [...]
> People did what they could. That was the tremendous contrast and paradox
> that the Germans had created.

Thus, instead of allowing the footage to read as an indictment against the better-off Jews, this commentary establishes their heroism for maintaining their dignity in the face of an impossible situation. Moreover, the survivor points to the fact—obscured by the footage—that the ones to blame for all of the misery are, in fact, the Germans themselves. A critical gaze is thus turned back on the Germans through this survivor's viewing of the "Das Ghetto" footage.

While the various forms of testimony do a great deal to expose Nazis' intentions, the propagandistic, dehumanizing gaze of the Nazi filmmakers becomes even more apparent when additional found footage is inserted into the film. In 1998, 44 years after the "Das Ghetto" footage was found in East Germany, filmmaker Adrian Wood discovered two additional reels from the Warsaw shoot on a US Air Force base. These reels included outtakes that, Hersonski's film asserts, the Nazis never meant to be seen. The outtakes visibly reveal that the Nazi film crew was not simply filming the reality of the ghetto as it spontaneously occurred but, rather, staging their own vision of that reality. Multiple takes of the same scenes, which Hersonski shows in succession, demonstrate that the film crew instructed Jewish people to perform particular acts in order to convey a preconceived image of the ghetto, one which emphasized the disparity between richer and poorer Jews and constructed a fictional vision of the richer Jews' uncaring attitude toward their poorer neighbors. For instance, we see several takes of a well-dressed woman ignoring a pair of boys dressed in rags as she enters a butcher shop. By staging these scenes as documentary evidence, the Nazis attempted to disguise their propagandistic gaze as the professional gaze. However, Hersonski's "misuse" of the outtakes makes the propagandistic, dehumanizing gaze explicit.

Although we can never really know with absolute certainty the intentions behind any text, *A Film Unfinished* suggests that we must nevertheless take intention into account in order to accurately evaluate the historical record. Indeed, Hersonski's film seems to fulfill an ethical imperative to demonstrate that the purported documentary intention to record the "real" may conceal more devious intentions, with the ostensibly professional gaze disguising the propagandistic gaze. When perpetrators produce images in order to dehumanize a group of human beings, it becomes a profoundly ethical act to "misuse" such images and establish a "countergaze." Yet nothing is ethically simple. To reuse these images may still seem unethical in relation to the people depicted in the images, most of whom are dead. Many, if not all, of them were coerced into being filmed. Certainly, those whose dead bodies were filmed never had any say in the matter. To look at these images could be considered a further violation of their dignity and humanity. Indeed, there is often a certain voyeuristic fascination in viewing the bodies of the poor, the starving, the dead, or the soon-to-be-dead. While the images are mostly anonymous—the names of most of the people filmed are unknown—they are not occluded. We see every detail of the emaciated corpses sliding into their mass grave. Yet there also seems to be an ethical imperative to bear witness; to occlude these images would obscure the extent of the horror of what the Nazis did. Thus, rather than occluding the unethical image, *A Film Unfinished* instead reasserts the humane gaze over and above the dehumanizing gaze of the Nazi filmmakers. In addition to directing our gaze to the German cameramen, Hersonski's use of freeze frames and slow motion also increases the duration of our own gaze at the Jewish subjects. By increasing the duration of the dehumanizing, propagandistic gaze, she asserts her own compassionate subjective responsiveness and thereby transforms the gaze into its opposite: the humane gaze that bears witness. Thus, through this palimpsest of gazes, footage intended to degrade and demean is reclaimed as a tribute to those who were filmed against their will and then—most of them—sent to die just months later. Viewing the Nazis' footage, which was meant to dehumanize in order to justify mass murder, may to some degree provoke a sense of voyeuristic complicity in the viewer. However, the "misuse" of the footage in the name of historical justice warrants its reuse. As she watches the Nazi footage of the dying and dead, one survivor weeps, saying, "Today, I am human. Today, I can cry."

Conclusion

Suitcase of Love and Shame and *A Film Unfinished* illuminate the multiple layers of interpretation involved in the viewing of appropriated footage and in determining the ethical valence of the appropriation as it is mobilized in the service of a documentary film. When private recordings are made public in a documentary, we may read the appropriation as voyeuristic unless the filmmaker's editing strategies adequately establish a sense of subjective responsiveness. When perpetrator footage structured through a dehumanizing gaze is appropriated into a documentary, the appropriation must establish an ethical countergaze in order for the appropriation to seem ethically acceptable. There may be many other, related structures in which two different gazes are juxtaposed within the viewer's experience of a single appropriated shot. In any case of appropriation, however, the ethics of the original gaze played against the ethics of the gaze of the appropriator will determine whether we read the appropriation as ethical or unethical. Documentary filmmakers now have access to an unprecedented amount of recorded material from an abundance of sources. With access, however, comes responsibility. Every reuse is, indeed, a "misuse." But the spectrum between a reuse as exploitation and as meaningful inquiry that adds to our understanding of our shared historical world must be further articulated so that we may distinguish between productive misuse and its destructive corollary: abuse.

Notes

1 Of course, when referring to audio recordings, the visual term "gaze" is not quite appropriate. However, our vocabulary for sonic activity is much more limited than for visual activity. Hence, the term "gaze" will have to stand in here for the act of listening as well as looking.
2 Phone interview with Jane Gillooly, September 20, 2014.
3 Again, the term "voyeuristic" is not quite appropriate, since voyeurism refers to sight and this film lets us hear but not see. However, there is no parallel word for the desire to hear.
4 In contrast, Werner Herzog's decision not to include the audio recording of Timothy Treadwell's and Amie Huguenard's deaths in his 2005 documentary *Grizzly Man* points to the fact that any appropriation of certain recordings may seem unethical and impossible to justify. As Herzog himself suggests in *Grizzly Man*, the aural voyeurism generated by that recording is too strong, so strong that Herzog tells Jewel Palovak, who possesses the tape, to destroy it.

Bibliography

Böser, Ursula. 2013. "*A Film Unfinished*: Yael Hersonski's Re-representation of Archival Footage from the Warsaw Ghetto." *Film Criticism* 37 (2): 38–56.
Durant, Mark Alice. 2014. "Jane Gillooly." *Saint Lucy*. Available online at http://saint-lucy.com/conversations/jane-gillooly/ (accessed September 16, 2014).
Gillooly, Jane. n.d. *Suitcase of Love and Shame*. Available online at www.janegillooly.com/films/suitcase-of-love-and-shame/.
Hirsch, Marianne. 2008. "The Generation of Postmemory." *Poetics Today* 29 (1): 103–28.
Liebman, Stuart. 2011. "The Never-Ending Story: Yael Hersonski's *A Film Unfinished*." *Cineaste* 36 (3): 15–19.

MacDonald, Scott. 2013. "Cine-surveillance: 3 Avant-docs Interviews with Amie Siegel, Sharon Lockhart, Jane Gillooly." *Film Quarterly* 66 (4): 28–40.

Nichols, Bill. 1991. *Representing Reality: Issues and Concepts in Documentary*. Bloomington and Indianapolis: Indiana University Press.

Sobchack, Vivian. 2004 [1984]. *Carnal Thoughts: Embodiment and Moving Image Culture*. Berkeley: University of California Press.

11

DOCUMENTARY, MULTI-PLATFORM PRODUCTION, AND COSMOPOLITAN DIALOGUES

Ib Bondebjerg

Two strong forces have had a clear impact on contemporary documentary film and television, as well as our societies and cultures in general, especially since the 1990s: mediatization through digital technologies and globalization. Mediatization refers to a situation in which media systems have been imbedded so deeply in our society, culture, and everyday life that they create a new logic of communication and interaction. The media become important and powerful institutions in themselves, influencing the way institutions and social, cultural, and political spheres function and communicate (Hjarvard 2013: 17). Mediatization gained prominence in the analogue era within national contexts, in which news, documentaries, and fiction were instrumental in nation building and the creation of an imagined community (Anderson 1983). Even with their origins within national contexts, media and documentary forms dealt with transnational issues and circulated within a global media culture. The combination, however, of mediatization on a larger scale, the rise of digital networks and platforms, and the intensified structures of globalization have profoundly influenced contemporary documentary culture.

Globalization has often been discussed in connection with theories of homogenization and the dominance of large capitalist corporations (Herman and McChesney 1997). While concentrations of power, authoritarian dominance over populations, and strong economic inequalities between different regions of the world should be of deep concern to all, there are also other aspects of globalization and mediatization that deserve attention. First, as Held et al. (1999: 15) have pointed out, globalization is basically a descriptive term, not a normative concept. Globalization as such should not be used for utopian or dystopian scenarios—it is the forms of globalization and our ability to control its forces and dynamics that are crucial. Second, globalization has been a developing phenomenon in many societies throughout history, pointing to a fundamental dynamic between the local, national, and regional on various levels of culture, and no society today can exist without some form of it. The question is not whether to be for or against globalization, but how globalization can be carried out in socially responsible ways and politically controlled. Mediatization and digitalization have created new platforms for the development of forms of transnational publics and dialogues. These mediated platforms are modern means of communication and forging new connections. Trade, religion, culture, and economic connections have always demanded some kind of communication, which modern media have made more instant and global. McLuhan's prophecy about "the global village" (McLuhan 1964) has not yet turned into a reality, but contemporary sociological, political, and media- and communication-based theories have increasingly dwelled on its potential, discussing the concepts of cosmopolitanism as well as a more globalized public sphere and media culture.

Cosmopolitan citizenship and global imaginaries

The notion of cosmopolitanism dates back to the Enlightenment, but the concept also has roots in antique Greek philosophy and non-Western religions and philosophy. Basically, *cosmopolitanism* is a way of thinking about human beings and citizens as defined by universal values and norms: We are much more alike than different, or rather the differences between us in terms of cultural dimensions are less important than what makes us alike. This concept is liberal and universalizing, and stands in opposition to *communitarianism*, which is the basis for conservative, national ways of defining citizens and humans by their specific cultural background. Communitarianism is linked to patriotism and to ethnic, cultural, and religious ways of thinking about and defining group identity. In the communitarian way of thinking, we are much more culturally different from each other than universally alike.

Although communitarian sentiments and ideas have a strong presence in contemporary societies as a way of defining national, religious, and ethnically defined cultures, sociological theories of globalization claim that culturally defined group differences cannot explain the fundamental dimensions of modern, networked societies. In *Cosmopolitan Vision*, Ulrich Beck claims that "the human condition has itself become cosmopolitan" (Beck 2006: 2), and offers the following formulation about the Enlightenment project:

> What is Enlightenment? To have the courage to make use of one's cosmopolitan vision and to acknowledge one's multiple identities—to combine forms of life founded on language, skin colour, nationality or religion with the awareness that, in a radically insecure world, all are equal and everyone different.
> *(Beck 2006: ii)*

Per this definition, cosmopolitanism is not negating difference, nor denying that humans primarily live in local, regional, and national settings, which frame and form their perspectives on the larger world. In a world as networked as ours, however, we need to have a global and cosmopolitan outlook, to think, act, and communicate in a way that resonates with others. By telling global stories, documentary film and television can help us establish global empathy and reflection. Documentary narratives can help us see the universally human behind difference and to understand distant others better (Bondebjerg 2014a, 2014b). Documentaries can also reverse global communication patterns dominated by Western media. The creators of *Why Democracy?* and *Why Poverty?* have striven to do this by inviting independent documentary filmmakers from all parts of the world onto the platforms of two of the major public service broadcasters in Europe.

Anthropologists such as Arjun Appadurai (1996) have long talked about a globalization of our cultural and media spheres. Appadurai sees migration as the double process involved in people moving around and creating a new diasporic reality, especially in the big cities around the world, and at the same time developing a media sphere that feeds into our ability to imagine a global reality. For Appadurai, media offer what he calls "scripts for possible lives" (3). Mediated stories in fictional or documentary form about the world can change our mental framework regarding the self and others. Appadurai furthermore points to the necessity of going beyond the discussion of imagined communities as only national entities. The national and local are not disappearing, but in a world of increased interconnectedness and communication, we need to develop an analytical and interpretive framework for understanding the transnational imagined communities or imaginaries established through migration and mediated global narratives. In Appadurai's words: "The diasporic public spheres [...] are no longer small, marginal or exceptional. They are part of the cultural dynamics of urban life in most countries and continents" (Appadurai 1996: 22).

Mediated cosmopolitanism and the global documentary

In *Mediated Cosmopolitanism* (2010), Alexa Robertson analyzes television news in a global perspective. One of her main points is that whereas "political cosmopolitanism" can be described as an often thin concept linked to the global elite and its institutions, media can potentially contribute to a thicker cosmopolitanism by communicating human realities within our world (Robertson 2010: 5). As I have argued in *Engaging with Reality: Documentary and Globalization* (2014a), documentary narratives are even better suited for this task than news reports, although news dominates our day-to-day experience of global events. Robertson's study is transnational in that she studies news reporting on specific networks across the national-global sphere (for instance, BBC World, CNN, and Deutsche Welle) and looks at how global issues are reported by national news organizations and global news channels. What is the image of the global on different types of television? Her starting point is to investigate whether cosmopolitan narratives, feelings, and sentiments are becoming more common in everyday life and in media stories.

Cosmopolitanism is often considered a highly elite form of ideology and attitude toward the realities of globalization. It is also linked, however, to basic cognitive, social, and emotional dimensions of group solidarity. This is what we see during coverage of large-scale disasters, whether natural, human-made, or social. As distant global citizens following disaster reports, we are moved, with emotional and social empathy appearing as the immediate and logical response. Based on her analysis of coverage of the Asian Tsunami of 2004, Robertson argues that while we are not automatically good cosmopolitans, the fact that cosmopolitanism can become a decisive, collective phenomenon when global disaster sets in shows that the normal and more rigid borders between "them" and "us" can be challenged (Robertson 2010: 79–80).

Robertson's study of global news confirms the role of mediatization as a kind of framing of our cosmopolitan imaginary. Although people travel more globally than ever before, and therefore have much more personal experience of certain aspects of global realities, the vast majority of us are still very much dependent on mediatized narratives and images of situations and events around the world. As John B. Thompson has pointed out, this fundamental function of the media has to do with the forming of our world beyond our immediate personal experience, in relation to both the present and the past:

> As our sense of the past becomes increasingly dependent on mediated symbolic forms, and as our sense of the world and our place within it becomes increasingly nourished by media products, so too our sense of the groups and communities with which we share a common fate is altered: we feel ourselves to belong to groups and communities, which are constituted in part through media.
>
> *(Thompson 1995: 35)*

Documentaries have a special status as narratives directly based on reality and thereby coming to us with a heightened sense of authenticity. This is especially important when we talk about broader transnational questions, such as global warming (see Bondebjerg 2014a, 2014c). The global climate issue attained greater visibility when Davis Guggenheim directed *An Inconvenient Truth* (2006), with former American Vice President Al Gore as the main narrator. As I have argued elsewhere (Bondebjerg 2014c), the global success of the film stemmed in part from the iconic status of Gore on the global stage, as well as from the power of the film's rhetorical, factual arguments. The narrative of global disaster and a personal life story combined to create a powerful emotional impact. *An Inconvenient Truth* illustrates how cosmopolitan sentiments can be created through film. The film has since been followed by literally dozens of films with a similar agenda and effect (Bondebjerg 2014a: 224ff.). The world success of BBC's series *Planet Earth* has also contributed to the global, cosmopolitan imagination of the earth as a complex and interdependent ecosystem.

Documentary narratives on global issues can potentially have a strong influence on our cosmopolitan attachments and emotions. The human dimensions of abstract problems matter, and personal stories that bring the distant other closer to us can increase our attention to their life situations. This is clearly illustrated by the numerous documentaries that have followed 9/11 and the wars in Afghanistan and Iraq (Bondebjerg 2014a: 77ff.). News reports often focus on combat, terrorist acts, or the political game, but many documentaries have tried to tell stories and show images of everyday life behind the frontlines. They have tried to show the human side of the distant others that the United States and its allies fight or claim to help. A poignant example of the latter is Phil Grabsky and Shoaib Sharifi's coming-of-age documentary *The Boy Mir* (2011). Over a period of ten years, the British Grabsky and his Afghan co-director filmed the life of a boy and his family in a remote province of Afghanistan. The production offers unique images of a unique life, in and out of poverty and geographically displaced because of the war. A Western audience can learn cosmopolitan empathy from films such as this, as well as an understanding of how universal family life is, despite social and cultural differences. The abstract image of the Afghan society and culture becomes concrete by being linked to the story of a single individual and his family.

A collaborative, multi-platform documentary project

In 2007 and 2012, BBC and the Danish public service broadcaster DR, together with the NGO Steps International, launched two major global media projects, based largely on documentary film, but with a broad digital platform of activities and texts related to the themes the films addressed. *Why Democracy?* (2007) and *Why Poverty?* (2012)—despite weaknesses in their attempts at global representation—are innovative multi-platform projects trying to establish a global public sphere and dialogue around important issues. In the first project, organizers asked ten filmmakers around the world to make films about democracy and what it meant to them. Ten one-hour films were made by independent filmmakers from Bolivia, China, Denmark, Egypt, India, Japan, Liberia, Pakistan, Russia, and the United States. They covered very different issues, from the American use of torture, to experiments with school democracy in China, to the Danish cartoon crisis, when a number of Muslim countries reacted against drawings of the Prophet Mohammed in a Danish newspaper. The films were shown simultaneously in more than 180 countries, placed on the project website, and screened in places around the world where documentaries were not normally available. The project also teamed up with newspapers around the world to establish global discussion on democracy.

The partners behind the project defined the main objectives of the two projects as the following:

1 To produce narratives which inspire people to think and be part of the solution
2 To involve the best filmmakers in the creation of bold and provocative factual films
3 To bring together broadcasters worldwide and engage with a wide and diverse audience through multiple media platforms
4 To create a global outreach campaign, supplementing the broadcasts with extra teaching materials
5 To engage with decision-makers and influencers to find solutions for change.

(Why Poverty? n.d.)

Why Democracy? is an advanced example of a cosmopolitan dialogue, a prototype of a global public sphere working to establish a form of global citizenship (Stevenson 2003). Establishing such a global citizenship is of course not fulfilled by an initiative such as this, but it is an example of what collaborative documentary projects can do on topics of urgent global interest. The producers followed many of the same strategies in the 2012 project *Why Poverty?*, with eight films dealing with the reasons for poverty in the world, as well as the imbalance between the disenfranchised people around the world and those in control of global power structures. The eight documentary films were made by independent film directors, each from a different country; a number of short pieces were also added to the website.

In the *Why Democracy?* project, the European broadcast partners represented 23 different countries. Africa was only represented by South Africa, and Latin America just by Mexico and Brazil, and from Asia and the Middle East we find only India, Japan, Taiwan, and Dubai showing the series. Canada, the USA, and Australia are represented as well. Although *Why Democracy?* is very global compared to other projects in terms both of broadcast partners and of production of films and outreach, the Western dominance is still clear.

The global reach to partners outside the Western world was significantly increased in the *Why Poverty?* project. Among the broadcasting partners we now also find Al-Rasheed-Iraq, MBC from Saudi Arabia, Al-Nahar TV from Egypt, Namibian NBC, Zimbabwean ZBC, EG from Ghana, E-Botswana, the Hong Kong-based RTHK channel, the Colombian channel Senal Colombia, and several others. Distribution increased significantly to the Middle East, Africa, and South America, while still keeping a large core of European participants.

If we take a closer look at the later series, *Why Poverty?*, and the way it uses digital platforms, we get a good picture of an advanced state of the art for documentary film projects in this area. If one clicks on the top button named "Resources," one arrives at a page where a global free-access principle is stated. The user can then watch the films for free on the website, embed them on a chosen site via the YouTube channel for *Why Poverty?*, download the films via Vimeo, or buy them on DVD online. There are certain conditions for the otherwise free use of the films; most importantly, any commercial use for profit is forbidden and there is also a warning: "NO ENDORSEMENT AND NO DEROGATORY USE: These films are not provided to allow you to use for campaigning and fundraising purposes or to defame others. Don't use it for illegal, offensive or fundraising purposes." The films and the rest of the material linked to the project are meant generally to sustain a free, democratic, and global debate on poverty. One further aspect of this is the sub-page under "Resources" dedicated to educators. Here it is possible to get the films in a package with supplementary material also found on the website, in the form of articles, comments, and information on global poverty. Since this is a global project, one also finds versions in multiple languages. The material is specifically linked to the various films.

I will look more specifically at three of the films on poverty: Ben Lewis's *Poor Us*, an animated history lesson on poverty through the ages which combines rhetorical argument and drama with a clear informative and educational purpose; Alex Gibney's *Park Avenue: Money, Power and the American Dream*, a classical critical documentary on the dark sides of the American dream; and Mona Eldaief and Jehane Noujaim's *Solar Mamas*, following an educational project in the Muslim world to liberate women through education. As well as taking up very different aspects of poverty and inequality, these three films also represent different subgenres in documentaries dealing with global issues.

Poor Us: global dialogue and the shaping of our cosmopolitan imaginary

Poor Us is in itself an example of a rather broad, global co-production, as is the whole series. While DR and BBC have the initial commissioning role of the whole project, each of the films has—with slight variations—the same co-production profile. *Poor Us* has an American co-producer, ITVS, which is a branch of the public service broadcasting system in the United States; its other main co-producers are the Japanese NHK, Swedish SVT, and German ZDF-Arte, all public service channels. Nordic public service broadcasters YLE (Finland) and NRK (Norway) are more minor co-producers, as are the Italian RAI and the Latin American network Television America Latina. The educational, informational intention of many of the films is secured by links to Open University International, and global foundations such as the Ford Foundation and the Bill & Melinda Gates Foundation. The global nature of the enterprise is furthered by its distribution to more than 180 countries and the later launch on digital platforms. This project uses all available technologies and communicative formats to create a global dialogue.

This global perspective is also clearly demonstrated in the making and construction of the film. *Poor Us* starts with a montage of images, involving human stories with different kinds of people in various parts of the world. The montage denotes the presence of global problems, conflicts, and social differences. The narrator takes us through the montage to a point when the film shifts to animation and we go back in time to discover the forms and roots of poverty in different epochs of the world. For the remainder of the film, these animated narrative sequences on poverty throughout history are combined with statements from historians and other experts expanding on what the animated story illustrates. As the film moves through the different historical phases and dimensions of global inequality and poverty, the animation is also gradually supplemented by other forms of still and moving images. There are references to paintings and drawings of historical episodes and persons. Photos, film, and television clips, and references to newspapers and books, illustrate different historical tendencies.

The film is akin to an animated history book with quotes and explanations from experts, and an animated storyline with increasingly complex visual storytelling that follows the increasing complexity of the explanations we get from the experts. The narrator of the film speaks from a contemporary perspective and thus to a contemporary audience with a clearly educational purpose. The film starts by addressing the viewer in the second person, and framing the story as a dream by the viewer. The film contrasts or compares the present with the past, addressing the viewer as a character in this story, as when the narrator comments on life in pre-historic times by saying that "you have no iPad and no fridge, but there are plenty of wild animals." Although the film uses animation and to a certain degree simplifies historical developments, it is not intended for children (see Figure 11.1). The simplification and the use of animation must be seen as part of a whole in which the expert statements add complexity to the underlying story.

The film is global not only in production and distribution, but also in the way it addresses the problem of poverty. One aspect of this globalization is that the film creates a dialogue between global experts from very different parts of the world: the United States, Europe, Latin America, and China. A multiplicity of voices analyzes global development. The narrative moves from global epoch to global epoch, from early hunter-gatherers to agricultural, industrial, and post-industrial societies. The animation, filmed visuals, and expert witnesses provide perspectives that deal with the regional consequences of global movements, from early colonization to the global economy after 1945. The message of the film seems to be that inequality and poverty have always been around, and that despite the development of the general welfare and the creation of a rather wealthy middle class, we still find massive poverty on a global scale and increased inequality.

The last part of the film focuses on a potential increase in global poverty and inequality. German philosopher Thomas Pogge points to the lack of global control over global issues and finances. He argues that the intention to help developing countries is mostly creating a situation in which most of the money spent flows back to the rich countries. American economist Joseph Stiglitz similarly criticizes the commonly held faith in "the trickle-down effect," the belief that growth in the global

FIGURE 11.1 An animated sequence from Ben Lewis's *Poor Us*, in the series *Why Poverty?* A quiz show on poverty in the last part of the film is used satirically.

economy will automatically also be of benefit to the poorest. The film ends on a rather pessimistic note, pointing to the new threats from world recession and global warming. Nevertheless, the last remark from the narrator to the viewer is: Well, this was all a dream, and it is time to wake up to a new day. The film is part of a global project, which the filmmakers want to be a global wake-up call to dialogue and action.

Park Avenue: the dark side of the American dream

The American dream is a concept that is familiar to most of us. It is a belief or an ideology that says that we can all make it, if we try hard enough. This story is behind many American films and television series that have been distributed to most of the world, even if it is not necessarily believed or accepted by all those who watch such films and series. It is a story, an imaginary dream that has actually sent people on the move toward the United States or other Western countries, as lands of opportunity. When Appadurai discusses the global mediascape in *Modernity at Large* (1996), he describes the capacity of mediated stories to create imaginary structures that actually function as scripts for actions and our wishes to live out dreams, such as those that start mass migration waves from the developing to the developed countries. The relationship between mass media and mass migration is thus, according to Appadurai, an important area of research for global studies. Fantasies, stories, and imagination are mobilizing forces; they can change concepts and frames of mind, and create hope—although often through quite unrealistic, if not false, hopes and expectations.

In *Park Avenue*, Gibney tears the American dream apart. The film as a whole deals with a broader, democratic problem linked to the fact that the 1 percent super rich have in fact turned the United States into a country where money can buy everything, including the political system. The film demonstrates how a small minority of super rich has become so powerful in America that they undermine the very foundation on which the American dream of individual freedom is built. Compared to *Poor Us*, this is not a film that is overtly global in scope. *Park Avenue*, however, deals with not just the American elite, but what amounts to a global elite operating around the world.

The film is a critical and authoritative documentary built on interviews with expert witnesses, but it also contains testimony by fallen members of the elite and those working for them, and factual documentation through statistics and visual evidence (see Figure 11.2). The beginning of the film shows us the contrast between the richer and poorer parts of Manhattan to visualize the extreme difference in America between the ultra-rich and the very poor. Statistics show that over the last 20 years, a new pattern has emerged in American society in which the distance in income between the richest 1 percent and the rest of society has grown tremendously. The middle-income group has stagnated whereas the rich have become even richer. At the same time, the lowered taxation of the rich and the assault on social programs have widened this gap further. In the film, 740 Park Avenue becomes a symbol of these elites and their excessive life style, underlined by interior shots of their apartments, and by following them around to social

FIGURE 11.2 From Alex Gibney's *Park Avenue: Money, Power and the American Dream.* An interior shot from the home of one of the 1 percent rich Americans who dominate financially and politically.

events. At this particular address, you find the residence of the richest Americans, those representing the golden winners in the competition for the American dream. The film points to the fact that this building used to be the home of the oil tycoons from the Rockefellers in the 1930s onward, but is now the home of the "hedge fund guys," the global financial capitalists.

The main focus of the film, next to showing that the American dream and the mechanisms behind it seem to produce a nightmare for poor and average Americans and the global economy, is the link between money and politics. The film uses numerous examples of how the rich try to buy politicians, the main case being the election of the Wisconsin governor Scott Walker in 2010, backed by the Koch brothers and others. The film explains in detail how Walker attacked unions and social welfare programs in order to reduce taxes, completely in line with those who financially supported his campaign. The film also draws a historical line back to the ideological influence of the Russian-American writer Ayn Rand on conservatives and Republicans to the present-day Tea Party movement and Paul Ryan, Mitt Romney's vice presidential candidate in the 2012 election. The film describes and shows clips from the film version of Rand's novel *Atlas Shrugged* (2011–12), a film clearly funded by this elite outside the normal Hollywood system.

Park Avenue—as a documentary film in the context of the *Why Poverty?* project—is very different from *Poor Us*, although they try to deal with the same question. Gibney's film undermines a powerful and nearly mythological concept in the globalized media world. The American dream is a psychological reality in the minds of millions of people around the globe, and there is no doubt that this imaginary dream has consequences for people's way of thinking about America and most of the developed world. It is a global image that is deeply questioned by the film. The dream is even undermined by a psychological test referenced in the film. According to the test, there is an element in winning that creates what the psychologist Paul Piff calls the "money-empathy gap." In a winner-take-all game played out in laboratory settings, winners start to care less about others. The film clearly offers a variety of provocative material for debate, and as with *Poor Us* and *Solar Mamas*, supplementary materials are rich in documentation and more data.

Solar Mamas: the power of education and mobility

Eldaief and Noujaim's film *Solar Mamas* (also released in a different version as an independent film under the title *Rafea: Solar Mama*) is completely different from the two films analyzed above. *Poor Us* and *Park Avenue* both belong to the authoritative documentary (Bondebjerg 2014a: 51ff.), or what Bill Nichols calls the expository documentary (Nichols 2001: 99ff.). *Poor Us* is clearly very didactic and rhetorical in its basic structure and form, but it also uses a dramatized format with the staging of an embedded "you" and an animated narrative universe on top of which arguments are provided by a variety of experts. The style and voice are relatively light, satirical, and ironic. *Park Avenue*, on the other hand, is based on a heavily critical position backed by experts, empirical data, and inside stories from the worlds of the rich and of the poor.

With *Solar Mamas*, we enter the format of the observational documentary (Bondebjerg 2014a; Nichols 2001), a documentary genre that gets us much closer to a slice of ordinary real life. An observational documentary offers a more anthropological approach to reality, in which no voice tells us what to think at a general level. Instead, the film's voice springs from the mixture of voices from within the diegetic world of the film. In a sense, we see life unfolding in front of our eyes, almost as if we were there in the middle of a distant reality. There is a narrative of some kind, but the film is much more open, and we have to interpret what we see ourselves.

The ethnographic dimension of the film, at least for a Western audience, is in the film's treatment of the lives of women in remote areas of Iraq, Jordan, and Africa, involving their families and everyday activities. The main character of the film, Rafea Anad, is a 32-year-old Jordanian mother of four, and her story is of a disenfranchised, uneducated woman. Together with a group of other women of a similar status, she is offered the possibility of getting an education as a solar engineer. The struggle to achieve this, the difficulties with her husband, and the conflict between family life, children, and education is a universal story. The social and cultural context for this specific story, however, is probably representative of many developing countries, with references to the particularities of a rural and highly patriarchal Middle Eastern family structure. The story in the film thus brings a modern world's cosmopolitan universalism in direct contact with a specific local culture that is deeply seated in tradition.

The funding and co-production structure of the film is also somewhat different from the profiles of the two other films. Funding institutions belonging to the global development culture provided support for the production. DANIDA, the Danish organization for aid to developing countries, and the Danish Ministry for Education helped to finance the film, as did the PPR Foundation for Women's Dignity and Rights, which is supported by the transnational Kering Foundation, which is dedicated to the global fight for women's rights. Contributions also came from funds dedicated to the creation of global communication and dialogue, such as the Skoll Foundation and the Sundance Institute's Fund for Stories of Change. The co-production profile of this film and the partners behind it thus clearly point to the multidimensional aspects of the *Why Poverty?* project. The project tries to establish global partnerships and dialogue across multiple platforms.

The overarching structure of the film is laid out directly from the beginning, when we meet a group of women in Iraq and Jordan, living in tents and simple houses. They meet with the Indian director of the Barefoot College, Bunker Roy, who is in charge of a solar project and its attempt to educate women. The opening sequences establish a link between women's roles in a Muslim society, in which men dominate and have several wives, and an alternative development organization trying to alleviate poverty and broaden women's opportunities. The organization develops a program to educate the women so they can become more independent and start working, or even launch their own businesses. The project trains them to become technicians and experts in solar energy, providing them with valuable skills (see Figure 11.3).

The film gives us a clear insight into family life in developing Muslim societies such as Jordan and Iraq, where women often have no formal education and no clear civil rights as individuals. The fight in this project to educate women is as much a fight against the personal problems the women encounter in leaving their children and families behind for six months as it is a fight against a male-dominated family culture. Raouf Dabbas, from the Jordanian Ministry of Environment, who is the local partner for the project with the Barefoot College, often has to mediate between the husbands, the families, and the women. Throughout the film, Rafea is caught between her family and children at home and her wish to become a solar mama. In the middle of her training, she feels forced to go back to take care of a sick child and a husband who has lost patience with her. The film has a happy ending as she finally gets her degree as a solar engineer. She returns to her village to establish solar energy and becomes a local heroine.

FIGURE 11.3 From Mona Eldaief and Jehane Noujaim's film *Solar Mamas*. The main character Rafea Anad is seen here in her Jordanian home.

As is usual in observational films, there is no clear voice speaking authoritatively on the social project *Solar Mamas* documents. The film, however, speaks clearly in itself and especially through the main character's story. Rafea speaks her mind from the beginning of the film and critiques the male-dominated Bedouin society to which she belongs. She has only had five years of primary education herself, because "it is shameful for a girl after ten to continue education." Sitting in front of her Bedouin tent with her four children behind her, she rather openly talks about the fact that it seems more shameful for women to live like this, "without any real education and purpose in life." She sees the solar project as a chance of getting into something that will give her that purpose, besides marriage and children, and help other women in the same situation. At the end of the film, when she has finished her education, arrives in triumph in her village, and finally starts working and installing solar energy, she still has to fight the authoritarian and traditional patriarchal culture, and even some of the elder women. The message of the film and its continued mission lie in the fact that Rafea is an important role model for women in traditional male-dominated societies, but there is a long way to go to improve women's lives in many parts of the world.

Cosmopolitan visions—global realities

Neither individual documentary films nor collaborative global projects such as *Why Democracy?* and *Why Poverty?* can change the world. Films about global realities and cultures in all their diversity, however, can create new dialogues. Such dialogues do matter, and they can potentially change our perception of, perspective on, and cognitive and emotional understanding of global others. Our global culture today is highly mediated, and cultural encounters are a way of shaping our understanding and cosmopolitan imagination. Because of the rise of more global and digital networks, national barriers mean less than in the previous century, and can be transgressed. This is what we see in the production and distribution strategy of the *Why Democracy?* and *Why Poverty?* projects. Although it may be difficult to measure the impact in simple, quantitative terms, it seems as if the projects have created multiple effects and set in motion several forms of communication, dialogue, and educational initiatives, and also potentially have changed attitudes and policies about politics and economics. On the websites of the two projects you can follow the afterlife of the films, and the kind of debates they have created.

On the website of *Why Poverty?*, it is possible to follow some of the reactions following the initial screenings of the films, and to learn what has happened to some of the characters portrayed in the film. In the case of *Solar Mamas*, Rafea experiences setbacks and problems in her initiative to bring solar energy to rural areas in Jordan, and to change the conditions for women. The director reports that not only is funding running out, but also Rafea's husband has been jailed for drug dealing (see www.pbs.org/independentlens/blog/amid-setbacks-the-solar-mamas-are-undeterred). Rafea continues, however, and the film has been screened all over the country. A key moment for *Solar Mamas* was when one of the directors, Mona Eldaief, presented the film and took part in a debate at the World Bank with several other global partners. The screening of parts of the film and the panel debate was part of World Day to Combat Desertification (www.connect4climate.org/blog/world-day-to-combat-desertification). As a film calling for the development of solar energy through the education of women, *Solar Mamas* offers a very concrete example of the effect of training women in parts of the world threatened with desertification.

The *Why Poverty?* project attempted to create a collective live global platform for debate in November 2012 as the project and films were launched. BBC World, for instance, broadcast from Johannesburg *BBC World Debate Why Poverty?*, which was simultaneously broadcast by 50 other stations around the world, reaching a potential audience of 500 million. The participants in this debate were high-ranking politicians, business people, intellectuals, NGO activists, and authors (see www.youtube.com/watch?v=KNIEb3injpc). Many programs like this can be found on *Why Poverty?*'s YouTube channel. DR made a similar program in English with an international panel of experts (www.youtube.com/watch?v=twTRq08QtaY).

It is impossible to fully follow the effect and potential impact of the *Why Democracy?* and *Why Poverty?* projects on regional, national, and global scales because of the wide distribution of the individual films and the very different agendas they raise. The three films I have discussed will probably be used differently by various audience groups and political, cultural, educational, and social institutions. Both DR and BBC estimate the active audience globally to be between 300 and 500 million, through traditional broadcast, online viewing, DVD sale, cinema, and festivals together (Christensen 2012). Each of the films has generated a significant response in both online and print media, a response that can be followed in part on the website of the project. One crucial aspect of the projects' success is the effect of co-producing and distributing in itself. Co-production and distribution create a network culture, and when this network culture transcends the usual global divides, a new system is developed that can hold promises for the future. People who work and discuss together, people who see different products from different countries made for the same agenda, may be able to continue their cooperation beyond the present projects.

A 2013 public debate contained a panel discussion of the *Why Poverty?* project. It was an interactive debate, in which audiences online could participate (www.odi.org/events/3171-bbc-poverty-project-aid-development-public-attitudes). The debate revealed some insights into the success of the series in different parts of the world. A total of 2.6 million Chinese actually managed to access the series, despite governmental blocking of the Internet, and the series had very high viewing shares in many European countries at the first broadcast, between 30 percent and 48 percent. In Denmark, the series garnered a viewing figure of 1.7 million out of a population of 5.5 million, and a share of 44 percent. The initial broadcasting must be seen as the tip of the iceberg, because the real effect is based on the long-term roll out of all the films and the contextual material through online media and downloads. On Danish YouTube (DK), around 1.5 million people have watched the films online. The project website, YouTube, participating broadcaster sites, and other portals create a snowball effect in terms of further distribution of the films and of interactive debate possibilities.

Documentary film and television are more important than ever in our globalizing world, and the possibility of dealing with global themes and actually reaching a global audience is better than ever before. I started out by pointing to Ulrich Beck's bold statement that "the human condition has itself become cosmopolitan" (Beck 2006: 2). Beck's main point here is not that we are now all thinking in a cosmopolitan way, but that the global realities are such that if we do not develop global policies based on a cosmopolitan vision, we will not be able to solve the global problems we are facing. Many individual documentary films have taken up this challenge, and the *Why Democracy?* and *Why Poverty?* projects have taken this global turn in documentary film and filmmaking even further. They are trying to empower us as global citizens by addressing global realities on multiple platforms. They use the strength of narratives of reality to promote cognitive and emotional insight into global issues and concrete aspects of the global human condition.

Beck's argument for a cosmopolitan agenda is shared by another sociologist, Gerard Delanty, in *The Cosmopolitan Imagination*:

> Inter-cultural communication is now more important than ever. But it needs to be given a more substantial basis than the conventional approach, which tends to separate cultural understanding from political action. [...] Inter-cultural communication conceived of in cosmopolitan terms has five main characteristics. First, it is a mode of communication that is deliberative. Second, it is reflective. Third, it is critical in its orientation. Fourth, it entails societal learning. Fifth, it concerns political practice that has global relevance.
>
> *(Delanty 2009: 261)*

Many new documentaries, including the *Why Democracy?* and *Why Poverty?* projects, are based on global communication, with practical and political agendas. Delanty, like Beck, maintains that such a cosmopolitan vision is not an impossible dream, but is indeed part of a new global reality. This reality is certainly characterized by many opposing forces and tendencies, and new transnational institutions have a hard time in a world where regional and national tensions seem to challenge the cosmopolitan vision. In such a reality, however, cosmopolitan voices and forms of intercultural dialogue on global issues are more important than ever. The contemporary documentary agenda is among other things a cosmopolitan, global agenda.

Bibliography

Anderson, Benedict. 1983. *Imagined Communities: Reflections on the Origin and Spread of Nationalism*. London: Verso.

Appadurai, Arjun. 1996. *Modernity At Large: Cultural Dimensions of Globalization*. Minneapolis: University of Minnesota Press.

Beck, Ulrich. 2006. *Cosmopolitan Vision*. London: Polity.

Bondebjerg, Ib. 2014a. *Engaging with Reality: Documentary and Globalization*. Bristol and Chicago: Intellect.

———. 2014b. "Cosmopolitan Narratives: Documentary and the Global 'Other'." *Nordicom Review* 35: 53–67.

———. 2014c. "Documentary and Cognitive Theory: Narrative, Emotion and Memory." *Media and Communication* 2 (1): 13–22.

Christensen, Bo Bech. 2012. "DR initiativtager til global mediebegivenhed." *DR DK*, September 24. Available online at www.dr.dk/DRPresse/Artikler/2012/09/24/094839. htm (accessed January 7, 2015).

Delanty, Gerard. 2009. *The Cosmopolitan Imagination*. Cambridge: Cambridge University Press.

Held, David, Anthony McGrew, David Goldblatt, and Jonathan Perraton. 1999. *Global Transformations: Politics, Economics and Culture*. Stanford: Stanford University Press.

Herman, Edward S., and Robert W. McChesney. 1997. *The Global Media: The New Missionaries of Corporate Capitalism*. London and Washington: Cassell.

Hjarvard, Stig. 2013. *The Mediatization of Culture and Society*. London: Routledge.

McLuhan, Marshall. 1964. *Understanding Media: The Extensions of Man*. Toronto: McGraw-Hill.

Nichols, Bill. 2001. *Introduction to Documentary*. Bloomington and Indianapolis: Indiana University Press.

Robertson, Alexa. 2010. *Mediated Cosmopolitanism*. London: Polity.

Stevenson, Nick. 2003. *Cultural Citizenship: Cosmopolitan Questions*. Maidenhead: Open University Press.

Thompson, John B. 1995. *Media and Modernity*. London: Polity.

Why Poverty? N.d. "The Project." *Why Poverty?* Available online at www.whypoverty.net/about-us/project/ (accessed October 2, 2014).

12

DOCUMENTARY AND VIDEO ACTIVISM

Daniel Marcus

Throughout the history of documentary, producers have sought to alert their audiences to social and political issues and problems. Implicitly or explicitly, they were seeking a response from viewers of their work that might affect the conditions and situations which they portrayed onscreen. Recently, some producers have pursued exhibition possibilities that would encourage audiences to become involved in the movements and conflicts they are documenting. The appeal to audiences to respond concretely to documentary subject matter has become more explicit and organized. Using social media and other Internet features that assist in reaching and organizing publics, documentary makers and video activists have pioneered new exhibition strategies to create engaged audiences (Schuler 2007).

This chapter will first present a history of the interaction among documentary, video activism, and political movements, and explore the new distribution methods that have emerged. I will then present two case studies that show the range of efforts by videomakers to reach politically engaged audiences. The Gulf Crisis Television Project and Robert Greenwald's Brave New Films production and distribution system demonstrate the technological and organizational changes in video activism over the past generation. With these changes, documentary's relationships to political movements, subjects, and audiences have moved toward closer models of participation and interaction.

Documentary and political organizations

Filmmakers have had a long but tenuous relationship with political movements and activist organizations. Since the Bolshevik government commissioned Dziga Vertov and other filmmakers to create Kino-Pravda and exhibit newsreel footage to audiences around the Soviet Union, many governments have subsidized and guided news, documentary, and propaganda production. The interaction between documentary and NGOs, however, has been more sporadic, subject to the vagaries of financing, levels of freedom of speech in given societies, the political inclinations of producers, and the interest in moving-image media by social movements. The 1960s and 70s saw the rise of politically committed video and film collectives that sought to intervene in the political controversies of the era, and a few explicitly collaborated with activist groups on the New Left, most notably the Newsreel collective (Nichols 1980; Boyle 1997). Other collectives and independent producers covered specific public events, such as anti-war and feminist protests. Given the interest in politics by groups such as the People's Video Theater, Videofreex, and TVTV, the paucity of official collaborations at the time between video experimenters and activist groups was striking. Many progressive political organizations demonstrated a pronounced skepticism about television as a whole, convinced that electronic visual media was coterminous with American commercial networks, and doomed to represent the ideology of imperialistic, patriarchal, corporate capitalism. Other activists saw sympathetic videomakers as obscure and powerless in a top-down media system, and concentrated their efforts at communicating through elite channels. Producers themselves prized their improvisatory organization and aesthetics, equating independence from larger organizations with authenticity and truth-telling, beholden to no one and nothing beyond themselves. The counterculture's valuation of personal vision, immediacy, and spontaneity worked against the establishment of ongoing links between videomakers and movement organizations.

After the splintering of both New Left groups and video collectives in the 1970s, a new period of media activism slowly arose in the 1980s. The ever-increasing conglomeration of mainstream media brought academic critique and activist work based on political economy to greater attention, while the presidency of Ronald Reagan in the United States inspired a national focus on the roles of semiotics, imagery, and symbolism in politics. Media began to seem central to notions of governance and power in contemporary society. Meanwhile, the advent of new video and digital technologies began to spread the ability to make electronic media across a wider array of social groups than ever. The movement to combat AIDS was noteworthy in its use of video, with both the Gay Men's Health Crisis and ACT-UP establishing production units for education and advocacy. (The latter's video work can be found in the 2012 documentary *How to Survive a Plague*.) Still, most progressive funding organizations were hesitant to fund media-centric projects, and a distaste for many forms of popular culture by older leftist political activists hampered the embrace of new production and distribution opportunities by anti-Reagan forces.

The documentary challenge to viewers

Documentaries inform audiences about the world around them, whether to celebrate, investigate, or berate their subjects. Because documentaries claim to represent real people and their conditions of life, they contain a challenge to viewers to respond appropriately. They explicitly or implicitly call for viewers to use their new knowledge. Bill Nichols includes documentaries in the "discourses of sobriety" such as scientific reports, public policy discussions, and economic analyses that speak directly to social and historical reality. As Nichols writes:

> They are the vehicles of action and involvement, power and knowledge, desire and will, directed toward the world we physically inhabit and share. Like these other discourses, documentary claims to address the historical world and to possess the capacity to intervene by shaping how we regard it. [...] To what kind of use do we put the knowledge a film provides? What we know, and how we come to believe in what we know, are matters of social importance. Power and responsibility reside in knowing; the use we make of what we learn extends beyond our engagement with documentary films to our engagement with the historical world represented by such films.
>
> *(2010: 37–8, 41)*

Documentary productions claim the moral seriousness of depicting the existing world, while also registering on an emotional level that is often absent in the other discourses of sobriety. They may not achieve the status of authoritative factuality that a medical or scientific report can, but films and videos may evoke more personal responses from audiences that imbue them with a sense of moral responsibility. The documentary provides its audience with knowledge about its world; what shall we do with such knowledge?

In recent writing on media activism, a participatory audience has often been taken as a major good, an improvement over the passivity that mainstream, corporate journalism often evokes. The potential for a responsive audience, however, has not always been defined as a positive phenomenon. The rise of documentary production in the 1920s coincided with the modern study of communication as a social force. Early communication theorists were concerned about the creation and shaping of public opinion; the rise of modern propaganda techniques in government, politics, and advertising created anxiety among theorists that film, radio, and other media could create an easily swayed, weak-minded public receptive to demagogic appeals (Lippmann 1925). A definition of communication sometimes called the "hypodermic-needle model" gained widespread circulation in the field, attributing great power to media content in creating public opinion, as if the public were simply injected with information, values, and opinions by media masters. The model was challenged by more complex theories in subsequent decades, and most documentarians preferred to not see themselves as propagandists anyway. The lack of widespread distribution of documentary productions in theaters in the post-World War II period surely contributed to filmmakers refusing to see themselves as strongly persuasive to audiences just waiting to take their orders; producers working in early television had to carefully avoid appearances of partisanship or advocacy of controversial positions in most cases. Yet for those working on political and social subjects, there remained a hope that their productions could make a difference in public attitudes, which could result ultimately in social change. For those producers coming of age amid the political struggles of the 1960s, a revitalized sense of political commitment and relevance stoked their ambitions for documentary to be a persuasive tool.

The political and social documentary ideal thus includes an audience that responds to a viewing of the film by actively intervening in the situation depicted in the work. Yet this ideal is often a chimera. Documentary producers have a limited window of interaction with audiences; their engagement with audiences rarely goes beyond the temporal and physical limits of the viewing experience itself. They do not control the types of viewers their work may attract, or the conditions of exhibition, or what audiences may do with their newfound knowledge. Few producers have tried to relate exhibition of their work with the activities of their viewers after the screening is finished. The early Lumière camera operators/exhibitors were present to contextualize their work and speak to audiences, as were those working with Dziga Vertov in the early days of the Soviet Union. This close interaction is sometimes replicated at film festivals, but the vast majority of viewing experiences have been marked by physical separation between producer and audience. Producers have sometimes created ancillary materials, such as educational study guides, to foment discussion and engagement among audiences after a screening, and to inspire preferred interpretations of their work, but most viewers have had only the documentary itself to inspire their involvement in putting their knowledge into action.

Documentary producers need not believe in a simplistic hypodermic-needle model of communication to hope that their work has some impact on their audiences, which can lead to greater public engagement with the subjects portrayed in their work. Most audiences have demonstrated some interest in the subject by their very presence at a screening or by choosing to watch the documentary at home amid a plethora of other viewing choices and activities. Given the limited size of audiences for most documentaries, there is already substantial self-selection of viewers, which increases the possibility that viewers will be amenable to the editorial positions taken by producers.

The single biggest factor in the ability of documentary makers to move viewers toward an activist response is the political context of reception. If the subject of a film relates to a broader social or political conflict or movement that has gained public visibility, the production may contribute to a process of ongoing politicization of its audience, and pathways to activism may be accessible to interested viewers. Viewers may come to recognize themselves as members of a larger engaged public, and take steps to join this public in its efforts to effect social change (Clark and Aufderheide 2009). Media may augment or mildly mimic the effect of personal social circles in influencing viewers to join political campaigns and social movements.

One method of propelling viewer involvement beyond the screening experience is to provide enabling information within the text itself. Enabling information provides suggestions for steps to be taken by viewers who wish to get involved in the issues discussed, and can include contact information for relevant organizations (Rosen 1999). The Gulf Crisis TV Project provided contact information for soldiers who wanted to refuse participation in the first Iraq–American war, so they could get legal advice and support (Halleck et al. 2002). Providing such information can make the work seem dated upon later viewing, and goes against traditional notions of objectivity that some distributors still wish to impose upon documentary makers, but the public journalism movement of recent decades has convinced some media organizations to approve inclusion of this kind of information. The creation of new exhibition platforms on the Internet allows for enabling information to accompany video work without having it placed in the work itself, creating the possibility of easily updating information over time. Producers can create links to a wide array of organizations and information resources, and offer specific, detailed suggestions for further action by viewers. New Internet frames can place the information within reach of those interested in pursuing it, without giving the video itself the stigma of being simply a recruitment video for specific organizations.

Types of political participation

What kinds of public participation can activist documentary inspire? Jessica Clark and Patricia Aufderheide assert that the key political efficacy of what they call Public Media 2.0 is the generation of problem-solving publics—that the act of viewership can create the sense of a collective public that empowers individuals to act within them. Clark and Aufderheide offer five types of engagement with new forms of activist media that constitute political action in the age of social media:

Creation: producing original and remixed content to offer views outside of
  mainstream media channels
Collaboration: crowdfunding, crowdsourcing journalism, and circulating petitions
Choice: audiences actively seeking out alternative media sources
Conversation: using comment sections and discussion boards
Curation: aggregating and sharing information and content across platforms
(Clark and Aufderheide 2009: 6–7)

These actions reinforce a sense of collective activity moving toward shared goals through the dispersal and retrieval of information. This media-centric vision of activism has been critiqued, with some reason, by Micah White, one of the initiators of the Occupy movement, as "clicktivism," a too-easy substitution of armchair pseudo-activity for real political engagement (White 2010). Yet Occupy grew into an important phenomenon through its wide exposure in both mainstream and alternative media outlets. YouTube clips of the original Zucotti Park protest in New York City circulated through the Internet with attendant commentary, playing an important role in furthering the physical commitment to occupy specific sites around the country and the world. Internet-centered activism may only be sufficient in and of itself in accomplishing Internet-related policy goals (such as the anti-censorship campaigns that have often been successful via Web organizing), but the use of alternative media to broadly promote interest in more embodied movements remains an enticing goal for producers.

Natalie Fenton has called for a move from the politics of protest to a politics of projects (Fenton 2008). This shift deemphasizes the concept of resistance to power as the goal of left politics, and instead values the positive creation of alternatives to dominant institutions. (Fenton's argument preceded Occupy New York's own move from street protest to hurricane relief and debt forgiveness.) Video activist projects can not only document this shift, but model it as well. Creating a film, a video, or new media content is a positive act that exemplifies the taking of power into one's own hands, to challenge entrenched hierarchies and powerful economic and cultural forces. While the goal of social change is not simply to allow everyone to become their own media producer, the demonstration of independent thought, political engagement, and collaborative creativity can be a powerful inspiration for viewers to envision their own abilities to effect change, attain personal fulfillment, and accomplish collective goals through social activism.

Political scientist David Whiteman asserts that we must look beyond a focus on the experience of the individual viewer, to a "coalition model" of the efficacy of political documentary (Whiteman 2004). Such a model looks at the impact that production has on activist organizations themselves, as they interact with producers to achieve common goals, and tallies the effects on political decision-makers once they know an issue has been raised and their actions are under scrutiny. Media productions can change the terms of discussion and debate among parties already actively involved in issues. Working in collaboration with media makers in production and distribution can clarify the policy goals of organizations, and offer additional avenues for active involvement by their members. Just as the making of an alternative media piece is a model for seizing control of one's own life, speaking up, and addressing problems creatively, the providing of assistance by activist groups in distributing and exhibiting media works is a performative act that exemplifies the intervention into the public sphere that can sustain group coherence and enthusiasm. Working with media producers reaffirms activist groups' relevance to the broader society, demonstrates the existence and power of allies across various spheres of activity, and provides a means for group members to reach out to other groups and potential recruits. Exhibition opportunities represent both outreach to get viewers newly engaged in issues and actions that can strengthen groups who are already involved.

The Gulf Crisis TV Project

The Gulf Crisis TV Project (GCTV) represented an effort to bring together the camcorder revolution, the video activist community, public access and public television channels, and progressive organizations to impact American foreign policy during the build-up to the first Persian Gulf War. GCTV benefited from some networked organizations already in place that could be used to distribute politically charged productions, while the Internet was still developing and the World Wide Web had yet to be created. GCTV combined these linked groups with newly diffused digital camera technology and its own organizing efforts to create an impromptu network that provided programming at odds with government policy and its support by corporate media. Ultimately, GCTV programming was swamped by the outpouring of support for the war by mainstream media sources. GCTV, however, left a legacy of networking among producers and exhibitors that influenced video activism as it embraced the camcorder and digital revolutions in production, and the Web and social media in distribution and exhibition efforts.

GCTV presented ten half-hour programs questioning American policy during the first Iraqi–American conflict in 1991 (Marcus and Stein 1996; Halleck et al. 2002). The shows covered anti-war activism, provided historical and political analysis, and presented entertainment vignettes critical of the administration of President George H. W. Bush. To gets its message across, the project utilized low-cost production equipment, extensive production and distribution contacts, support by anti-war organizations, and high levels of public attention and controversy during the war. Public access and public television channels throughout the country telecast the shows, which were also distributed internationally.

The project was initially organized by veteran public access producers associated with Paper Tiger Television (PTTV) and the Deep Dish Television Satellite Network (DDTV), two groups who had been using access television resources for a decade to challenge the ideologies and practices of corporate media outlets (Stein 2001; Halleck et al. 2002). A largely volunteer collective founded by documentary maker and activist Dee Dee Halleck, Paper Tiger had been producing a weekly show in New York City and elsewhere on media treatment of political issues; it had spawned Deep Dish, a national organization that provided satellite distribution of progressive documentary material on subjects such as AIDS, housing and homelessness, and the health care crisis. As the build-up to war intensified in the fall of 1990, unsolicited tapes began arriving at the offices of the two groups, made by amateur or low-budget professional videomakers from around the country, who were familiar with the abilities of the organizations to distribute leftist programming to interested public access stations. A number of Paper Tiger producers took it upon themselves to quickly organize the material, solicit more videos, raise money, arrange for distribution, and contact potential exhibitors, creating the Gulf Crisis TV Project (Lucas and Wallner 1993). The work of the GCTV coordinators combined three of the functions Aufderheide identifies as the marks of activism in the current age: the Project collected and curated material from a wide range of sources; commissioned and created original content as well; and relied on crowdsourcing for its reports. At the time, however, with the Internet in its early stage, the World Wide Web not yet created, and today's social media nonexistent, the multiplicity of platforms to distribute content that Aufderheide also highlights was not yet available. The project could concentrate only on its video distribution to established outlets in the televisual sphere.

The new technological capabilities of the time, however, were crucial to the production and distribution of the GCTV. Camcorders had become popular, with the Hi-8 video format marking a significant improvement over the older VHS recordings, enabling independent producers to meet broadcast technical standards for picture quality. The use of satellites to send television signals across the continent had grown to the point where rental costs were no longer prohibitive for activist organizations. Satellite signals could be picked up by home dish owners, public access and public television stations, and other institutions such as universities and churches that possessed dishes to receive signals. A month after putting out a call for tapes, GCTV had received more than 120 contributions, and organized excerpts into four 30-minute programs on themes such as the history of the Middle East, energy policy, and the activities of anti-war groups. Deep Dish handled distribution to public access channels, and claimed that more than 300 local stations telecast the series. A small public television station in Philadelphia, WYBE, sponsored the series on a specialized Public Broadcasting Service satellite feed, raising the visibility of the programs within the broadcasting network. About forty PBS stations ran shows just before and during the start of the war in January 1991, covering about forty percent of the country's population (Lucas and Wallner 1993).

Channel Four in Britain picked up the series, which provided a spark to public debate in Great Britain about the war. Channel Four's financial support allowed GCTV to organize a second series of six programs, distributed in the spring of 1991. The second series continued to reach a large number of access stations, but lost its PBS imprimatur, which reduced the number of broadcast stations that ran it. The seemingly successful conclusion of the war, and the patriotic spectacles that had attended it, made some television programmers less enthusiastic about running reports critical of Bush administration strategies.

Crucially, however, it was not just the diffusion of camcorder and satellite resources that made the series possible. GCTV benefited from years of networking by Paper Tiger and Deep Dish among video producers, media activists, and public access channel staff. The two groups had developed a reputation for outspoken work, and had assembled valuable mailing lists of stations and other institutions interested in exhibiting low-tech video on controversial subjects. While PTTV and DDTV had small staffs and operating budgets, they had built a consistent organizational presence in the alternative media field that made them magnets for producers who were looking for outlets to distribute their tapes, and provided instant credibility among a loose network of public access activists and PBS programmers. Before the rise of the Internet, independent producers needed to negotiate a terrain full of gatekeepers that restricted access to media venues. In later decades, as the Internet increasingly became the venue for distribution and exhibition of independent work, the need to get past traditional gatekeepers was replaced by the need for effective promotion to let potential audiences know of the availability of these productions. Paper Tiger, Deep Dish, and the Gulf Crisis TV Project provided models for sharing work and creating series that made finding audiences easier than could individual producers of isolated works, who needed to continually start from scratch in building attention and credibility.

GCTV reached out to the anti-war community, hoping to work with organizers of popular protests against impending war. The anti-war movement was split between two groups, the National Campaign for Peace in the Middle East and the Coalition to Stop U.S. Intervention in the Middle East, which differed in political orientations. Both groups had devised strategies to gain mainstream media attention; neither group had given much thought to alternative media before being approached by GCTV, though the Campaign did collaborate with the alternative Pacifica radio network to broadcast a teach-in about the war. The two groups each agreed to cooperate with GCTV, by putting producers in touch with possible interview subjects and publicizing screenings of shows to their members. In return, GCTV referred activists around the country to local GCTV contributors to enhance coverage of local actions. Local activists and producers sometimes collaborated on "wrap-around" segments on their own activities that accompanied screenings of the GCTV series, which sometimes led to completely new series being created on a local basis. Two other groups, the War Resisters League and Veterans for Peace, were directly involved in production; the WRL collaborated with the GCTV in making one episode, while a show completely produced by Veterans for Peace was added to the GCTV satellite transmission schedule at the end of the second series (Halleck et al. 2002).

Collaboration between activists and producers was limited by several factors. All of the groups were acting under severe time pressures as the march toward war advanced. GCTV had a hard deadline for finishing shows before satellite upload, and thus had restricted opportunities for consultation with outside groups that might take considerable time. Producers also prized their editorial independence from any larger group, especially because the two main anti-war groups did not work together and GCTV did not want to take sides in their frosty relationship (Halleck et al. 2002).

Moreover, the goals of the activist organizations and GCTV did not completely coincide. The organizations believed that stopping the war necessitated reaching as many Americans as possible in a short amount of time, and thus concentrated their publicity efforts on mainstream media able to deliver large audiences. They were slow to realize that changes in the media environment had created greater opportunities for activists to control their own message without facing corporate media gatekeepers. Progressive groups had thought "it was impossible to break into TV," said Leslie Cagan, coordinator of the National Campaign for Peace, and "our thinking has not caught up with the technology that now exists" (Cagan 1993). GCTV was aware of its own limited reach, and rather than producing programming to reach a mass audience, instead chose strategies to appeal to those already sympathetic to anti-war views, hoping to catalyze greater activism among them and maintain morale. GCTV could inform isolated individuals in pro-war areas that an oppositional movement did indeed exist, and sometimes was able to publicize ways that individuals could get involved in local activities. "[Our audience] was people sitting at home frustrated, not knowing that they were not alone," stated Simone Farkhondeh, a GCTV series coordinator (Farkhondeh 1993). Ultimately, Cagan identified a similar process as the most successful element of the movement's work. "What we did best was mobilize our base […] and gave support they needed to express their opposition to the war" (Cagan 1993). As the war started and movement morale flagged, working with GCTV gave activists concrete tasks to fulfill, by having them organize interviews, produce wrap-around shows, and call local programmers to urge the running of the series. As David Whiteman theorizes, media activism can bolster identification with a cause and strengthen ties among groups of activists.

GCTV demonstrated that production of activist-oriented video could be contemporaneous with important events, and that crowdsourcing, curation, and promotion efforts could benefit by building on established organizations and networks. These lessons were applied to the work of the Independent Media Center (IMC), created in conjunction with protests against the World Trade Organization (WTO) in Seattle, Washington, in 1999. The first major anti-globalization protests in the United States, the Seattle gathering was documented by an alliance of media activist organizations and freelancers, who during the week of protests created a daily newspaper, audio reports, and a continuous Web feed, one of the first uses of the World Wide Web to offer alternative coverage of a major news event (Kidd 2003). The IMC also produced a nightly television program carried by access stations and Free Speech TV, a distributor of progressive video with a dedicated channel on the DISH TV subscription service. The programming provided a pointed alternative to mainstream media's usual emphasis on violence and property damage within the protests, instead providing discussions of global economics, the history of the WTO, and interviews with many participants in the anti-globalization movement. (The video results can be seen in *Showdown in Seattle* from Paper Tiger TV (1999) and *This Is What Democracy Looks Like* from Big Noise Films (2000).) The success of the IMC in Seattle inspired the creation of a network of Indymedia centers around the world, through which local producers could document human rights struggles, political protests, and organizing efforts. The creation of ongoing platforms for alternative productions, the building of group identities shared by disparate networks of videomakers and Web activists, and closer collaboration among producers and nongovernmental organizations (NGOs) were all legacies of the Gulf Crisis TV Project's efforts in the early 1990s.

Robert Greenwald and Brave New Films

Michael Moore's success with *Roger & Me* (1989) heralded new public interest in political documentaries. Throughout the 1990s, Moore personified left-wing documentary filmmaking for American audiences, joined eventually in the 2000s by Morgan Spurlock and a number of other producers who enjoyed momentary successes. Moore and Spurlock presented themselves as entertainment entrepreneurs, able to negotiate the commercial terrain of theaters and television networks, and political provocateurs, using constructed situations and their celebrity status to put forward their arguments. While Moore and Spurlock each took on important issues of the time, from unemployment and immigration to gun violence and food politics, they did so generally without coordinating with activist groups. They were solo acts, entering into public debate by virtue of their creative representations of fissures in American society and the attractions of their personae in a celebrity-suffused culture.

Robert Greenwald, whose work rose to prominence in the 2000s, offers a different model for reaching audiences. Rather than building an Internet profile for himself,

Greenwald and his associates use digital resources to create contacts and entrance points for interested activists and audience members. Further, instead of developing strategies to use the corporate entertainment complex against itself, Greenwald has developed a loose network of collaborators which has allowed him to largely bypass corporate media altogether. Greenwald bases his strategy on the use of house parties and screenings, in which small audiences can watch his productions and make contact with local activists across a range of issues; this strategy has been abetted by Greenwald's coordination with national progressive organizations that have provided financial and logistical support. His work is not to be consumed as entertainment as much as utilized to launch political participation, using the physical act of attending a screening to avoid the dangers of passive clicktivism.

Greenwald was a veteran film producer and director when he began making a series of topical documentaries in response to the policies of President George W. Bush. Greenwald had previously worked in an array of entertainment genres, from crime films to family dramas to sports sagas, and had addressed social issues such as alcoholism and, most notably, domestic abuse, in the acclaimed television film *The Burning Bed* (1984). The coming to power of Bush in the disputed 2000 presidential election inspired Greenwald to turn to argument-driven documentary, and he collaborated with producer-directors Richard Ray Perez and Joan Sekler to release *Unprecedented: The 2000 Presidential Election* (2002), which combined narration, interviews, and archival news footage to argue that Republicans had effectively stolen the presidency. (Sekler had been a co-founder of the Los Angeles Independent Media Center (Rampell 2005).) This commenced a series of over two dozen productions made by Greenwald and his associates that have directly addressed contemporary political controversies, from Wal-Mart's poor wages to Bush administration policies in Iraq (Haynes and Littler 2007).

Most of Greenwald's productions offer little that is new in terms of documentary aesthetics or form.[1] They are quickly put together, highly polemical, and unashamedly agit-prop in tone and progressive in politics. The innovations of Greenwald and his company, operating by 2004 under the name Brave New Films (BNF), are in the realms of distribution and exhibition, and in working in cooperation with activist organizations on specific issues. As identified by Christian Christensen, they revolve around several key developments: the ability to obtain partial funding for production via Internet appeals; the ability to circumvent gatekeepers for DVD sales and public screenings by use of the Internet, thereby avoiding commercialized retail and theatrical outlets; and the ability to coordinate screenings with activist communities (Christensen 2009: 79–80). Greenwald's model for each production can include some or all of the following: coordination at the conceptual stage with an activist organization, to better tailor the content to the organizing needs of the latter, without giving up all editorial control, as in a work commissioned in a simple client–producer relationship; funding appeals to viewers of trailers and teasers on YouTube and other sites; assistance by an activist organization in publicizing the documentary and arranging for local screenings all over the country; exhibition in churches, schools, private homes, and other alternative spaces, often accompanied by local speakers and organizers; DVD sales available at screenings, on websites of Greenwald, the collaborating organization, and conventional Web retailers; mass distribution of DVDs to activist organization members; and streaming possibilities on YouTube, Netflix, Hulu, and other major digital services.

Greenwald's approach can be considered as in conjunction with broader trends in distribution and exhibition of both fiction and nonfiction independent film, of what Peter Broderick has called the "New World of Distribution" (Broderick 2008). Producers can no longer rely on making simple deals with one theatrical distributor and one domestic television exhibitor, and a few international deals, while giving up control of how and where their work gets displayed. They must chase many revenue streams, parceling out rights in a complex web with themselves at the center, maintaining the overall control while pursuing various strategic partnerships, and all the while identifying a core audience for their work. Greenwald adds the occasional but often crucial participation of non-media groups to the mix, building a brand based on quick, polemical works as likely to be screened at house parties and activist meetings as sold to individual viewers on DVD or through streaming.

The scale of the Brave New Films operation has been impressive. BNF claims that *Wal-Mart: The High Cost of Low Price* (2005) has been screened 8,000 times in North America, and been seen by at least 700,000 viewers in the United States (Christensen 2009: 89). *Uncovered: The War on Iraq* premiered with 2,600 house party screenings on a single day in 2003 (Musser 2009). *Outfoxed: Rupert Murdoch's War on Journalism* sold 100,000 DVDs in 11 days in 2004 (Rampell 2005). In more recent years, BNF has not had the big commercial successes it enjoyed during the Bush years—politically minded work in the United States tends to run counter-cyclically to political tides, gathering the most support when in opposition to the visible political leadership of the country. Bush was good for left-wing media businesses, and right-wing opposition to Obama generates more commercial momentum than support for his policies. Brave New Films has also been concentrating more recently on producing shorter works for free distribution. The vast majority of its income now comes from foundations and major gifts (Brave New Films 2014). Its reach, however, remains estimable: As of 2013, it had over 20,000 Facebook followers, over 300,000 Facebook likes, and an extensive email list (Brave New Films 2014). Its social media presence may seem to be just another example of clicktivism, but the group continues to organize public screenings as well, with greater emphasis on exhibition on college campuses. Greenwald's emphasis on public screenings may seem counterintuitive or archaic in the era of ubiquitous electronic and social media. By soliciting attendance at public and semi-public events, however, BNF can promote the sense of physical embodiment, of acting in physical space, that remains a key way to instill commitment to a cause, and for audience members to see themselves as members of engaged publics rather than as isolated individuals. Through its use of the public screening model, BNF can also launch big one-day events that gain publicity and attain a scope that attracts participation, while also flexibly allowing for gradual roll-outs or later screenings that can accommodate latecomers to an issue.

Many of Greenwald's biggest successes have come through collaboration with significant activist groups. *Outfoxed* got half of its budget from the pioneering Web political group MoveOn.org and the Center for American Progress (CAP), a Democratic-leaning Washington think tank (Bettig and Hall 2008). MoveOn members also helped prepare the archival footage from Fox News and other sources used in the film's criticism of the Murdoch media empire (Bettig and Hall 2008). The two groups also helped to distribute *Uncovered* and other Greenwald productions, urging members to host and attend viewing parties, providing publicity, and distributing DVDs. With its close connection to former Clinton administration officials and congressional Democrats, CAP was also useful in bringing Greenwald's work to political elites, another part of the producer's strategy in creating changes in national policy (Haynes and Littler 2007). Unions helped organize screenings for the *Wal-Mart* documentary, and Greenwald worked with the American Civil Liberties Union (ACLU) on *Unconstitutional: The War on Our Civil Liberties* (2004), which questioned the post-9/11 Patriot Act and Bush administration policies. Greenwald later produced a television series, *The ACLU Freedom Files* (2005–07), with the group, and produced another series, *Sierra Club Chronicles* (2006), with the longstanding environmental organization (Hirsch 2007).

Karen Hirsch argues that for successful use of activist groups to organize screenings, national groups have to have an active network of local chapters that they can call upon to arrange for facilities, local publicity, and telephone, email, and social media contact lists (2007). Local chapters can also arrange for speakers to accompany film screenings, and use the events for local organizing efforts. For citizens interested in a topic but not yet fully committed to engaging in activism, a free film screening may be a more inviting prospect than a straightforward organizing or recruitment meeting. Attending a screening promises some entertainment value and a chance to learn more about an issue, without making an explicit commitment to take further action (Christensen 2009). For the organizers, it is a chance to create a relationship with newcomers attracted by the screening, to turn their quest for knowledge into inclusion in a social network of activists (Haynes 2007). Screenings also can be used to bring different groups into contact with each other, building local coalitions. For the national headquarters of activist groups, it offers the opportunity for strengthening contact with local chapters and to provide them locally useful materials on a national basis. For some films, Greenwald and national groups have provided national satellite hook-ups to allow for simultaneous transmission of a wrap-around segment with live discussion of the issues presented in the film at the conclusion of the screening. Whereas the Gulf Crisis TV Project included some local wrap-arounds for television audiences featuring local activists, Brave New Films emphasizes wrap-around discussions for physically present audiences, featuring both local and national speakers.

Brave New Films can offer publicity materials and advice on screening logistics. As Greenwald's films became familiar productions to progressive voters, his own reputation could also inspire attendance at screenings, and his group eventually compiled its own contacts lists, lessening reliance on other groups to organize successful local screenings. BNF also solicits feedback from screening hosts and attendees, so screenings serve as focus groups providing information on audience responses to both the films and the contexts of their exhibition. BNF has launched a college outreach distribution effort, and has found that screenings are more successful when framed as information providers and conversation starters, rather than as explicit invitations to join an activist group (Jones 2014).

Along with the television series he has produced with the ACLU and the Sierra Club, Greenwald has also moved beyond the single-production model of his earliest documentaries. During the 2008 presidential campaign, he launched *The Real McCain*, an Internet series focused on inconsistencies in Republican candidate John McCain's statements and votes on public policy over his career. Using the Internet as the distribution venue allowed for a continually renewed presence during the campaign, and the series of videos received millions of hits (Musser 2009). BNF productions in recent years have fluctuated between longer pieces, usually about war and the national security state, and smaller videos on economic justice, criminal justice, and immigration issues, which are available on BNF's YouTube channel. In *Rethink Afghanistan* (2009), Greenwald combined short forms with a larger structure, releasing short videos on specific subjects about Afghan society and American involvement in the war and ultimately putting them together into one collection. As Chuck Tryon states, this strategy "allows the film to be viewed not as a final product but as a mutable object, capable of being changed as the situation in Afghanistan changes or as new information becomes available" (Tryon 2011). In treating a subject as ambiguous as the Afghan war, Greenwald may have found smaller, less definitive statements more appropriate; also, as an anti-war activist now investigating a war run by a Democratic president, Greenwald may have valued the flexibility and nuance available in a more fragmented treatment than he usually employed.

Conclusion

With the diffusion of video and digital recording technology in recent decades, the ability to document political issues has become available to a wide array of producers, activists, and NGOs. With production hurdles more easily transcended, successful propagation of political ideas through documentary has become centered on networks of distribution and exhibition. How can producers traverse the multiplicitous terrain of modern distribution? How do filmmakers get the word out and build interest in their productions? The ability to call on networks of activist communities and other interested individuals can be a crucial determinant of successful distribution and the gaining of public interest. In turn, the field of documentary can help sustain activist organizations and movements in their political efforts, by both publicizing their issues and providing a focal point for their organizing efforts.

In recent years, Brave New Films has attempted to share its model of distribution with the creation of Brave New Theaters, through which BNF launched a Web platform that could be used by other progressive producers to organize public screenings and develop promotional materials. Producers using Brave New Theaters did not create successful campaigns on the scale of Greenwald's work, however;

the explosion of production has perhaps contributed to the difficulty of gaining traction for a low-budget project without already established links to larger groups. Other companies, such as Participant Films and SnagFilms, have had more success in distributing politically charged documentaries and/or increasing their impact through innovations in digital technologies and social media, most notably in Participant's release of *An Inconvenient Truth*, former Vice President Al Gore's treatise on global warming, which featured extensive follow-up materials and organizing links on the Web (Tryon 2011). These initiatives are not only in the United States; numerous groups have used digital platforms to help produce, distribute, and publicize political documentaries around the world. In the field of human rights and social change advocacy, Witness, EngageMedia, video4change, and other groups have provided production equipment and distribution resources to local producers documenting human rights abuses and struggles to hold political authorities accountable (Gregory 2006; Notley 2014). Indigenous communities have increasingly used video production to promote their claims for cultural autonomy and control of land resources under threat by settler governments. Globally, documentary forms have been taken up by performance artists, street artists, hoaxers, and hacktivists to promote causes and investigate malfeasance by authorities (Kara 2015). These "artivists," with their propensity for colorful performance, pithy phrase-making, and public outrageousness, rely on the virality of the Internet to magnify their reach. Many are too anarchic to coordinate with larger movements in an organized way, but the work of the previous generation of art world provocateurs, such as the feminist Guerrilla Girls, may point the way toward sustainable activity, now imbued with the power of digital and social media.

The ability to shoot video is within reach of millions; the successful use of such material depends on the ability to create and sustain networks and communities who can extend the reach of producers in promulgating their work. Activist groups have grown in their appreciation for contemporary media, and the opportunities for closer coordination between media makers and NGOs and other politically active groups exist as never before. It only happens, however, when significant effort and commitment are made by parties on each side of the relationship to provide what is needed by the other.

Note

1 For analyses of the content, style, and aesthetics of Greenwald's documentary productions, see Haynes 2007 and Fallon 2013.

Bibliography

Aufderheide, Pat. 2003. "In the Battle for Reality: Social Documentaries in the U.S." Washington: Center for Social Media. Available online at http://cmsimpact.org/sites/default/files/Battle_for_Reality3.pdf (accessed February 28, 2015).

Bettig, Ronald V., and Jeanne Lynn Hall. 2008. "Outfoxing the Myth of the Liberal Media." In *The Rhetoric of the New Political Documentary*, ed. Thomas W. Benton and Brian J. Snee. Carbondale, IL: Southern Illinois University Press. 173–204.

Boyle, Deirdre. 1997. *Subject to Change: Guerrilla Television Revisited*. New York: Oxford University Press.

Brave New Films. 2014. *Annual Report 2013*. Culver City, CA: Brave New Films. Available online at https://d3n8a8pro7vhmx.cloudfront.net/bravenew/pages/8568/attachments/original/1420618215/BNFAnnual_Report_2013rs.pdf?1420618215 (accessed February 28, 2015).

Broderick, Peter. 2008. "Welcome to the New World of Distribution." *Indiewire*, September 15–16. Available online at www.indiewire.com/article/first_person_peter_broderick_welcome_to_the_new_world_of_distribution_part1and_part2 (accessed February 28, 2015).

Cagan, Leslie. 1993. Interview by author. Tape recording. New York City. November 5, 1993.

Christensen, Christian. 2009. "Political Documentary, Online Organization and Activist Synergies." *Studies in Documentary Film* 3 (2): 77–94.

Clark, Jessica, and Pat Aufderheide. 2009. "Public Media 2.0: Dynamic, Engaged Publics." Washington: Center for Social Media. Available online at http://cmsimpact.org/sites/default/files/documents/pages/publicmedia2.0.pdf (accessed February 28, 2015).

Fallon, Kristopher. 2013. "Where the Truth Lies: Digital Media and Political Documentary Film, 2000–2010." PhD dissertation. University of California, Berkeley.

Farkhondeh, Simone. 1993. Interview by author. Tape recording. New York City. November 5, 1993.

Fenton, Natalie. 2008. "Mediating Hope: New Media, Politics and Resistance." *International Journal of Cultural Studies* 11 (2): 230–48.

Gaines, Jane M. 2007. "The Production of Outrage: The Iraq War and the Radical Documentary Tradition." *Framework* 48 (2): 36–55.

Gregory, Sam. 2006. "Transnational Storytelling: Human Rights, WITNESS, and Video Advocacy." *American Anthropologist* 108 (1): 195–204.

Halleck, Dee Dee, Simone Farkhondeh, Cathy Scott, and Marty Lucas. 2002. "The Camcorder Goes to War: Making Outrage Contagious." In Dee Dee Halleck, *Hand-Held Visions: The Impossible Possibilities of Community Media*. New York: Fordham University Press. 169–88.

Haynes, John. 2007. "Documentary as Social Justice Activism: The Textual and Political Strategies of Robert Greenwald and Brave New Films." *49th Parallel* 21 (autumn). Available online at https://fortyninthparalleljournal.files.wordpress.com/2014/07/3-haynes-documentary-as-social-justice.pdf (accessed February 28, 2015).

Haynes, John, and Jo Littler. 2007. "Documentary as Political Activism: An Interview with Robert Greenwald." *Cineaste* 32 (4): 26–9.

Hirsch, Karen. 2007. "Documentaries on a Mission: How Nonprofits Are Making Movies for Public Engagement." Washington: Center for Social Media. Available online at www.cmsimpact.org/sites/default/files/docs_on_a_mission.pdf (accessed February 28, 2015).

Jones, Laurie. 2014. Interview by author. Seattle. March 21, 2014.

Kara, Selmin. 2015. "Rebels Without Regret: Documentary Artivism in the Digital Age." *Studies in Documentary Film* 9 (1): 42–54.

Kidd, Dorothy. 2003. "Indymedia.org: A New Communications Commons." In *Cyberactivism: Online Activism in Theory and Practice*, ed. Martha McCaughey and Michael D. Ayers. New York: Routledge. 47–69.

Lippmann, Walter. 1925. *The Phantom Public*. New York: Macmillan.

Lucas, Martin, and Martha Wallner. 1993. "Resistance by Satellite: The Gulf Crisis Project and the Deep Dish Satellite TV Network." In *Channels of Resistance: Global Television and Local Empowerment*, ed. Tony Dowmunt. London: BFI Publishing. 176–94.

Marcus, Daniel, and Laura Stein. 1996. "Radical Uses of Public Access Television." *Peace Review* 8 (1): 81–8.

Musser, Charles. 2009. "Political Documentary, YouTube and the 2008 US Presidential Election: Focus on Robert Greenwald and David N. Bossie." *Studies in Documentary Film* 3 (3): 199–218.

Nichols, Bill. 1980. *Newsreel: Documentary Filmmaking on the American Left, 1969–1974*. New York: Arno Press.

——. 2010. *Introduction to Documentary*. 2nd ed. Bloomington and Indianapolis: Indiana University Press.

Notley, Tanya. 2014. "Video for Change Impact Evaluation Scoping Study: A Summary of Key Research Findings." Video4change Network.

Rampell, Ed. 2005. *Progressive Hollywood: A People's Film History of the United States*. New York: Disinformation Books.

Rosen, Jay. 1999. *What Are Journalists Good For?*. New Haven: Yale University Press.

Schuler, Kate. 2007. "Making Your Documentary Matter: Public Engagement Strategies That Work." Washington: Center for Social Media. Available online at www.cmsimpact. org/sites/default/files/MYDM_rapporteur_report_2007.pdf (accessed February 28, 2015).

Stein, Laura. 2001. "Access Television and Grassroots Political Communication in the United States." In John D. H. Downing et al., *Radical Media: Rebellious Communication and Social Movements*. Thousand Oaks, CA: SAGE. 299–324.

Tryon, Chuck. 2011. "Digital Distribution, Participatory Culture, and the Transmedia Documentary." *Jump Cut* 53 (summer). Available online at www.ejumpcut.org/archive/ jc53.2011/TryonWebDoc/text.html (accessed February 28, 2015).

White, Micah. 2010. "Clicktivism Is Ruining Left Activism." *The Guardian*, August 12. Available online at www.theguardian.com/commentisfree/2010/aug/12/clicktivism-ruining-leftist-activism (accessed March 3, 2014).

Whiteman, David. 2004. "Out of the Theaters and into the Streets: A Coalition Model of the Political Impact of Documentary Film and Video." *Political Communication* 21: 51–69.

INDEX

CPSIA information can be obtained
at www.ICGtesting.com
Printed in the USA
JSHW021808071119
2327JS00002B/6

9 781138 849549